AF600562

Canonical Precedence

This dissertation was approved by the Reverend Frederick R. McManus, A.B., J.C.D., as director, and by the Right Rev. Monsignor Clement V. Bastnagel, S.T.L., J.U.D., and the Rev. John Rogg Schmidt, A.B., J.C.D., LL.B., as readers.

THE CATHOLIC UNIVERSITY OF AMERICA
CANON LAW STUDIES
No. 408

Canonical Precedence

A DISSERTATION

Submitted to the Faculty of the School of Canon Law of the Catholic University of America in Partial Fulfillment of the Requirements for the Degree of Doctor of Canon Law

BY

REVEREND PAUL F. SCHREIBER, A.B., J.C.L.
A Priest of the Diocese of Dodge City

THE CATHOLIC UNIVERSITY OF AMERICA PRESS
WASHINGTON, D. C.
1961

Nihil Obstat:

FREDERICK R. MCMANUS, J.C.D.
Censor Deputatus

Washingtonii, die 5 septembris, 1959

Imprimatur:

✠ JNO. B. FRANZ, D.D.
Administrator Dioecesanus

Dodgepoli, die 10 septembris, 1959

Printed by

ST. JOSEPH'S PROTECTORY PRINTING DEPARTMENT
Pittsburgh 19, Pennsylvania

TO THE MEMORY OF

THE RIGHT REVEREND MONSIGNOR

EDWARD G. ROELKER

WHOSE INTEREST

INSPIRED THIS STUDY

FOREWORD

There are some whose notion of humility has prompted them to decry the effort spent by legislators, past and present, to determine proper precedence among people in the various strata of society. A total lack of precedence in any form would correspond to their notion of the equality of men as they came from the hands of their Creator. Yet it is from this very same Creator that the basic principle of precedence comes, as Gratian noted: it is found in the divine provision for the various ranks of angels and archangels who differ from each other in power and rank.[1]

The rules of precedence, then, are intended to preserve public order and avoid confusion when the various groups within the Church meet simultaneously in a public function or assembly. The public nature of such a function provides all the more reason for its being an orderly meeting. In the past, even with some norms of precedence established by various legislators, there were still dissensions and confusion: this shows only too well how important it is that these norms be as exact as possible. In them, each will have as justification for his stand some authority other than his own mere desire for higher place, or his unwillingness to accept what is his right.[2] Both personal humility practiced immoderately, and dislike for honor and position, are incompatible with the common good and its demand for peace and order; they must be set aside.

---

1 ". . . Quia vero quaeque creatura in una eademque qualitate gubernari vel vivere non potest, coelestium militiarum exemplar nos instruit, quia dum sunt angeli et sunt archangeli, liquet, quia non sunt aequales, sed in potestate et ordinem (sicut nostis) differt alter ab altero."—c. 7, D. 89; from a letter of Pope Gregory the Great to France (595)—Philippus, Jaffe, *Regesta Pontificum Romanorum ab condita ecclesia ad annum post Christum natum MCMCVIII,* ed. G. Kattenbach, F. Kaltenbrunner, P. Ewald, S. Loewenfeld (2. ed.; Lipsiae, 1885-1888), no. 1375 (hereafter cited as Jaffé).

2 Ojetti, *Commentarium in Codicem iuris canonici* (4 vols.; Romae, 1927-31), II, 203, note 2 (hereafter cited as *Commentarium*).

As some contribution to the creation of this peace and order at assemblies and other public functions, in some way connected with the Church, this work is undertaken.

Much time and effort was devoted to the problem of the precedence of laymen in many of the sources consulted. These discussions were largely concerned with the precedence of the lay patron. The norms of precedence for this institute have been deliberately excluded from this study because of their limited application in the present day.

A rather large portion of the discussion about lay precedence was concerned with the special problems connected with the precedence of pious associations of the faithful. These too, have been omitted from this study. They were thought to be of limited interest in this country as far as precedence is concerned because of the wide-spread failure to observe the basic requirements of their right of precedence: appearance in a uniform and under a proper banner. In addition, the topic is sufficiently broad in itself to warrant a special independent study.

Similar reasons obtain in part for the omission of any detailed consideration of the cathedral chapter and other chapters of canons. It was felt that a treatment of this institute in the Church would not be of any great value or interest to the English-speaking readers of this dissertation.

The writer has endeavored, after treating briefly of the historical development of the notions of precedence and its various sources, to give a detailed commentary on the precedence of nearly every type of physical or moral person in the Church. This has entailed, first, a thorough treatment of the general principles of precedence as found in canons 106 and 491; secondly, a study of the special norms alluded to in canon 106 was then in order to see how the general norms were either applied, or derogated from, in specific cases. Frequently a discussion is terminated with a schematic outline of the conclusions reached in that particular division of the dissertation. These outlines the reader could profitably advert to when noting the special conclusions at the end of the dissertation.

The writer wishes to express his appreciation to His Excellency, the Most Reverend John B. Franz, D.D., Bishop of Peoria, formerly Bishop of Dodge City, for the opportunity to pursue graduate studies in Canon Law, and for the encouragement given by him during the course of these studies. To the Most Reverend Marion F. Forst, D.D., present Bishop of Dodge City, the writer wishes to express his sincere gratitude for His Excellency's permission and support in publishing this work. He acknowledges his gratitude to the staff of the Mullen Library, particularly the photo-duplication department, for its assistance, as well as to the Reverend Joseph Gallagher, archivist of the Baltimore Archdiocesan Archives, for his help in procuring necessary historical facts and figures. To his fellow priests in the Diocese of Dodge City, to his professors, classmates and friends at the Catholic University of America, to his parents and others whose suggestions, encouragement and prayers helped to bring this dissertation to its completion, the writer expresses his most sincere thanks. A special expression of gratitude is due the Reverend Frederick R. McManus, under whose judicious and kind direction this work progressed. The writer is also indebted to the Right Reverend Monsignor Clement V. Bastnagel and the Reverend John Rogg Schmidt for their interest shown as the second and third readers.

TABLE OF CONTENTS

PART I

Historical Synopsis

CHAPTER I

PRE-TRIDENTINE CONCEPT OF PRECEDENCE

Article 1. The Definition of Precedence

The essence of nearly every definition of precedence offered by canonists through the years has been the greater excellence of one person over another, called *maioritas*.[1] These early canonists were equally unanimous in correlating the notion of obedience with that of superior rank, in imitation of the Decretals of Gregory IX wherein the thirty-third title of his first book of decretals was labeled *de Maioritate et Obedientia*.[2]

The two notions of obedience and superiority were combined as a result of their development by the glossators. In no one place was a principle set down that whoever is a superior must consequently be held in esteem and reverence. Instead, in individual cases laws or rulings were made with a view to meeting a specific need. These came to be applied to similar situations with increasing frequency until there was a common practice, from which

1 Henricus Cardinalis de Segusio (Hostiensis), *Summa Aurea* (Venetiis, 1570), Lib. I, tit. xxxiii, *de maioritate et obedientia*, s.v. *in quibus obedientia;* this title (I, 33) from the Decretals of Gregory will be cited as *de M. et O.*: Alphonsus Stickler, *Historia Juris Canonici*: *Historia Fontium* (Augustae Taurinorum: Apud Custodiam Librariam Pontif. Athenaei Salesiani, 1950), p. 251 (hereafter cited as Stickler, *Hostoria Fontium*); Petrus Leurenius, *Forum Ecclesiasticum in quo ius canonicum universum librorum ac titulorum ordine explanatur* (Venetiis, 1729), p. 378, q. 905 (hereafter cited as Leurenius, *Forum Ecclesiasticum);* Ludovicus Engel, *Collegium Universi Iuris Canonici servato ordine Decretalium* (9.ed.; Beneventum, 1760), p. 83, §1 (hereafter cited as Engel, *Collegium);* Gaetanus Verano, *Iuris Canonici Universi Commentarius Paratitlaris* (5 vols., Monachii, 1703-1708), I, p. 583 §I, n. 1 (hereafter cited as Verano, *Commentarius Paratitlaris*); Anacletus Reiffenstuel, *Ius Canonicum Universum* (6 vols., Venetiis, 1735), II, 40, n.2; Franciscus Schmalzgrueber, *Ius Ecclesiasticum Universum,* (5 vols. in 12, Romae, 1843-1845), I, part II, 267, § I, n.1; Philippus De Angelis, *Praelectiones Iuris Canonici ad Methodum Decretalium Gregorii IX Exactae* (5 vols. in 9, Romae, 1877-1891), I, 299 (hereafter cited DeAngelis, *Praelectiones*). The term *maioritas* will be rendered throughout as "superior rank."

2 *Decretales D. Gregorii Papa IX, suae integritati una cum glossis restitutae* (Romae, 1582), Liber I, tit. xxxiii.

commentators derived a principle as from a custom. Sometimes, however, reason showed that the general principle either could not be applied exactly, or could easily be extended; here adaptations were made by these commentators, sometimes even by later legislators. Often they made the application by combining two or more general principles, and suiting them to the present given case.

But a person could reasonably be considered deserving of greater reverence because of an excellence founded on some basis other than those of power or jurisdiction. Such a basis might be the individual's personal dignity as derived from various sources. Concerning these sources, there was considerable, but not complete agreement. However, it is not always clear precisely what they meant even when they did agree, for their descriptions were often quite short. More frequently they explained their point by citing an example. Confusion enters in when the same cleric and office are cited as an example of several different bases for precedence, as was the case with the archdeacon. A comparative study of the main commentators of this period will clarify some notions. It will be left to the later commentators after the Council of Trent to clarify the matter further by definition and example.

Article 2. The Sources

Henricus de Segusio (+1276), the Cardinal of Ostia (hence the more common name, Hostiensis), one of the earliest commentators (1250) on the decretals of Gregory IX, concluded that there were five major sources from which one could derive superior rank: (1) the sacrament of Orders; (2) episcopal consecration; (3) dispensation (his term for the superior rank of someone with power or jurisdiction); (4) antiquity (priority in time), and (5) the time of ordination.[3]

Later (ca. 1271), in his larger commentary on the five books of the decretals, Hostiensis added the notion of *praelatio* as a source of superior rank, and changed the order for the items mentioned earlier in his *Summa* as follows: (1) dignity; (2) age;

---

[3] *Summa Aurea*, Lib. I, *de M. et O.*, n. 1, s.v. *in quibus consistat obedientia.*

(3) dispensation; (4) *praelatio;* (5) consecration; (6) the rank of the ordaining prelate, and (7) the time of ordination.[4]

No explanation seems satisfactory when one tries to account for the omission of ordination as a source of precedence in this second listing. It is possible that Hostiensis concluded that, since he was concerned only with the precedence of those in Orders, and since this was the oldest of the norms of precedence and well known to everyone, there was no need to mention it. It could not have been included under the notion of *dignitas,* for the commentators indicate that the main component of this source of precedence was an office whose chief charge was some form of administration.[5] It likewise could not come under the notions of dispensation or prelacy, which Hostiensis used interchangeably to refer to the prerogative of an office aside from the Orders which the official had, as in the classic example of the archdeacon.[6] In fact, the distinction between dispensation and *praelatio,* as also the character of either of these as compared with *dignitas,* is not clear. It must be remembered that no definite principles as such were given by the early lawmakers as they are now found in modern legislation. From the decisions made in several similar cases to determine the precedence of a certain cleric in any given rank, commentators drew their conclusions and established a principle. This, in turn, began to be used by the lawmaker in making his decisions, as well as by the writers of the early manuals of church law.

The rank of the ordaining prelate was not mentioned in Hostiensis' first list, although it was already included in the

---

4 *Commentaria in Quinque Libros Decretalium* (Venetiis, 1581), Lib. I, *de M. et O.*, n. 2, ad c. 15, s.v. *maioritas multiplex est,* p. 175 (hereafter cited as Hostiensis, *Commentaria*).

5 *Glossa ordinaria* ad c. 3, X, III, 4, s.v. *dignitas*; et ad c. 5, X, I, 3, s.v. *maiores et digniores;* et ad casum ad c. 1, D. 25 — *Decretum Gratiani, emendatum et notationibus illustratum una cum glossis,* 2 vols. (Romae, 1582) (hereafter cited as *Decretum Gratiani*); Innocent IV, *In V. Libros Decretalium Commentaria* (Venetiis, 1570), ad c. 28, X, III, 5, s.v. *personatus;* Heintschel, *The Medieval Concept of an Ecclesiastical Office,* The Catholic University of America Canon Law Studies n. 363 (Washington, D.C.: The Catholic University of America Press, 1956), p. 87.

6 *Commentaria,* Lib. I, *de M. et O.,* ad c. 15, n.2, p. 174.

Decretals of Gregory IX at that time.[7] It cannot be said that Hostiensis intended to list these sources in the order of their importance as norms of precedence; for the *dignitas* of the archdeacon in that case would have out-ranked the consecration of his own ordinary.

However, Henricus Boich (+1350) in his commentary on the decretals of Gregory IX gave a presentation which more clearly stated these bases which more closely paralleled the modern notions about the sources of superior rank, and, consequently, about the bases for precedence. He lists them in this order:

1) consecration (the peak of dignity exemplified in the preference given a bishop over a priest);

2) *dignitas,* which was called prelacy by Boich (preferring a person with such a rank to those with any of the forms of superior rank to follow, and exemplified in the dignity of the archdeacon compared with that of the archpriest, on the basis that the former had the greater power or jurisdiction, in spite of his lower rank in sacramental Orders: this was a principle concluded from the common practice);[8]

3) ordination (which gave preference to someone over all those who had any of the lower forms of superior rank to follow, as exemplified in the higher rank given to a priest rather than to a deacon, both of whom were in Orders);

4) the ordaining prelate's rank (and this form of superior rank outclassed seniority of time and age, but only when comparing one person with another in the same sacramental Order; it was exemplified in the higher rank given to a priest ordained by the Pope in preference to one ordained by the local ordinary);

5) the time of ordination (the earlier date of which produced a

---

7 C. 7, I, 33 and the *glossa ad hoc* s.v. *subdiaconatus.*

8 "Nota in quibus de jure communi consistit officium archdiaconi. Item nota quod imperat subdiaconibus, et levitis. Item sollicitudo et ordinatio parochiarum pertinet ad ipsum. Item audire debet causas singulorum. Item decani rurales subsunt ei. Item major est post episcopum et ejus vicarius reperitur. Item dicitur oculus episcopi et loco ejus corrigit excessus subditorum. Item institutio corporalis in beneficiis et dignitatibus ad ipsum pertinet. Item examinatio clericorum qui ad ordines promoventur, ad ipsum pertinet et eos debet episcopo praesentare."—*casus* ad c. 7, X, I, 23.

higher rank than did that of birth if two were ordained to the same order);

6) age (which came last as a final resort in determining the superior rank of one over the other, all other criteria being equal).[9]

SECTION 1—THE EARLIEST BASIS: ORDERS

The clearest listing of the Orders, in the same order in which they are usually given today, is found in a letter of Pope St. Cornelius (251-253) to Bishop Fabius of Antioch in the year 251.[10] Five years later, St. Cyprian when writing to a certain Rogatianus warned deacons to be mindful that, while Christ chose bishops and priests to be His ministers, it was only after His ascension that the apostles chose deacons to be theirs.[11] The official teaching of the Council of Trent makes St. Cyprian's position untenable today as far as his reasoning went.[12]

The Decree of Gratian includes a canon which is allegedly derived from the *Constitutum Silvestri* (324). It states:

> . . . A subdiacono usque ad lectores omnes subditi sint diacono cardinali viro reverentissimo, in ecclesia representantes ei honorem. Porro pontifici presbyter, presbytero diaconus, diacono subdiaconus, subdiacono acolythus, acolytho exorcista, exorcistae lector, lectori hostiarius, hostiario abbas, abbati monachus in omni loco represente obsequium sive in publico, sive in gremio ecclesiae . . .[13]

---

9 *In Quinque Decretalium Libros Commentaria* (Venetiis, 1576), Lib. I, *de M. et O., ad* c. 15, p. 143 (hereafter cited as Boich, *Commentaria*).

10 Kurtscheid, *Historia Iuris Canonici, Historia Institutorum,* I (ab Ecclesiae Fundatione usque ad Gratianum) (Romae: Officium Libri Catholici, 1941), p. 47.

11 C. 25, D. 93 — *Corpus Scriptorum Ecclesiasticorum Latinorum,* 70 vols. (Vindobonae, 1866—), II, 469, Epistle IX (hereafter cited as *CSEL*).

12 Sess. XXIII, *de ordine,* c. 4, can. 6 — Schroeder, *Canons and Decrees of the Council of Trent* (St. Louis: Herder, 1955), p. 163 (hereafter cited as Schroeder, *Council of Trent*).

13 C. 5, D. 93—Joannes Mansi, *Sacorum Conciliorum Nova et Amplissima Collectio* (53 vols. in 60, Parisiis, 1907-1927), II, 626 (hereafter cited as Mansi). This canon is derived from a decree of a council supposedly presided over by Pope St. Sylvester and the Emperor Constantine (324); the decree is one of

The I Ecumenical Council of Nicaea (325) specified that deacons were not to sit in the midst of the priests, because it was "... *praeter ordinem et canonem* ..."[14] Again on the basis of Orders, the Council of Laodicaea (343/381) declared that a deacon should not occupy his seat before a priest, except at his bidding, and that similar honor should be paid to the deacon by the lower clergy.[15]

A letter of St. Jerome (410) also stated that priests should have preference to those in lower Orders,[16] as did another of Pope Gelasius (494) to the Bishops of Lucca, Italy.[17]

Other early legislation giving precedence to priests over deacons on the basis of a higher sacramental Order is found in the Council of Agde (506), [18] in the II Council of Tours (567),[19] and in the Council of Trullo (692).[20]

---

the group called Symnachian forgeries, and was circulated during the first years of the sixth century by over-zealous followers of Pope Symnachus (498-514) with a view to strengthening his position, which had been so greatly compromised during the schism of Laurentius. The original text reads: " . . . ut a subdiacono usque ad lectorem omnes subditi essent diacono cardinalis urbis Romae, in ecclesia honorem repraesentantes tantum; pontifici vero presbyteri, diaconi, subdiacones, acolythi, exorcistae, lectores in omni loco repraesentant obsequium, sive in publico sive in gremio ecclesiae, tantum pontifici." — Stephan Kuttner, "Cardinalis: The History of a Canonical Concept," *Traditio,* III (1945), 189.

14 Can. 18—Mansi, II, 675.

15 Can. 20, cited as c. 15, D. 93—Bruns, *Canones Apostolorum et Conciliorum Saeculorum IV-VII,* (2 vols., Berolini, 1839), I, 75 (hereafter cited as Bruns).

16 *Epist. ad Evangelium,* Ep. 146, cited as c. 24, D. 93—*CSEL,* Vol. LVI, Sect. I, Pars III, p. 308.

17 C. 6, 7, 8, Epist. XIV, cited as c. 7, D. 75—Jaffé n. 636; Migne, *Patrologiae Cursus Completus, Series Latina,* (22 vols., Parisiis, 1844-1855), Vol. LIX, col. 50-51 (hereafter cited as *MPL*).

18 Can. 2, cited as c. 21, D. 50—Bruns, II, 146; can. 23, cited as c. 5,. D. 74—Bruns, II, 150; can. 65—Bruns, II, 159.

19 Can. 4—*Monumenta Germaniae Historica,* Legum Sectio III, *Concilia,* Tomus I, (ed. A. Boretius et V. Krause; Hannoverae et Lipsiae, 1896), p. 123 (hereafter cited as *MGH, Concilia*).

20 Can. 7—Mansi, XI, 943-946. This is the famed *Quini-Sextum* council of questionable authority. This particular canon contained only ancient law; hence, it very easily entered the legislation of the Latin Church. This canon is cited in Gratian's *Decretum* as c. 26, D. 93.

The classic source for the precedence of clerics among themselves, however, is found in a letter of Pope Gregory IX to the archpriest of St. Mary Major in Rome about 1230:

> Statuimus, ut presbyteri primum locum, diaconi secundum, subdiaconi tertium, et sic de reliquis obtineant ordinatim, etiamsi posterius admittantur. Et qui major est ordine, etiamsi postea sit receptus, in portione percipienda esse volumus potiorem, ac minores facere servitia consueta.[21]

SECTION 2—TIME OF ORDINATION AS A BASIS

Among the earlier notions of the bases for precedence was the priority of the conferral of Orders. One of the first instances is found in the letter of Pope St. Gelasius (494) to the Bishops of Lucca (Italy).[22] The same idea was put into legal form by the Council of Agde (506).[23] But the legal principle really took its origin from a letter of Pope Gregory I (590-604) to the Bishop of the Angles.[24] The summary of this chapter in the Decretals, *Prius ordinatus, ceteris paribus, prior et major habendus est,* succinctly summed up the basic notion of this letter.[25]

This principle of priority was intended to solve the problem of precedence between persons of equal rank, as in the case of two bishops, two priests or two deacons. Whichever one was ordained earlier was to be considered greater in matters of precedence. The decretalists found various ways in which the words *"ceteris paribus"* of the famous chapter were left unrealized, and therefore pointed to cases wherein priority of ordination did not give precedence. Hostiensis cited what was later to become another basis for precedence as one of the exceptions or cases of

---

21 C. 15, *de M. et O.*—A. Potthast, *Regesta Pontificum Romanorum inde ab anno post Christum natum MCXCVIII ad annum MCCCIV* (Berolini, 1874-1875), n. 9566 (hereafter cited as Potthast).

22 ". . . nec cuiuslibet utilitatis, seu presbyterum seu diaconum his praeferre, qui ante ipsos fuerint ordinati."—Epist. XIV, cap. II, cited as c. 7, D. 75—Jaffé, n. 636.

23 Can. 23, cited as c. 5, D. 74—Bruns, II, 150; can. 65—Bruns, II, 159.

24 C. 1, X, *de M. et O.*—Jaffé, n. 1829.

25 Although these summaries were added by various canonists of the XII and XIII centuries, they have no binding force. However, there is some historical value in them. Cf. Stickler, *Historia Fontium,* p. 248.

inequality namely, when the one was ordained by a higher ranking prelate, even though the second was ordained earlier.[26] Likewise, stated Hostiensis, a contrary custom or special privilege could intervene to render the priority rule inapplicable: for instance, the Patriarch of Constantinople outranked the other Oriental patriarchs by special privilege;[27] likewise the Church of Ostia outranked the suburbicarian Churches of Rome, and therefore also did its bishop. In either case, earlier ordination or consecration did not furnish a valid basis for precedence.[28] But he ruled out any custom which gave precedence to someone ordained later over someone ordained earlier, or which put a man of lower Orders ahead of a man in higher Orders, without the justifiable basis of higher dignity or office, or greater merits easily recognizable, a principle enunciated by Innocent IV (1243-1254). In both his enumerations of the bases of precedence, Hostiensis adopted the time or priority of ordination as a last-resort criterion. Boich, on the other hand rated it second last in his list, with the age of the person as the last criterion.

Later decretal legislation from Pope Boniface VIII (1294-1303) put into legal form as a rule of law what had been only a summary of a chapter in the decretals of Gregory IX: "Qui prior est tempore, potior est iure."[29]

SECTION 3—CONSECRATION AS A BASIS

Early legislation on this basis simply acknowledged precedence to a bishop over the other clergy, without stating specifically why. For instance, the Council of Laodicaea (343-381) forbad priests to enter the synod before the bishops.[30] The late date at which such norms were given may be an indication that there had been no particular problem prior to that date regarding the matter of precedence. But shortly after this example of the need for such legislation, the IV Council of Carthage (398)

---

26 *Commentaria,* Lib. I, *de M. et O.,* ad c. 1, s.v. *ordinatus,* p. 170.

27 Cf. *infra,* pp. 36 ff.

28 *Commentaria, loc. cit.,* s.v. *habeatur.*

29 Reg. 54, R.J. in VI°; Joannes Andreas indicated that this principle was applicable to questions of precedence, in his *glossa ad casum,* ad Reg. 54.

30 Can. 56, cited as c. 8, D. 95—Bruns, I, 79.

found it necessary to reaffirm that right of bishops over their priests.[31]

The I Council of Braga (Portugal) in 561 helped to establish the relative precedence of a bishop over his fellow bishops according to the date of their consecration, an early example of the priority rule established some forty years later by Gregory I.[32] Before giving this now famous rule of precedence, Gregory had insisted that bishops take their proper place, whether in council or in any other matter wherein order was demanded.[33]

The IV Provincial Council of Toledo (Spain) in 633 assigned to bishops a preferential place in synods, with the priests sitting behind them, and the deacons standing in sight of the bishops.[34] The gradation of clerics according to their rank, as found in the *Constitutum Silvestri,* gave first place to the bishop.[35]

With the coming of the period of the decretists and decretalists, reasons were sought for this precedence of the bishop over his clerics. Rufinus (1158) maintained that it was because of their power to consecrate, and that the episcopate was more properly a dignity (implying administration) than an Order.[36] Bernard of Pavia (+1213), on the other hand, attributed the superior rank of the bishop to his consecration.[37] And Hostiensis (ca. 1270) maintained a third position: that the superior rank of a bishop was attributable also to his prelacy or a special dispensation, citing as proof the power of a bishop to punish and administer in matters not requiring consecration, even before he had been consecrated, provided his election had been at least confirmed.[38]

31 Can. 35, cited as c. 10, D. 95—Bruns, I, 145.

32 Can. 6, cited as c. 1, D. 18—Bruns, II, 34. This cannon is given in a *Palea* in the *Decretum,* and is cited as drawn from a Council of Chalon sur Sâane (France); but, as the *Correctores Romani* noted, it was actually drawn from the I Council of Braga.

33 "Episcopus secundum ordinationis suae tempus sive ad consedendum in concilio, sive ad subscribendum vel in qualibet alia re, sua attendere loca decernimus, et suorum sibi praerogativum ordinum vindicare."—cited as c. 5, D. 17—Jaffé, n. 1265.

34 Can. 4, cited in the *glossa* ad c. 20, D. 93—Bruns, I, 222.

35 Cited as c. 5, D. 93—Mansi, II, 626.

36 *Summa Decretorum* (ed. H. Singer, Paderbornae, 1902), pp. 45-46.

37 *Summa Decretalium* (ed. Th. Laspeyres, Ratisbonae, 1860), p. 20.

38 *Commentaria,* Lib. I, *de M. et O.,* p. 174.

He agreed with the earlier decretalists, however, that the episcopal consecration was also a source of precedence.[39] Boich in his commentary on the decretals acknowledged precedence to a bishop solely because of his consecration. This he regarded as that something which made a bishop greater than a priest; he did not offer any definite statement with reference to the nature or the cause of this difference.[40]

SECTION 4—DIGNITY AS A BASIS

There is no express or general rule in the *Corpus Iuris* to the effect that one who has authority over another also has the prerogative of precedence over that person; the glossators and commentators on the *Corpus* developed this rule as a juridical conclusion, based on the legislation which permitted reverential honors to certain persons in authority, in virtue of that authority.

The fifth canon of Distinction 93 acknowledged preference to someone in higher Orders, but the glossator mentioned the exception: unless the one in lower Orders held an administrative post over the one in higher Orders, as in the case of the archdeacon over the archpriest.[41] The same exception was mentioned by Rufinus (1158)[42] and by Bernard of Parma (+1263).[43] Bernard of Pavia (+1213) agreed with the earlier commentators, but he explained the preferential position of the archdeacon as deriving from dispensation,[44] in the much the same way as Hostiensis (ca. 1270) was to do, while interchangeably referring to this basis also as *potestas*. As an example he cited not only the customary archdeacon-archpriest relationship, but likewise the precedence of an archbishop over a bishop, a primate over an

---

39 *Loc. cit.;* Cf. c. 9, X, *de consecratione ecclesiae vel altaris*, II, 40. The letter (1233) referred to was directed by Pope Gregory IX to the Bishop of Astorga (Spain) and clearly indicated that the power of consecrating was part of the episcopal power of Orders, not of jurisdiction.—Potthast n. 9203.

40 *Commentaria,* Lib. I, *de M. et O.*, ad c. 15, n. 7, s.v. *praelatura triplex*, p. 143.

41 *Glossa ordinaria* ad c. 5, D. 93, s.v. *honorem*.

42 *Summa Decretorum*, pp. 185, 189.

43 *Glossa ordinaria* ad c. 15, X, *de M. et O.*, s.v. *consueta*.

44 *Summa Decretalium*, p. 20.

archbishop, and a papal legate over a primate. All of these were bishops by Orders; therefore, any basis for precedence was necessarily to be sought outside this standard. This led the decretalists and other commentators to look to the notion of superiority also by reason of a greater administrative position or authority.[45] In his commentary, when discussing this point, Hostiensis designated this basis as *praelatio,* and pointed to the new example of the elected but un-consecrated bishop's precedence by reason of his election and confirmation.[46]

---

45 *Summa Aurea, de M. et O.,* s.v. *in quibus consistat maioritas,* p. 81.

46 Lib. I, *de M. et O.,* c. 15, n. 2, p. 174.

CHAPTER II

PRECEDENCE FROM THE COUNCIL OF TRENT TO THE PRESENT CODE OF CANON LAW

Preliminary Notions of the Sources

Article 1. The Development of the *Corpus Iuris Canonici*

With the completion of Gratian's Collection the *Concordia Discordantium Canonum* (1140), a new era began for the science of canon law; it gave jurists the most complete collection of earlier legislation thus far compiled. With its acceptance as the *Decretum Gratiani,* there remained for later collectors only such norms as had been not included by Gratian in his collection, or such as were issued after the completion of the *Decretum.* These two groups of norms Pope Gregory IX ordered collected into one volume and promulgated as an exclusive collection in 1234.[1] Although originally known as the *Liber Decretalium Extravagantium,* or the *Liber Extra* (X), this collection is more commonly known today as the *Decretales Gregorii Papae IX,* despite the fact that not all the documents contained therein are decretals.[2]

In a similar way, later pontiffs made collections of their own legislation and of other decretals not yet found in an earlier collection: in 1298 Pope Boniface VIII issued his *Liber Sextus;*[3] Pope Clement V died before the promulgation of his *Liber Septimus (Clementinae),* which was later published by Pope John XXII.[4] These two collections were authentic, and considered as general laws all promulgated at one time. The *Liber Sextus* of Boniface VIII was also an exclusive collection: any laws promulgated between the time of Gregory IX and the time of

---

1 Bull, *Rex pacificus,* 5 sept. 1234—*Corpus Iuris Canonici,* ed. Lipsiensis secunda, post Aemiliii Richteri curas . . . instruxit Aemilius Friedberg, 2 vols. (Lipsiae: Tauchnitz, 1879-81; [ed. anastatice repetita; Graz: Akademische Druck-u. Verlagsanstalt, 1955]), II, pp. 1-4 (hereafter cited as Friedberg).

2 Stickler, *Historia Fontium,* p. 242.

3 Bull, *"Sacrosanctae Romanae Ecclesiae,"* 3 mart. 1298— Friedberg, II, 933-935.

4 Bull, *Quoniam nulla,* 25 oct. 1317—Friedberg, II, 1129-32.

this collection but not incorporated in the latter were considered abrogated. Both of these collections abrogated any previous legislation contrary to decretals contained in them.[5]

Two more collections were made, but they had private authority only: the *Extravagantes Joannis XXII* (edited by John Chappuis in 1500) and the *Extravagantes Communes* (published in 1503).[6]

The *Corpus Iuris Canonici* was the sum total of these six component collections; they have been so called since Gregory XIII referred to them as such in promulgating the Roman edition in 1580.[7]

Although this collection of all collections was complete before the Council of Trent (in pre-Roman editions), it is proper that it be treated in this period for after the Council of Trent the *Corpus Iuris* was the basic canonical collection. It served as a transition from the pre-Tridentine period to that following the Council, when much attention was given to its correction and new promulgation. It was to serve, too, as the main source of legal norms throughout the present period, for the majority of the commentators used it as the basis for their canonical studies.

Gratian's collection was so honored and respected that it seemed to become the prevailing law. This was due to the richness of its matter, its scientific method, and its influence on judges and teachers, according to Stickler's analysis of it.[8] It was famous, too, for its harmonization of conflicting canons and its teaching utility. Because of the *Decretum Gratiani,* canon law came to be taught as a separate subject apart from theology. During the reign of Pope Gregory XIII (1572-1585) the revision of this collection was completed. This text of the Roman Correctors was approved by Gregory in a brief of July 1, 1580.[9] When this corrected version was finally printed in 1582, a second brief

---

5 Alphonsus Van Hove, *Commentarium Lovaniense in Codicem Iuris Canonici,* Vol. I, Tomus 1, *Prolegomena* (ed. altera; Mechlinae-Romae: Dessain, 1945), pp. 363-66 (hereafter cited as Van Hove, *Prolegomena*).

6 Stickler, *op. cit.,* pp. 270-71.

7 *Cum pro munere pastorali,* 1 iul. 1580—Friedberg, I, pp. LXXIX—LXXXII.

8 *Op. cit.* p. 217.

9 *Cum pro munere pastorali*—Friedberg, I, p. LXXIX.

from the Pope prohibited any changes in the text and forbad the use of any other text.[10]

The reported approval of Pope Eugene III (1145-1153) lacks historical foundation; according to Van Hove (1872-1947), neither the revision made by order of the Roman Pontiffs in the XVI century, nor custom, gave this collection as a whole the force of law. The juridic value of legislation found therein was the same as if it had never been included. However, many of the texts of the decree (even though particular or spurious legislation), as well as some of the maxims *(dicta)* of Gratian obtained the force of universal law by the fact that the *Decretum* was taught publicly in the schools, commented upon, and received by the popes and various tribunals in many phases of law.[11] Cicognani does not hold this opinion; he states that

> . . . the schools have never had the power thus to attribute legal force to canons. It is true that the courts can give the force of juridic interpretation to canons; but they usually quote them in the light of their own proper force and not because they are included in the *Decretum.*[12]

Wernz (1842-1914) followed a middle course. He stated:

> . . . If we deny the entire collection of Gratian the force of an official collection of universal law, we can by no means refuse to admit that not a few canons or texts of Gratian have become in various ways in the course of time authentic and therefore universal law.[13]

A final, but unofficial, opinion was expressed by Gasparri (1852-1934):

> Gratiani Decreto publica nullo tempore accessit auctoritas. Quamvis enim illud emendandum edendumque Apostolica Sedes haud semel curaverit, nunquam tamen authenticum declaravit, nec vim legis omnibus et singulis contulit canonibus qui in eo referebantur . . .[14]

---

10 *Emendationem,* 2 iun. 1582—Friedberg, *loc. cit.*

11 Van Hove, *Prolegomena,* pp. 345-46.

12 *Canon Law,* trans. Joseph M. O'Hara and Francis J. Brennan (2 ed. rev.; Westminster, Maryland: Newman Press), p. 288.

13 Franciscus X. Wernz; *Ius Decretalium* (6 vols., Romae et Prati, 1898-1914), I, p. 349, in note 39.

14 *Codex Iuris Canonici,* Praefatio, p. xxi.

Article 2. The Development of Later Sources

SECTION 1—PAPAL LAW

Because of the internal unity of the legislation contained in the *Corpus Iuris Canonici,* it is easy to see the importance it was to have in this period of Church legislation and legislative development. It was the acme of legislative and doctrinal activity of that classical and golden period of law, the period of the *ius decretalium.* It was to be the foundation on which Church discipline would be built for centuries.[15]

In his excellent treatment of this period of juridical development, Stickler states that the *ius decretalium* of the pre-Tridentine period was a composite of pure Christian, much Roman, and some German elements, all solidly built into a single structure, the *Corpus Iuris.* Despite its defects, it came very close to meeting the needs of jurists of that day. This explains its continued use and influence for centuries after its appearance. However, with the passing of the centuries it became less and less perfectly suited to the changing needs of the Church, needs that arose from extraordinary necessities and circumstances. It became imperative that new norms be developed while the old had to be adapted to keep pace with life inside the Church. For this reason, the Pontiffs looked for new norms and new compilations to assist them.[16]

But, because of the same elements that led to the so-called Reformation, the authority of the Church was being rejected more and more, especially in regard to its discipline. With the coming of the heresiarchs, there was an even more urgent need for disciplinary reform—their own battle cry. The "deformed reformation" brought about a new order: it demanded a new evolution and new activity in legislation; it necessitated a new organization of the Catholic communities in the lands of the apostates, and new norms to regulate the relations of Catholics with heretics; in Catholic regions a territorial organization had to be formed to counteract the new demands for greater liberty; most especially the central authority of the bishop had to be

15 Stickler, *op. cit.,* p. 275.

16 *Ibid.,* pp. 277-78.

restored and confirmed. The institutes of the earlier period which had effected decentralization of the episcopal power had to be tempered. For the same reason, the religious and their exemptions had to be given more definite limits; procedural law and its workings had to be speeded up. In general, the acceptance of the authority of the Roman Pontiff needed reconfirmation.[17]

Much of the new legislative activity came because of demands from the regions outside Europe. Although the Faith was lost in much of Europe, it rose up strong in the mission lands. But, for such lands and peoples in their Christian infancy, the laws governing European Catholics could not be invoked in their entirety, or with full vigor. For them, a new set of criteria and norms arose, which became a substantial addition to the *ius decretalium*. This new juridic activity, the *ius novissimum,* was of greater importance in this epoch of juridical history than the adaptation of the *ius decretalium*. It was this new set of juridic norms that immediately preceded the present day Code of Canon Law.[18]

All the general laws of this period flowed from two universal sources: the Roman Pontiffs and the general councils of Trent and the Vatican. Insofar as the authority of the council is joined indivisibly with the Pope by reason of its convocation, continuation or suspension, and approval, even the conciliar canons can be reduced in some way to the basic *ius pontificium*.

The work of the needed counter-reformation had to be carried out by a general council for two reasons: the need for reform was so widespread that nothing less than an ecumenical council could be expected to be successful; the acceptance of papal authority was at such a low point as to be almost totally ineffective for such a measure. It was probably for these reasons that the Council of Trent was called in 1545 in an effort to bring the needed reform. Therefore, the *ius novissimum* could also be called the *ius Tridentinum*.

But the further development of the reform law still depended upon the pontiffs, because the Council itself recognized the exclusive right of the Papacy to authentically promulgate, interpret,

---

[17] *Ibid.*, pp. 278-81.

[18] *Loc. cit.*

derogate, extend or change any of the decrees of the Council. With the legislation for the mission lands reserved to the Holy See, even the *ius novissimum* and the new juridic institutes added to the *ius decretalium* were evolved and developed exclusively by the Holy See.[19] This was to be done in great part by means of the papal constitutions, briefs, letters, and other forms of papal documents that were issued for the purpose of meeting the specific needs as they arose.

SECTION 2—THE ROMAN CONGREGATIONS

Prior to the time of the Council of Trent (1545-1563) papal legislation consisted largely of constitutions, bulls, briefs and decrees coming more or less directly from the Roman Pontiff. The new law as formed in this post Tridentine period was to come from delegated sources to a greater extent. The spread of Christianity and the increased burdens of administration in a more highly centralized ecclesiastical government made it necessary for the popes to enlist help from various organs; the extra arms to help with the extra work were to be those of the Roman Curial offices, either created anew, or given new duties: the Sacred Congregations, Tribunals and Offices. Of particular importance at this early stage were two congregations, one for the interpretation of the Council of Trent and its legislation, the other for the Propagation of the Faith. These were the chief instruments in the hands of the Pontiffs as they reformed and adapted the old law and developed the new.

A. The Sacred Congregation of the Council

With a full realization that it was of very little help to establish laws, unless there was someone to effectively carry out their application by means of a proper interpretation, Pope Pius IV (1564) established the Sacred Congregation of Cardinals for the Interpretation of the Council of Trent.[20] To St. Charles Borromeo

19 *Ibid.*, pp. 281-82.

20 Motu proprio, *Alias nos nonnullas*, 2 aug. 1564—*Bullarum Diplomatum et Privilegiorum Romanorum Sanctorum Pontificum Tauerinensis Editio.* (ed. A. Tomasetti et F. Gaude, 24 vols. et Appendix, Augustae Taurinorum, 1857-1872; 5 vols., Neapoli, 1867-1885), VII (pt. 1), 300 (hereafter cited as *Bull. Rom. Taur.*).

(1538-1584) as its prefect, along with his eight episcopal helpers, was given this commission:

> . . . quatenus ipsi seu eorum major pars, conjunctim vel divisim, eorum arbitrio etiam tamquam executores dictarum literarum, constitutionum, et decretorum praedictorum, constitutiones et ordinationes ac decreta praefata, juxta tenores eorum ac literarum desuper confectarum, per quoscumque poenitentiariae, vicariae, et camerae ac rotae curiarum ac tribunalium praedictorum judices et officiales, sub excommunicationis latae sententiae, ac privationis officiorum et aliis eisdem cardinalibus benevisis, etiam pecuniarum, eo ipso incurrendis poenis, firmiter observari faciant . . .[21]

Inasmuch as the Council of Trent legislated for some forms of precedence, this Congregation had competence in that field.[22]

B. The Sacred Congregation for the Propagation of the Faith

The history of this Congregation began under Pope Pius V in 1568 with the erection of a Congregation of Cardinals for the spread of the Faith, both in the countries which had defected from the Faith, and also in the countries across the seas. Pope Gregory XIII in 1576 instituted another congregation of Cardinals to do the same work for the Oriental schismatics. Only in 1599 was there to be a congregation for this purpose with the name and organization as it is found today, set up by Pope Clement VIII (1592-1605).

Finally, in 1622 the Congregation was definitely established by Pope Gregory XV (1621-1623).[23] This Congregation was given full competence in matters and cases in those mission lands which were subject to its jurisdiction. In more important matters, the consent of the Roman Pontiff was required.[24] It was re organized and given a very definite field of operation by the Constitution

21 *Ibid.*, no. XCIX, §1.

22 Sess. XXV, *de regularibus*, c. 13.

23 Const., *Inscrutabili*, 22 iun. 1622, § 8—*Codicis Iuris Canonici Fontes* (9 vols.: Vols. I-VI, ed. P. Gasparri; Vols. VII-IX, ed. I. Serédi; Romae: Typis Polyglottis Vaticanis, 1923-1939), n. 200 (hereafter cited as *Fontes*).

24 Franciscus Wernz—Petrus Vidal, *Ius Canonicum*, (7 vols. in 8; Vol. II, 3 ed.; Romae: Apud Aedes Universitatis Gregorianae, 1943), II, 504.

Sapienti consilio[25] and the *Ordo Servandus*,[26] both of which were issued in 1908 by Pope St. Pius X (1903-1914).

C. *The Sacred Congregations of Rites and Ceremonies*

In January, 1588, Pope Sixtus V (1585-1590), with the promulgation of the bull *Immensa aeterni,* created fifteen congregations in a complete re-arrangement of the Roman Curia.[27] The fifth of these was created with the intention that ". . . veteres ritus sacri ubivis locorum . . . a quibusvis personis diligenter observentur."[28] This was the Congregation for Sacred Rites and Ceremonies. Its eight purposes, included the solution of controversies over precedence.[29]

An allied congregation dealing with matters of precedence was the Ceremonial Congregation, whose origin is somewhat indefinite. It seems that this Congregation did not begin with its being named in the bull *Immensa aeterni,* in 1588. McManus explains its origin in this way:

> Because of the fact that the Ceremonial Congregation as such is not mentioned in the bull *Immensa,* authors have more often stated that it was founded subsequently by Pope Sixtus, or that it gradually assumed a separate existence, distinct from the Congregation of Sacred Rites. A final alternative, and perhaps the most reasonable, is based on the assertion of Haine (1815-1900) that the S. Ceremonial Congregation antedated the Congregation of Rites, and was in fact founded by [Pope] Gregory XIII in 1572 . . .
>
> The best explanation of the relation between the two congregations that can be offered now is that Pope Sixtus V included in the new Congregation of Sacred Rites what had belonged to the Ceremonial Congrega-

---

25 *Fontes,* n. 682.

26 *Ordo servandus in S. Congregationibus, Tribunalibus, Officiis Romanae Curiae,* 29 sept. 1908—*Fontes,* n. 6459 (hereafter cited as *Ordo Servandus*).

27 *Bull. Rom. Taur.,* VIII, 985-999.

28 *Ibid.,* p. 989.

29 Controversias de praecedentia in processionibus aut alibi ceterasque in huiusmodi sacris ritibus et caeremoniis incidentes difficultates cognoscant, summarie termminent, et componant.—*Ibid.,* p. 990.

tion prior to 1588, but that the latter regained its separate status shortly thereafter.[30]

The Congregaion of Ceremonies had as its field of activity the liturgical ceremonies of the Popes and Cardinals, other ceremonies of a profane nature in the Papal Court, and the matters of precedence involved in either place.[31]

D. The Sacred Congregation for Bishops and Regulars

In 1572 Pope St. Pius V (1566-1572) had instituted the Congregation for the Consultations of Bishops and Other Prelates. The reorganization undertaken by Sixtus V in 1588 resulted in another congregation, the Congregation for the Consultations of Regulars,[32] and an accurate definition of the powers of both. The former had the faculties to hear the petitions of patriarchs, primates, archbishops, and their inferiors with the exception of regulars, and to respond *sedule humaniterque* to the propositions, difficulties, questions, controversies, and whatever else they submitted for consultation. The Congregation was to look to the preservation of their dignity, jurisdiction, exemption, immunity, rights, privileges, and laudible customs, insofar as they did not come under the jurisdiction of the Congregation for the Council, or within the scope of judicial procedure.[33] The S. C. for Regulars was to be concerned with the doubts, controversies, and consultations proposed by Regulars, Mendicants, non-Mendicants, Hospitallers and all religious in general. Any internal difficulties were to be considered proper matter for the superiors to settle according to their special institutes. In 1601 Pope Clement VIII united these two into one Congregation for the Affairs of Bishops and Regulars.[34] This Congregation was suppressed by Pope St. Pius X in 1908. In its place he created the completely new Congregation for Religious.[35] This new Congre-

---

30 *The Congregation of Sacred Rites,* The Catholic University of America Canon Law Studies, n. 352 (Washington, D. C.: The Catholic University of America Press, 1954), p. 34.

31 Stickler, *Historia Fontium,* p. 336.

32 Bull, *Immensa aeterni—Bull. Rom. Taur.,* VIII (pt. 2), p. 993, §1.

33 *Ibid.,* pp. 994-95.

34 Stickler, *op. cit.,* p. 333.

35 Const., *Sapienti consilio,* 29 iun. 1908—*Fontes,* n. 682, § 5.

gation was to be competent in those matters which concerned any of the various groups of religious and in all matters so concerning them: whether between different religious bodies, or between bishops and religious, or between religious and others, as long as it was in disciplinary matters.

SECTION 3—THE ROMAN ROTA

There were three tribunals through which the Holy See exercised and had her judicial power since the XII century: the Sacred Roman Rota[36] and the Apostolic Signatura exercised that jurisdiction in the external forum; the Sacred Penitentiary exercised it for the internal forum. Of these three, the Rota was most important for its contribution to the development of the juridical norms of this era.

As the number of causes submitted for decisions by the Holy See grew larger, it became increasingly necessary for the Pontiffs to hear these cases through delegates, especially after the XII century. It was from the XIV to the XVIII centuries, however, that the Rota was to see its greatest judicial activity. This can be explained by the fact that during that period the Rota heard causes as a court of first instance as well as a court of appeal from the instance of some other tribunal. The more serious causes involving ecclesiastical discipline (except the criminal causes and others of the same type) were heard: this included the causes dealing with benefices, and others dealing with jurisdiction, exemptions, betrothals, adoptions, legitimations, preeminence and precedence, the rights of patrons, and other honorary

36 Ioannes XXII, bulla *Ratio iuris exigit,* 16 nov. 1331—M. Tangl, *Die päpstlichen Kanzleiordnungen von 1200-1500* (Innsbruck, 1894), Const. XI, p. 86. However, Bouscaren-Ellis state simply that the Rota was established in 1424.—*Canon Law, Text and Commentary* (2. rev. ed.; Milwaukee: Bruce Publishing Co., 1951), p. 165. Metz states that nothing is known for certain about the time of the foundation of the Rota, but it seems safe to say that it existed as an actual collegiate tribunal only for a comparatively short time before the issuance of the *Ratio iuris* of John XXII in 1331.—*The Recording Judge in the Ecclesiastical Collegiate Tribunal,* The Catholic University of America Canon Law Studies, n. 287 (Washington, D.C.: The Catholic University of America Press, 1949), p. 6.

rights of nomination, election, and confirmation of candidates for ecclesiastical offices.[37]

With the erection of the Sacred Congregation of the Council in 1564, the activity of the Rota was somewhat limited, since this Congregation also exercised judicial jurisdiction.[38] With the creation of other new congregations and the new definition of their various powers, the Rota began to slip notably from its XV century climax of activity. One by one its powers were transferred to various congregations: whatever had been dealt with by the Council of Trent automatically came under the jurisdiction of the Congregation of the Council, such as benefices, betrothals, and the rights and obligations of bishops; disciplinary causes of precedence were made the concern of the Sacred Congregation of Rites and Ceremonies, leaving only the judicial causes to the Rota; to the Congregation for the Propagation of the Faith were assigned former Rota activities concerning the mission lands, with the exception of causes which required pure judicial procedure.

The fruit of the labor of the Rota was of fundamental importance for the history of ecclesiastical law. In its decisions and its competence, the Rota jointed the skill and learning of its auditors to the authority of the Holy See to form the highest jurisprudence, from which there was no appeal. Many times this was done through a combination of both the supreme judicial and legislative powers of the Church. It is true that these decisions became law only for the litigant parties, and did not bind future decisions of the Rota, nor the judges of the lower courts. Nevertheless, they were received throughout the world with the greatest reverence, as supreme doctrinal and juridical norms which could be safely applied and used in the schools, or in the courts. In this way, these decisions helped determine the evolution of ecclesiastical law.[39]

---

[37] Benedictus XIV, const., *Justitiae et Pacis*, 6 oct. 1746—*Magnum Bullarium Romanum a beato Leone usque ad S.D.N. Benedictum XIV, seu eiusdem Continuatio*, 19 vols. (Luxemburgi, 1727-1758), XVII, 88-93 (hereafter cited as *Bull. Lux*).

[38] Stickler, *op. cit.*, p. 339.

[39] *Loc. cit.*

The fields of operation of these various congregations soon overlapped, despite their definitive reorganization by Pope Sixtus V in 1588.[40] To correct this confusion, Pope St. Pius X instituted the reform of the Roman Curia in 1908, which even more clearly outlined the specific areas in which each congregation was to be competent.[41]

Matters which were concerned with sacred rites in only a remote way, such as precedence, were withdrawn from the competence of the Congregation of Sacred Rites[42] and placed within the competence of the Congregation of the Council;[43] causes of a judiciary nature were reserved to the Rota.[44] Judgment of controversies regarding the precedence of religious was reserved to the Congregation for Religious.[45] If the controversies concerned the precedence observed in the Papal Chapel or Court, or that of the cardinals anywhere, they were reserved to the Congregation for Ceremonies.[46]

---

40 Bull, *Immensa aeterni—Bull. Rom. Taur.* VIII, 985-99.

41 Const., *Sapienti consilio,* 29 iun. 1908—*Fontes,* n. 682.

42 *Ibid.,* § I, n. 8°, 1.

43 *Ordo servandus,* Pars II. *Normae peculiares,* cap. VII, art. IV, n. 5°.

44 *Loc. cit.;* Pius X, const., *Sapienti consilio,* § I, n. 4°, 3, 4.

45 *Ibid.,* n. 5°, 2.

46 *Ibid.,* n. 9°; *Ordo servandus,* Pars II, *Normae peculiares,* cap. VII, art IV, n. 5°; art IX—*Fontes,* n. 6459.

CHAPTER III

THE BASES FOR PRECEDENCE AFTER THE COUNCIL OF TRENT

Article 1. General Notions of *Maioritas*

With the promulgation of the Decretals of Gregory IX canonists could more easily see the relation of one juridical notion to the other because of the arrangement of the decretals and canons of councils according to subject matter. This brought about a greater understanding of many phases of Church law such as rescripts, custom, elections, and obedience, to name only a few. In the first book of decretals, Gregory began in the twenty-third title to develop notions about various offices, such as the archdeacon and archpriest; he followed this with a treatment of judicial matters. Prior to this twenty-third title he had treated of prelates, the transfer of bishops, authority in general and the use of the pallium. Many of these earlier titles of the first book treated of people in authority, and the titles explained some of their obligations. It was a natural sequence, then, to devote the thirty-third title to the notions of superior rank and of the obedience due someone because of that rank *(de maioritate et obedientia).*

For these four centuries from the Council of Trent to the promulgation of the Code of Canon Law, the arrangement of Gregory's decretals was to serve as a basic outline for nearly all commentaries, precisely because it was on this book of decretals that most authors chose to comment. In these commentaries on *maioritas et obedientia* are found the basic notions of precedence.

That which makes one person greater because of his authority over another creates an obligation of obedience in the inferior or subject. It will be readily admitted that the people who have a right to a subject's obedience likewise have a right to his reverence and respect, at least in the ideal situation. With this same notion in mind, several commentators of this period defined superior rank *(maioritas)* as ". . . excellentia unius [personae] prae alia ex qua oritur obedientia debita superioribus . . ."[1]

Aside from this very evident example of superior-subject relationship, there are times when all will admit that there is an obligation of respect and reverence even to someone who has no particular authority over others, or any right to demand their obedience to his will. This leads to the conclusion that there must be other sources of superiority than that based on authority.

Boeckhn (1690-1752) was one of the earliest commentators of the post-Tridentine period to make note of these other sources in his work; but he did so just in passing: "Cum vero majoritas etiam latius pateat, et aliquando illis competat qui nulla jurisdictione pollent. . . ."[2]

DeAngelis (1824-1881), too, distinguished between a true superiority that begot the corresponding obligation of obedience, and a form of superiority or excellence which begot a form of obedience *improprie dicta,* or simply some act of reverence.[3]

Gradually the idea developed that there was a right to precedence from any kind of superiority, whether it was based on jurisdiction or some other form of power, or on neither. Leurenius (1646-1723) was one of the earliest to note this specifically when he defined *maioritas* as ". . . excellentia unius personae ecclesiasticae prae alia: unde oritur praecedentia, qua una aliam praecedit. . . ."[4] This understanding of superiority was taken up very shortly by Schmalzgrueber (1663-1735), who defined it as ". . . excellentia unius personae . . . et ante omnia attendenda est excellentia dignitatis."[5]

With the acquired notions of the past at his disposal, Wernz (1842-1914) was able to summarize the notions of his predecessors and point out specifically that which others had only alluded to:

---

[1] Engel, *Collegium, de M. et O.,* n. 1; Reiffenstuel, *de M. et O.,* n. 2; Verano, *Commentarius Paratitlaris, de M. et O.,* p. 583, n. 1; DeAngelis, *Praelectiones, de M. et O.,* p. 299.

[2] *Commentarium in Ius Canonicum Universum* (3 vols., Salisburgi, 1776), I, *de M. et O., in initio* (hereafter cited as Boeckhn, *Commentarium*).

[3] *Praelectiones,* I, *de M. et O.*

[4] *Forum Ecclesiasticum,* I, *de M. et O.,* q. DCCCCV; cf. S. B. Smith, *Elements of Ecclesiastical Law* (3 vols., Vol. I, 6. ed.; New York, 1887), n. 438.

[5] *Ius Ecclesiasticum Universum,* I (pt. 2), *de M. et O.,* § I, n. 1,

"*Maioritas* hoc loco intelligitur complexus iurium honorificorum, quae omnibus et *solis clericis* vi status clericalis sive ratione potestatis sive ratione ordinis propria sunt."[6]

It is proper, then, to proceed to an investigation of the ways in which this superior rank *(maioritas)* could be acquired by clerics. It must be recalled that it could be in connection with a true form of authority that required obedience along with reverence, or only in connection with some honor or dignity, not necessarily connected with authority, but nevertheless requiring some form of reverence.

In taking up the individual sources of superior rank, this study will limit itself to those sources which are proper to clerics in conformity with Wernz' definition of superior rank as a . . . *complexus iurium honorificorum quae omnibus et solis clericis . . . propria sunt.* . . . The sole exception will necessarily come in the treatment of religious, where lay persons will be considered also, because of their religious profession.

An attempt will be made in this study of the individual sources to clarify what was often less than clear in any one author. Sometimes by comparing or contrasting the different commentators' definitions and examples, it was possible to get a more accurate idea of the matter under discussion. For the sake of orderliness, these sources have been carefully divided into clear-cut sections. It will be noted very readily, however, that in many instances such a division cannot be made in actual fact; as a result some repetition will be found from section to section. It is hoped that this division will more readily point out the development toward the later, more accurate divisions of the basis of precedence in the Code of Canon Law.

Article 2. Dignity as a Basis for Precedence

With the development of ideas concerning superior rank and precedence, the pre-eminence of Orders gradually gave way to a rather undefined source of superior rank called variously *dispensatio, iurisdictio, potestas, praelatio,* and *dignitas.* Of the many commentators who were consulted, none gave a satisfactory definition of any of these terms, although each used one or the

6 *Ius Decretalium,* II, n. 160.

other. They did provide an example in most cases, however, in order to illustrate their meaning.

Although Hostiensis listed dignity as one of the sources of superior rank, he acknowledged it as such only in connection with an office to which was attached some form of administration; his examples usually referred the reader to the dignity of the archdeacon, as compared with that of the archpriest.[7] Henry Boich likewise equated dignity with prelacy in some form, and again the archdeacon was the example.[8] Earlier Bernard of Pavia (+ 1213) had gone beyond the archdeacon-archpriest example and explained the basis of power, jurisdiction, or dignity by applying it to the archbishop: it would give him precedence over a bishop; in the case of the papal legate, it would give him precedence over a primate.[9]

But in later centuries the notion of dignity as a source of superiority became more definite. Although there probably was no doubt about the pope's rights of precedence and those of others superior to the bishop, the early commentators of the Decretals did not treat of these persons specifically or as thoroughly as they treated the problem of precedence for the bishop and his inferiors.

Sabelli, relying heavily on private decisions of the Rota, also listed dignity as one of the sources of precedence.[10] This was taken up and given even more prominence by Schmalzgrueber, who stated that ". . . ante omnia attendenda est excellentia dignitatis."[11] Boeckhn listed dignity as a primary source of precedence: "Desumitur imprimis a propria dignitate vel excellentia, etiam ab Ordine. . . ."[12] Wernz maintained that dignity was the first basis for superior rank, citing canon 18 of the I General Council of Nicaea (325).[13] This canon gave a proper place to each cleric in the sanctuary apart from the people. The practical

7 *Commentaria,* Lib. I, *de M. et O.,* n. 2, ad c. 15.

8 *Commentaria,* Lib. I, *de M. et O.,* ad c. 15, p. 143.

9 *Summa Decretalium,* p. 20.

10 *Summa Diversorum Tractatuum* (4 vols., Venetiis, 1692), § *Praecedentia,* XXXII, n. 1 (hereafter cited as Sabelli, *Summa*).

11 *Ius Ecclesiasticum Universum,* Lib. I, *de M. et O.,* § I, n. 1.

12 *Commentarium,* I, *de M. et O.,* p. 247, n. 1.

13 Mansi, II, 675.

purpose of this was to distinguish the clerics from the laymen by way of place inasmuch as they were otherwise indistinguishable; for Wernz continued: "Praeterea clerici paulatim obtinuerunt titulos honorificos et habitus sibi solis proprios."[14] With the different and proper garments it became possible to distinguish the clergy from the laymen by external appearances. With that, a place set aside for the clergy became in time purely honorary. In the next paragraph, Wernz listed ordination, the priority of ordination, ordination by the Roman Pontiff, and jurisdiction as sources of superior rank. These apparently applied only to the clergy below the rank of bishop, for under the title of dignity he had already included the pope, cardinals, patriarchs, primates, metropolitans, and bishops. Other prelates, said Wernz, were first arranged according to the hierarchy of their jurisdiction: the other norms were to be used as secondary criteria.[15]

From what has been said, added to the examples given by the commentators, something of a definition can be offered for the basis chosen to represent all these various notions under one name—dignity. Dignity was that rank which a cleric enjoyed by reason of his office or position, over and beyond his power of Orders, because of which a special reverence was due him in view of his greater jurisdiction, special privilege, or custom.

On the basis of this definition the study of dignity as a source of superior rank will be divided into three parts: (1) dignity as a source with jurisdiction attached; (2) dignity attached by custom to an office or position to which jurisdiction need not be attached; (3) dignity attached to an office by reason of privilege.

SECTION 1—DIGNITY WITH JURISDICTION

In comparing the various authors of the post-Tridentine period, one notes that all the institutes given precedence because of dignity can be divided into three classifications: those with jurisdiction, those without it, and those whose dignity was a privilege granted them by a superior.

There is no dispute over the greatest dignity in the Church to which jurisdiction is attached. The papacy has commonly

14 *Ius Decretalium,* II, n. 161.

15 *Ibid.,* n. 162.

been acknowledged as possessing this dignity and as deserving of special reverence.[16] The supreme position acknowledged for the pope is further demonstrated by the fact that it was the practice in the Church that the pope confirm the election of bishops, if he did not actually appoint them himself. The Oriental patriarchs at various times had the custom of applying to the pope for a confirmation of their election, and of asking him for the pallium.[17]

The next institute considered as a criterion for precedence because of dignity while at the same time having some jurisdiction attached, was the archbishopric. Commentaries of this post-Tridentine period often spoke of the archbishop as a primate, more often as a metropolitan. The Provincial Council of Tours (1849) explained the superiority of the archbishop in this way: "Etsi omnes episcopi aequales sint ratione ordinis, nonnulli aliis praecellunt ratione jurisdictionis."[18]

DeLuca (1614-1683) listed archbishops immediately after primates. Because of the title of metropolitan given them by the law, he described them as twofold persons: as ordinaries in their own dioceses; as metropolitans, to whom as appellate [sic!] judges it was possible to have recourse [sic!] from the bishop, other prelates, and ordinary ecclesiastical judges in the province. Such a person certainly had to have greater power or jurisdiction if he was to strive for the purpose of an appeal from a bishop.[19]

Considering dignity with jurisdiction, all authors agreed that in rank immediately after the archbishops came the bishops of dioceses. About this there was no problem:

> Extra omnem controversiam est, primum et spectabiliorem locum deberi episcopo, juxta textum Tridentinum, sess. 25, c. 6, de reform.: "Episcopis praeterea ubique is honor tribuatur, qui eorum dignitati par est, eisque in choro et in capitulo, in processionibus et alliis

---

16 Engel, *Collegium, de M. et O.*, § I, n. 3.

17 Verano, *Commentarius Paratitlaris, de M. et O., Commentarium*, § 1, n. 2.

18 *Acta et Decreta Sacorum Conciliorum Recentiorum Collectio Lacensis* (7 vols., Friburgi Brisgoviae, 1870-1892) IV, col. 256 (hereafter cited as *Coll. Lac.*).

19 *Theatrum*, tom. III, disc. I, n. 17.

> actibus publicis sit prima sedes et locus, quem ipsi elegerint, et praecipua omnium rerum agendarum auctoritas.[20]

The power of the bishop was divided, however; in addition to his ordinary jurisdiction, he had also the power of Orders from his ordination and consecration. With this latter power he could confirm, ordain, and consecrate. For these reasons, the bishop was on several bases to be considered greater than someone not a bishop: because of his greater consecration he had higher rank in Orders; from his office as ordinary he had greater jurisdiction; because of the combination he had greater dignity than anyone else in the diocese. Anyone of these bases was sufficient to oblige anyone of a lower rank than a bishop to give him proper reverence, which could be shown by conceding precedence.

With the discussion of the bishop the study has reached the diocesan level, and herein lay the greatest amount of confusion since the very beginning of the problem of clerical precedence. This is not surprising, when one reflects that in the early Church there was far less communication between dioceses to create a problem between bishops and their superiors with precedence, except at councils. The legislation for these occasions was soon to be forthcoming, as will be seen later. Only in Rome itself was it to be expected that several of these institutes would be in close juxta-position at the same time at some large function, and Rome had its own rules of precedence. These served as a basis for norms to regulate precedence outside the city.

Giraldi (1692-1775), among others, noted that ". . . in dioecesi primum locum obtinet episcopus: hunc de jure communi sequitur vicarius generalis, archidiaconus, archipresbyter et alli canonici . . ."[21] How the principle of dignity with jurisdiction applied to each of them, will be seen in its proper place. Giraldi

---

20 Benedictus XIV, *De Synodo Dioecesana* (2 vols., 2. Parmensis ed.; Parmae, 1764), Vol. I, Lib. III, c. X, § 1.

21 *Expositio Iuris Pontificii*, I, Appendix to *de M. et O.*, p. 128 . . . Cf. also S.R.C., *Andrien.*, 25 sept. 1610—*Fontes*, n. 5257: *Decreta Authentica Congregationis Sacrorum Rituum* (7 vols., Romae, 1898-1927), n. 287 (hereafter cited as *D.* with decree number); Leurenius, *Forum Ecclesiasticum*, I, q. DCCCCXI; Schmalzgrueber, *Ius Ecclesiasticum*, I, *de M. et O.*, § I, n. 10; Benedictus XIV, *De Synodo Dioecesana*, Lib. III, c. X, § II.

was careful to note that although sometimes precedence was owed by reason of dignity, some were not strictly to be obliged to give this reverence, although they were lower in Orders, or dignity. This obtained by reason of jurisdiction, of some particular office, or of the fact that they were acting as proxy for someone of higher rank. Such was the case of the archdeacon, who, though less than the archpriest by way of Holy Orders, had precedence over him because of higher jurisdiction. It was disputed whether this precedence of the archdeacon was due because of custom, or from the common law. [22]

When two people of equal dignity had to determine their precedence rights, they had to resort to the prerogative of Holy Orders, according to Schmalzgrueber.[23]

Although the dignities here discussed had jurisdiction attached to them, and cardinals very often could be included in this category by reason of their holding the office of Ordinary of some diocese, the more common notion of the cardinalate pointed to it as a dignity without jurisdiction attached. It will, therefore, be discussed as such in the very next section. Though some patriarchs did have a special jurisdiction, the nature of their superior rank was traceable to a privilege, and it will be discussed in the third section on dignity.

SECTON 2—NON-JURISDICTIONAL DIGNITY

The high dignity of the cardinal today has not always been a mark of the cardinalate. Up to the XI century a simple bishop took precedence over a cardinal, at least on one occasion, in the signing of a constitution of Pope John XV.[24] The same was true of the four major Oriental patriarchs before the XI century.[25] Prior to that time, precedence was determined largely by the concept of Holy Orders, rather than by the notion of dignity. But with regard to cardinals at least, this gave way as the office

---

22 *Ibid.*, p. 129.

23 Vol. I (pt. 2), *de M. et O.*, § I, n. 2: Boeckhn, *Commentarium*, I, *de M. et O.*, n. 5.

24 Vincentius Petra, *Commentaria ad Constitutiones Apostolicas* (5 tomes in 2 vols., Venetiis, 1729), I, 78 (hereafter cited as *Commentaria*).

25 Engel, *Collegium*, de M. et O., § IV, *in initio*.

of cardinal was gradually exalted by increasingly important roles in Church affairs:

1) in 1059 Pope Nicholas II (1059-1061) made the cardinals the principal electors of the pope;

2) more and more frequently cardinals were sent as legates of the pope to councils. On these occasions they were given precedence over bishops in the signing of the acts, although they themselves were only priests or deacons. Cardinal bishops gradually began to precede all who were not cardinals. Then cardinal priests and deacons began to precede all other priests and deacons;[26]

3) Pope Innocent IV (1243-1254) shortly after the I General Council of Lyons (1245) granted cardinals the insignia of honor and dignity, the red hat.[27]

In giving an explanation of the great dignity attributed to the cardinals, Verano (1648-1713) adverted to these reasons: (1) the notion of the high offices given them; (2) the titles with which they were formerly decorated; as well as the many privileges and prerogatives which they enjoyed as papal advisers, such as the robes of royal purple.[28] He concluded that for these reasons cardinals deservedly preceded all prelates, bishops, archbishops, primates, and patriarchs. No one else had higher precedence that they, for ". . . nec inter membra et caput sit separatio . . ."[29] As will be seen in the next section, special prerogatives of honor were granted the four major patriarchs; by reason

26 Petra, *op. cit.*, I, 89.

27 N. Hilling, *Procedure at the Roman Curia,* trans. from the German (New York, 1907), p. 29. Citing Thomassinus (1619-1695), Rupprecht (+ 1763) stated that in 1244 Pope Innocent IV gave some red hats to cardinals whom he invited to be willing to shed their blood for the Church. It was thought that these cardinals were then confirmed at the Council of Lyons in 1245. Raynaldus (1595-1671) (n. 29) was also cited by Rupprecht as reporting that about 1316 Pope John XXII (1316-1334) refused a request of King Philip V of France (1316-1322) to send the red hat to a newly created cardinal instead of having him come to Rome for it, on the basis that ancient custom did not permit such a procedure.—*Notae Historicae in universi iuris canonici* (Venetiis, 1764), *de M. et O.*, nos. 12-13. No other source consulted in this study revealed any more accurate information.

28 *Commentarius Paratitlaris,* I, *de M. et O.*, § XIII, n. 5.

29 *Ibid.*, § XIV, n. 6.

of these honors, only the patriarch of Rome, the Pope, would have outranked them; the cardinals, logically, should have been preceded by these patriarchs.[30]

In this regard, Manrique (+1649) stated:

> . . . de jure praecedere debuissent S. R. E. Cardinales, sed consuetudo contrarium Romae servatur. . . . est rationabilis consuetudo; nam si cardinales sunt pars corporis Papae et fratres ejus, inconveniens esset et monstruosum inter fratres et unum corpus, alterum inserere; unde praedicti patriarchae nec cardinales praecedunt; imo postponuntur.[31]
>
> . . . sed quod dixi de praeferendis cardinalibus patriarchis intelligendum est de consuetudine Romanae Curiae cum alias sciam secundum plurium D.D. opinionem dubium esse de jure communi, praecipue illis quattuor patriarchis . . .[32]

Some archbishops, because of their dignity, were given a higher title with an accompanying higher rank and greater precedence. These were the primates. The notion of a primate was not too clear until the latter part of this past century, when it became increasingly evident that it was a merely honorary title. As Engel (1634-1674) noted:

> Sed quod aliquis patriarcha minor vel primas appellatur nihil in effectu tribuere, sed tantum augere titulum, quae vero alias in jure de patriarchis leguntur, de quatuor principalibus intelligi debere.[33]

The fact that very little is found about primates in the decisions of the Sacred Congregations, or in those of the Rota, is some indication that the status of a primate was not a very widespread

---

30 C. 23, X, *de privilegiis,* V, 33, citing c. 5 of the IV General Council of the Lateran (1215)—Henry Schroeder, *Disciplinary Decrees of the General Councils* (St. Louis: B. Herder Book Co., 1937), p. 564 (hereafter cited as Schroeder, *Disciplinary Decrees*).

31 *Tractatus de Praecedentiis et Praelationibus Ecclesiasticis* (Lugduni, 1635), q. xxxiii, *de praecedentia patriarcharum,* n. 3 (hereafter cited as Manrique, *De Praecedentiis*).

32 *Ibid.,* q. xiii, *de pracedentia cardinalium,* n. 2.

33 *Collegium, de M. et O.,* §IV, n. 23.

institute. DeLuca (+1683) recorded that in his day there were no primates in Italy.[34]

Verano regarded the fact that a primate had greater jurisdiction as the exception rather than the rule:

> Primates sunt quidam archiepiscopi potentiores, ut in Hispania Toletanus, in Germania olim Magdeburgensis, hodie Salisburgensis; quod vero vocetur aliquis primas vel patriarchae minor, parum in effectu tribui, sed tantum titulum auget.[35]

Only one commentator provided special norms for precedence among primates; he determined it according to the special privileges given not to them, but to their churches. In the absence of such a criterion, priority of promotion to the dignity was to be the deciding factor.[36]

Titular archbishops and bishops were also given precedence because of dignity without jurisdiction. The Congregation of Sacred Rites in 1656 declared that an archbishop, simply because he was an archbishop, had a higher rank than a bishop. On this particular base, precedence was given to a titular archbishop *(in partibus infidelium)* over the residential bishop of Leitmeritz (Litomerice) (Czechoslovakia).[37]

SECTION 3—DIGNITY BY WAY OF PRIVILEGE

Although other groups would seem at first to come under this division of dignity such as cardinals or primates, the commentators both before and after the Council of Trent referred solely to the patriarchs of the four major Oriental Sees when discussing precedence by way of privilege. Although commented on by decretalists and later commentators, the basis for this privilege goes back to a period many centuries before the decretals or the Council of Trent.

The I General Council of Nicaea (325) acknowledged that like the bishop of Rome, the bishops of Alexandria, Antioch, and

34 *Theatrum,* III, Disc. I, n. 15. Evidently he intended to say that Italy had no primate other than the Pope. However, none of the authors consulted named the Roman Pontiff as primate of Italy.

35 *Commentarius Paratitlaris,* I, *de M. et O.,* § XV, n. 2.

36 Leurenius, *Forum Ecclesiasticum,* I, q. DCCCCXI, n. 1.

37 S.R.C., *Pragen,* 29 ian. 1656—*Fontes,* n. 5484: *D.* 999.

Jerusalem had the dignity of being a type of supervisor of the surrounding provinces.[38] In 381 the I General Council of Constantinople also declared that it was fitting and proper, now that the city of Constantinople was the new capital of the Roman empire, that the bishop of that city should be second only to the bishop of Rome, as far as a primacy of hnor was concerned.[39] As will be seen in its proper place, this developed to the point where the IV General Council of the Lateran (1215) and Pope Innocent III recognized the primacy of honor of the patriarch of Constantinople among the other patriarchal sees.[40] It was acknowledged as a privilege which as such came from the Roman Pontiff.[41] Citing Barbosa, Manrique agreed that the discussions between the patriarchates as to which was the oldest for the purpose of determining precedence were missing the point. He concluded with Barbosa that ". . . eorum praecedentiam non tam ex antiquitate quam ex pontificum pendere privilegiis . . ."[42]

One of the reasons which justify the cardinalitial dignity today by custom, formerly gave higher rank to the patriarchs also: namely, their closeness to the Holy Father; but the patriarchs had their postion by a specifically-granted special privilege.[43] This higher rank put them immediately after the Roman Pontiff in rank as Engel noted:

> Quamvis olim post summum pontificem ante cardinales primum locum obtinuerint patriarchae, hodie

[38] Canons 6, 7—Schroeder, *Disciplinary Decrees*, pp. 29, 33.

[39] Canon 3—*Ibid.*, p. 65.

[40] Canon 5—*Ibid.*, p. 246.

[41] Leurenius, *Forum Ecclesiasticum*, I, *de M. et O.*, q. DCCCCX citing c. 6, D. 22, which is taken from c. 36 of the Quini-Sextum Synod of 692—Mansi, XI, 943-46; citing also c. 23, X, *de privilegiis*, V, 33, which is taken from c. 5 of the IV General Council of the Lateran (1215)—Schroeder, *Disciplinary Decrees*, p. 564; Manuel Gonzalez-Tellez, *Commentaria perpetua in singulos textus quinque Librorum Decretalium* (5 vols.; Lugduni, 1673), I, *de M. et O.*, ad c. 1, n. 5 (hereafter cited as *Commentaria*); Eugenius IV, bull, *Laetentur coeli*, 6 iulii 1439—*Bull. Lux.*, I, 335-36.

[42] Manrique, *De Praecedentiis*, q. xxxiii, *de praecedentia patriarcharum*, n. 3.

[43] "Propter privilegium major habetur ille cuius personam sedemve pontificis specialis concessio praetulerit, veluti patriarcha Constantinopolitanus Alexandrino. . ."—Gonzalez-Tellez, *Commentaria*, I, *de M. et O.*, *commentarium* in c. 1, n. 5.

> tamen cardinales *de consuetudine et iuris ratione* praesunt patriarchis tanquam unum corpus constituentes cum summo pontifice, et primarii ecclesiae catholicae directores.[44]

It is true that the major Oriental patriarchs, both past and present, had true jurisdiction, and in a higher degree than their subordinates;[45] therefore, they could be said to have precedence by reason of higher jurisdiction also. The determination of precedence within a grade or rank was ordinarily based on the priority of promotion to that rank. In the case of patriarchs, however, it was determined first by reason of the privilege given the four major sees;[46] this privilege, in turn, was largely based on the antiquity of these sees and their early importance in the Oriental Christian world. The patriarchs of the minor Oriental sees and the Latin patriarchs in this post-Tridentine period determined their precedence according to the date of promotion, unless some special privilege had been given their Church.[47]

The only other example of precedence by reason of privilege as listed by the commentators was that of the Cardinal Bishop of Ostia. He was given precedence by reason of the privilege given his Church, and from the fact that he was the consecrator of any new pope not yet consecrated.[48]

Article 3. Holy Orders and Consecration as Bases for Superior Rank and Precedence

As was seen earlier, the first norm of precedence was that of Holy Orders, which distinguished the cleric from the layman. For this reason clerics were set aside from the people in a separate

44 *Collegium, de M. et O.*, § IV, *in initio.*

45 . . . et sensu stricto denotavit solummodo Praesules Ecclesia, qui ex officio et vi sedis episcopalis haberent superiorem quandam judisdictionem ecclesiasticam in omnes Episcopos et Metropolitas et Primates sive Ecarchas vel Catholicos adicuius regionis. . . ."—Wernz-Vidal, *Ius Canonicum,* II, n. 517.

46 ". . . via privilegii seu Papae voluntate patriarcham Constantinopolitanum etsi antiquitate et origine Antiocheno et Alexandrino posteriorem supra eos principem locum obtinere."—Leurenius, *op. cit.,* I, q. DCCCCX.

47 "Post hos veniunt patriarchae minores, et primates, habita inter eos in ordine ad praecedentiam ratione specialium privilegiorum competentium illis ratione ecclesiarum suarum, et ubi talia non sunt, habita ratione majoris antiquitatis promotionis ad illas dignitates."—*Loc. cit.*

48 Schmalzgrueber, *Ius, Ecclesiasticum Universum,* Lib. I, *de M. et O.*, § I, n. 5.

part of the church [49] called the *presbyterium*.[50] It seems that legislation from the Council of Laodicaea (343/381) was the first to acknowledge that any person in a higher Order had greater rank than someone in a lower Order: the Council instructed deacons to show proper reverence to priests by not occupying their own places before the priests occupied theirs, but only afterwards, and at the bidding of the priests. The same canon required that greater respect be paid to the deacon by the lower clergy.[51] Legislation along similar lines was enacted in later councils.[52]

The classical text for the superiority of one in higher Orders is found in a decretal of Pope Gregory IX to the archpriest of St. Mary Major in Rome about 1230: "Statuimus ut presbyteri primum locum . . . et qui major est ordine, etiamsi postea sit receptus, in portione percipienda esse volumus potiorem."[53]

To understand the principle given above, it is necessary to know something about the canons and cathedral or collegiate chapters. It had become the custom at the time of Gregory IX for some cathedral and collegiate chapters to accept clerics in minor Orders as prospective canons. These served a sort of apprenticeship for three or four years while awaiting an opening in the college of canons. During this waiting period, these canons-to-be performed what the commentators referred to as the *servitia consueta* of cleaning the church, caring for the candles, and ringing the bells. When a vacancy did occur, the prospective canon who had been in the preparatory school the longest time, that is, who had been accepted or received first, was chosen to fill the

49 Canon 18 of the I General Council of Nicaea (325)—Mansi, II, 675.

50 The presbyterium of a later period was described as "... illa prima mansio quae prope altare majus solet cancellis includi, et tale seu diaconium appellatur . . ."—*Pampilonen.*, 3 febr. 1700—*Sacrae Romanae Rotae Decisiones Nuperrimae* (10 vols., Romae, 1751-1771), VI, 442, *Decisio* 245 (hereafter cited *S.R.R. Decis. Nuper.*).

51 Canon 20 cited as c. 15, D. 93—Bruns I, 75.

52 Canon 2 of the Council of Agde, France (506)—Bruns, II, 146; canon 23—*Ibid.*, p. 150; canon 65—*Ibid.*, p. 159; canon 4 of the Council of Tours, France (567)—*MGH, Concilia*, I, 123; canon 7 of the Council in Trullo (692) —Mansi, XI, 943-946.

53 C. 15, *de M. et O.*,—Potthast, n. 9566.

opening in the college. There was no regard for his higher or lower rank in Holy Orders compared with others who had been received at a later time. In this way, even though a priest had been waiting to join the chapter, a deacon or subdeacon who had been waiting longer would be chosen. As a result of this, many such clerics could go through their whole life without one of the motives for completing their preparation for and being ordained to the priesthood. Gregory had hoped that, by giving promotion to the cleric in highest rank in Holy Orders, he could entice more of the lower-ranking clerics to complete their preparation for ordination to the priesthood. For in this way they could have a better chance to obtain an office as canon in one of the chapters.[54]

It has been said that it was unthinkable to prefer a person in minor Orders to someone in major Orders, with all other things equal,[55] unless for the one exception commonly made: the archdeacon had come by custom to have superior rank over the archpriest, by reason of his greater office and dignity in the diocese. Now, however, some authors maintained that the custom of letting the *prior receptus* have first chance at promotion to the chapter should be respected,[56] since custom had always been respected as one of the greatest norms for determining precedence. But, in Gonzalez-Tellez words, it was this very thing which Gregory reproved when he ordered ". . . ut maior in ordine, licet posterior in receptione, praeferatur antiquioribus sed gradu inferioribus; quia temporis prioritas quoad praecedentiam attenditur inter aequales eiusdem gradus, non vero inter maiorem et inferiorem gradus obtinentes consideratur . . ."[57]

Boeckhn also maintained that Orders were to be used as a criterion for superior rank only if all other things, such as dignity and office, were equal.[58] That these other things were criteria or

---

54 Leurenius, *Forum Ecclesiasticum,* I, *de M. et O.,* q. DCCCCVI.

55 E. Pirhing, *Universum Ius Canonicum secundum titulos Decretalium distributum et nova methodo explicatum* (5 vols. in 4; Dilingae, 1674-77), I, *de M. et O.,* Sect. I, § I (hereafter cited as Pirhing, *Ius Canonicum*).

56 Felinus Sandeus (1444-1503), cited by Pirhing, *loc. cit.* Cf. Reg. 54, R.J., in VI°: *Qui prior est in tempore potior est in iure.*

57 *Commentaria,* I, *de M. et O.,* in c. 15, X, I, 33, n. 4.

58 *Commentarium,* I. *de M. et O.,* n. 3.

bases more important than Orders can be deduced from the fact that the prerogative of Orders was considered greater only than the prerogative of time or priority.[59] For only if both were ordained could priority of ordination come under consideration. If the time of ordination was the same for two clerics, then the next criterion was to be their ages, with the older having precedence. The sole exception occurred if one of the two who were ordained on the same day had been ordained by the pope. Even if such a one was the younger, he enjoyed superior rank and precedence over his senior by reason of this special privilege.[60] On the other hand, dignity and office were considered higher norms for superior rank when compared with Orders.[61] In this sense, dignity or office was to be considered first, regardless of Orders. If both persons had equal dignity, then the one in higher Orders had superior rank. If both were ordained or consecrated, then the date of ordination (priority) or the rank of the ordaining prelate was the distinguishing norm.

The early lists of the sources of superior rank included episcopal consecration.[62] It was originally the sole norm for determining the precedence of bishops over members of the clergy who were not consecrated. But by the year 561, the I Council of Braga had recognized the time-of-consecration norm to determine a bishop's precedence in relation to his fellow bishops.[63] By 1270, when Hostiensis wrote his commentary, superior rank was acknowledged for a bishop also because of his special power to administer as a bishop-elect those affairs of the diocese which did not require episcopal consecration.[64] However, he did not rule out episcopal consecration as a basis for superior rank completely. Whatever his precedence, the bishop did not lose it by his resignation from his episcopal benefice, however, according to a decree of

---

59 Leurenius, *Forum Ecclesiasticum, de M. et O.*, q. DCCCCVI.

60 Benedictus XIV, *De Synodo Dioecesana*, I, lib. III, c. X, § VIII, based on cap. 7, X, I, 33, a letter of Innocent III to the Bishop of Florence in 1206—Potthast, n. 2738.

61 Engel, *Collegium, de M. et O.*, § VI, n. 63; Boeckhn, *loc. cit.*

62 Hostiensis, *Commentaria*, lib. 1, *de M. et O.*, n. 2 ad c. 15 s.v. *maioritas multiplex est;* Boich, *Commentaria*, lib. I, *de M. et O.*, ad c. 15.

63 Canon 6—Bruns, II, 34.

64 *Commentaria*, lib. I, *de M. et O.*, p. 174.

the Congregation of Sacred Rites in 1606: ". . . titulum et ordinem semper retinere; et consequenter debere praecedere omnibus aliis episcopis post ipsum electis et consecratis. . . ."[65]

By the XVII century commentators, such as Pirhing (1606-1679), did not mention consecration specifically as a basis for precedence; he merely included it in the notion of *ordo,*[66] as did Leurenius (1646-1723)[67] and Reiffenstuel (1642-1703) at the beginning of the XVIII century.[68] But the Provincial Council of Rome (1725) stated that the precedence of archbishops and bishops was to be determined . . . *secundum suae ordinationis tempus* . . .[69]

From 1596 to 1904 several decrees came from the Congregation of Sacred Rites, each stating definitely that the precedence rights of a bishop were determined in these specific instances by the date of his preconization or nomination and confirmation in consistory.[70] An example of using consecration as a secondary criterion, however, was listed by DeHerdt (+1883): he called for its use when there was some bishop-elect who was not yet consecrated and some other bishop who was named in the same consistory with him but already was consecrated. The consecrated bishop then took precedence over the bishop-elect.[71] This case, according to DeHerdt, was to be considered as providing an exception to the *ceteris paribus* clause understood in the decree of

65 S. R. C., *Minerbina,* 4 martii 1606—*Fontes,* n. 5219.

66 *Ius Canonicum*, I, *de M. et. O.,* Sect. II, § I; see also Verano, *Commentarius Paratitlaris,* I, *de M. et O.,* § XIV, n. 2.

67 *Op. cit.,* I, q. DCCCCV.

68 *Ius Canonicum Universum,* II, *de M. et O.,* n. 3.

69 Tit. XVI, cap. 1, a—*Coll. Lac.* I, col. 372. This Council based its legislation on c. 1, D. 18, from Gratian: "Placuit, ut conservato metropolitani primatu ceteri episcopi, secundum suae ordinationis tempus. . . ."

70 S.R.C., *Aquileien.,* 30 sept. 1596—*Fontes,* n. 5176: *D.* n. 60; S.R.C., *Segobricen.,* 21 mart. 1609—*Fontes,* n. 5274: *D.* n. 270; S.R.C., *Regni Sardiniae,* 2 mart. 1641—*Fontes,* n. 5393: *D.* n. 734; S.R.C., *Pragen.,* 29 ian. 1656—*Fontes,* n. 5484: *D.* n. 999; S.R.C., *Ephesina,* 8 apr. 1656—*Fontes,* n. 5485: *D.* n. 1006; S.R.C., *Terulen.,* 20 nov. 1677—*Fontes,* n. 5623: *D.* n. 1606; S.R.C., *Iaren.,* 15 apr. 1904—*Fontes,* n. 6329: *D.* n. 4133.

71 *Praxis Pontificalis, seu Caeremonialis Episocoporum Practica Expositio* (3 vols., ed altera; Lovanii, 1873), I, 108 (hereafter cited as DeHerdt, *Praxis Pontif.*).

1609 cited above: all bishops under discussion were considered as having been already consecrated when the date of promotion was given as a criterion. If they were not, those who were consecrated had precedence over those who were not, which divided them into two classes. Each of these classes then looked to the priority of promotion in consistory to determine their precedence among themselves, according to DeHerdt.

Boeckhn maintained that it was necessary to consider consecration or blessing in the same way he had considered Orders: a secondary criterion for determining superior rank . . . *inter plures qui similem dignitatem obtinent*. . . .[72] Smith (1854-1895)[73] also held that consecration could be used as a secondary criterion for ecclesiastics in the same Order, but he insisted that it was the *time* of consecration that was to be the criterion, not the *fact* of consecration.[74] It is not clear that Boeckhn intended the time element to be important; it seems he did not, since he stated: ". . . benedictus vel consecratus praeponatur non benedicto vel non consecrato. . . ."[75] This was consistent with DeHerdt's exception to the *ceteris paribus* clause understood in all decrees about episcopal precedence.

But strangely, DeHerdt had just previously cited consecration as a normal criterion for precedence:

> Archiepiscopi, etiam titulares in partibus infidelium, praeferuntur episcopis et archiepiscopis consecratione junioribus, nec non aliis episcopali charactere senioribus sed gradu archiepiscopali posterioribus.[76]

DeHerdt considered as supporting his view, two decrees from the Congregation of Sacred Rites as cited above: the one sent to Prague, January 20, 1656, and the second, sent to Ephesus, April 8, 1656. These two are also cited in the footnotes of the Code of Canon Law to canon 280, which deals with the precedence of patriarchs, primates, archbishops, and bishops. Careful study of these two decrees will show that they support the norm of the code for episcopal precedence, namely the date of preconization

72 *Commentarium*, I, *de M. et O.*, n. 4.

73 *Elements of Ecclesiastical Law*, I, n. 611.

74 *Ibid.*, n. 439 (italics supplied).

75 *Loc. cit.*: cf. Reiffenstuel, *Ius Canonicum Universum*, I, *de M. et O.*, n. 5.

76 *Loc. cit.*

in the consistory, and that they were misunderstood by DeHerdt. For the sake of showing a pattern in these decrees of the Congregation in 1656, both earlier and later decrees on the basis for episcopal precedence will be quoted.

In 1596: "Coadjutores cum futura successione in Synodo Provinciali sedeant *juxta tempus eorum promotionum.*"[77] In 1609: "Circa praecedentiam inter episcopos *nullam aliam* rationem esse habendam, *nisi temporis electionis* seu promotionis ad episcopatum."[78] In 1641: "Praecedentiam regulandam esse *a die decreti consistorialis* super expeditione Eccesiae."[79] Then there are the two in 1656: "Ad archiepiscopum, *uti archiepiscopum majoritate gradus* supra episcopum praecedentiam spectare." This was in answer to a question concerning the right of precedence of a titular archbishop over a residential bishop. No mention was made of earlier consecration.[80] The second one seems to have been the one which most misled DeHerdt: "Num archiepiscopi titulares in aliena dioecesi existentes praeferri debeant episcopis, et archiepiscopis *consecratione junioribus,* nec non aliis episcopali charactere senioribus, sed *gradu archiepiscopali posterioribus,* ut puta ad ecclesiam archiepiscopalem post ipsius oratoris ordinationem translatis? Et EE. PP. praedictae [Sacrorum Rituum] congregationi praepositi, ad relationem Emi D. Card. Azzolini, 'Affirmative responderunt, extra tamen Ecclesiae ambitum intra quam Ordinario privative quoad omnes episcopos et archiepiscopos etiam seniores, praecedentia competit.' "[81]

Close examination of the wording of this decree will lead to these two conclusions: (1) a titular archbishop has precedence over bishops and archbishops who are his juniors by consecration; (2) a titular archbishop also has precedence over bishops who are his senior by consecration, but his junior according

77 S.R.C., *Aquileien.,* 30 sept. 1596—*Fontes,* n. 5176 (italics supplied): *D.* n. 60.

78 S.R.C., *Segobricen.,* 21 mart. 1609—Fontes, n. 5247 (italics supplied): *D.* n. 270.

79 S.R.C., *Regni Sardiniae,* 2 mart. 1641—*Fontes,* n. 5393 (italics supplied): *D.* n. 734.

80 S.R.C., *Pragen.,* 20 ian. 1656—*Fontes,* n. 5484 (italics supplied): *D.* n. 999.

81 S.R.C., *Ephesina,* 8 apr. 1656—*Fontes,* n. 5485 (italics supplied): *D.* n. 1006.

to the time of their promotion to the rank of archbishop. The second conclusion definitely rules out any application of this decree as proof that bishops derive precedence from the date of their consecration, because here someone who was consecrated earlier must concede to someone consecrated later, but promoted earlier to the archiepiscopal rank. As for the first conclusion, it does not follow that, just because those over whom an archbishop has precedence are his juniors by consecration, his priority of consecration is the reason for his precedence. In some cases this will, in fact, be true, at least in regard to bishops, but not always; even less often will it be true of the archbishops over whom another archbishop has precedence. It may or may not be maintained that the Congregation intended to change its policy in this matter; but in 1677, another decree states: "*Attendendum est tempus promotionis,*"[82] and, finally, another in 1904 which confirmed two earlier decrees: "*Praecedat ille qui prius in consistorio propostitus fuit,* iuxta decreta n. 270 Segobricen., 21 martii, 1609, et n. 1606 Terulen., 20 nov. 1677." [83] From this decree it is apparently safe to conclude that the principle of precedence derived from prior promotion has been presupposed during the intervening centuries. There seems to be no other conclusion than to say the DeHerdt misunderstood the 1656 decree to Ephesus.

It was because of the earlier notion of the bishop's precedence from the fact of his consecration that he was given precedence over cardinals prior to the XI century; for as often as not the cardinals were not consecrated bishops. Sometimes they were not even priests. The relative superior rank of both cardinals and bishops will be treated in more detail in its proper place.

Article 4. Seniority or Priority as a Basis for Superior Rank

In his *Summa Aurea* Hostiensis seemed to equate *antiquitas* with priority of ordination.[84] Later, in his commentary, he men-

---

[82] S.R.C., Terulen., 20 nov. 1677—*Fontes,* n. 5623: *D.* n. 1606.

[83] S. R. C., Iaren., 15 apr. 1904—*Fontes,* n. 6329: *D.,* n. 4133 (italics supplied by the writer).

[84] Lib. I, *de M. et O.,* n. 1, s.v. *in quibus consistat obedientia.*

tioned only the time of ordination, omitting any mention of age (*antiquitas*).[85] Boich had listed them both, definitely stating that the time of ordination gave higher rank than did age, and that age was to be the very last resort as a criterion to determine superior rank.[86] Panormitanus (Nicolaus de Tudeschis, Abbas Siculus, 1386-1453) was one of the first commentators to mention priority in regard to the receiving or conferring of an office as a possible criterion for superior rank,[87] in addition to priority of ordination or consecration.

The basic notions of these pre-Tridentine commentators were taken up with little change by commentators after the Council of Trent. Despite some differences in application, these commentators all derived their notions of priority primarily from a letter of Pope Gregory I to the Bishop of the Angles, found in the decretals as the chapter *Cum certum*.[88] Most of these commentaries proceeded to discuss and solve what looked like contradictions between this chapter of Gregory and other legislation, both earlier and later. From these discussions evolved a clearer notion of just what could be concluded from the decretal.

In regard to the priority of ordination, Gonzalez-Tellez' commentary on the chapter *Cum certum* offered one of the more detailed considerations,[89] and will be greatly relied upon in the treatment of superior rank as a basis for precedence. This decretal succinctly stated: ". . . sit vero inter Londoniae et Eboracae civitatis Episcopos in posterum honoris ista distinctio, *ut ipse prior habeatur qui prius fuerit ordinatus*."[90] It becomes evident from the briefest study of this text that the decretal dealt specifically with the time of the two bishops' consecrations, and the resultant rank or honor. It was not thought out of place for the decretalists to extend this same principle to priests and the

---

85 Lib. I, *de M. et O.*, n. 2, ad c. 15, s.v. *majoritas multiplex est.*

86 *Commentaria*, Lib. I, *de M. et O.*, ad c. 15.

87 *Commentaria in Quinque Libros Decretalium* (5 vols. in 7, Venetiis, 1588), Tom. II, *de M. et O.*, in c. 1, n. 4, s.v. *quid autem si non* (hereafter cited as *Commentaria*).

88 C. 1, X, *de M. et O.*,—Jaffé n. 1829.

89 *Commentaria*, I, *de M. et O.*, ad cap. 1, nos. 4-6.

90 Italics have been supplied by the present writer.

time of their ordination; it was frequently cited as a criterion for determining superior rank among those of equal grade or dignity. This extension of the original principle is another indication of the pattern followed by commentators after the Council of Trent: little distinction was made between Orders and episcopal consecration as norms for determining precedence. The one was included under the term of the other when the bases for superior rank were listed. Perhaps they justified this extension by combining *Cum certum* with the rule of law found in Boniface VIII's *Liber Sextus: Qui prior est in tempore, potior est in iure.* [91]

Gonzalez-Tellez (+ after 1673) studied this principle of *Cum certum,* the superior rank deriving from the earlier ordination by raising several possible objections. Some, confusing the spiritual with the juridical, might object that merits should be considered in any determining of the person to whom greater honor should be given, and not priority of ordination or some such mechanical norm. The matter was thought to be further complicated by the conclusion that the rule of priority or antiquity should result in a consistent preference of the older to the younger. But this was not always the case in actual fact.[92] It was objected, further, that this principle was inconsistent with ecclesiastical discipline and clerical modesty. The commentator recalled the scriptural reprimand of the Pharisees who enjoyed first places at banquets and in the synagogues as well as the public acknowledgment that came from a greeting in the forum.[93] It might be objected, too, that superior rank was properly being determined not according to this principle of priority, but rather by the degree of dignity of certain persons. For proof, Gonzalez-Tellez cited the canon *A subdiacono* of Gratian (1140),[94] which set up the principle that someone in higher Orders has precedence over someone in lower Orders. In addition, there was the chapter *Statuimus* of Gregory IX (1127-41), which established that

---

91 Reg. 54, R. J., in VI°.

92 Gonzalez-Tellez, *ibid.*, n. 4.

93 Matt., XXIII: 6-7.

94 C. 5, D. 93—Mansi, II, 626.

" . . . *qui maior est ordine,* etiam si postea receptus etiam in portione percipienda potiorem esse volumus. . . ."[95]

Having made these possible objections Gonzales-Tellez offered to defend the principle of Gregory in *Cum certum.* The objections raised were similar to those raised today by people who profess a lack of interest in places and signs of honor and dignity, forgetting that the primary purpose of observing precedence is to maintain peace and order in the Church, especially on public occasions. The answers given by Gonzalez-Tellez were similar to those expressed in the foreword of this work: the Pope was dealing with a human situation, in which human beings with their limitations were trying to establish a human norm by which someone could be said to deserve to go first, and another have the right only to be placed second or third in line. Against those who chose to cite the Scriptures in disproof of precedence, there was offered St. Paul's passage requiring that all proceed ". . . *decenter et secundum ordinem.* . . ."[96] If heaven needs to have a form of organization according to the ranks of the angels, how much more humankind here on earth?[97]

It was found agreeable to give superior rank to the person ordained earlier, for it was generally agreed that whoever received a dignity or office earlier should be presumed the more worthy, even though he was younger in years.[98] An important point was stressed by Gonzalez-Tellez in his mention that the familiar condition, *ceteris paribus,* had to be considered as presupposed in this principle of priority of ordination ". . . cum majoritas contenditur inter *aequali gradu* [therefore, all higher norms of precedence gave the parties concerned an equal rank—*ceteris paribus*] pollentes; non vero si una majori dignitati decoratur."[99]

This removed the chapter *Cum certum* from any conflict with the chapter *Statuimus (qui maior est ordine . . . potiorem esse volumus)* and the canon *A subdiacono,* which listed the major and minor Orders according to their relative superior rank. It

95 C. 15, X, *de M. et O.* Italics have been supplied by the writer.

96 I Cor., XIV: 40.

97 C. 7, D. 89—Jaffé, n. 1375.

98 *Glossa ordinaria* ad c. 7, D. 17.

99 *Commentaria,* I, *de M. et O.,* ad c. 1, 7 (Italics supplied).

will be recalled that in the treatment of these two chapters under the notion of precedence from Orders or consecration, it was stated that, if two people had the same rank from Orders or consecration, the time of the reception of their rank determined their superior standing, unless the ordination or consecration had been conferred by the Pope.

It can be seen, then, that the principle should now read: he who is ordained (or consecrated) earlier, should have superior rank over someone ordained (or consecrated) later, all other things being equal. Therefore, if A was ordained earlier than B, but B held an office considered more important because of the dignity or jurisdiction attached to it, or because of some special privilege, then, despite B's rank as junior by ordination (or consecration), he held superior rank by reason of his office, or privilege. It can be seen, then, how ordination (consecration) and the time of ordination (consecration) served truly as secondary criteria in any determining of the relative rights of precedence on the part of clerics among themselves.

Although there were particular occasions when the priority of ordination to minor Orders was used as a criterion,[100] the normal practice was to consider only the date of major Orders[101] or, more frequently, the Order of priesthood only.[102] Thus, if ordination was the highest criterion available (for simple clerics without any office or special dignity), the grade of Orders was the first criterion for superior rank. Only when both had the same rank in Orders could the priority of ordination rule be invoked as a criterion. However, allowance always had to be made for the exception or privilege to be discussed immediately: superior rank because of ordination by the Roman Pontiff. Adone further determined precedence rights for those in the same Order when also ordained on the same day by giving

---

100 S.R.C., *Comen.*, 18 apr. 1682—*Decreta Authentica Sacrorum Rituum Congregationis,* (7 vols. ed. Gardellini) Romae, 1807-1827), III, n. 2980.

101 Aloysius Adone, *Synopsis Canonico-Liturgica* (Neapoli, 1886), Lib. III, cap. VII, § III, n. 1997.

102 *Manuale Decretorum Sacrorum Rituum Congregationis* (Ratisbonae, 1873), cap. XX, art. VIII, § 7.

superior rank to the one who was named first and ordained first in his group.[103]

Priority of age or birth was the very last criterion, listed by a few of the commentators as a final resort, based more on reason than any juridical foundation.[104]

Article 5. Superior Rank Because of the Ordaining Prelate

Gonzalez-Tellez, writing in the XVII century, noted that superior rank resulting from ordination by a higher prelate was of rare occurrence in his day;[105] it is equally rare today, for the Holy Father to ordain a cleric to either minor or major Orders. Historically, it did happen in at least one instance which provided the occasion for a special decretal in that regard. A subdeacon of the diocese of Florence, Italy, had been ordained by the Roman Pontiff. His notions about this privilege were so exaggerated as to lead him to think that he was thereby exempt from the obligation of obedience to his local ordinary, the Bishop of Florence. In answer to an inquiry from the bishop, Pope Innocent III (1198-1216) gave in a reply in 1206 that was to serve as almost the sole basis for this criterion of superior rank, a letter known from its opening words, *Per tuas.*

The inquiry: ". . . utrum quis per ordinem subdiaconatus a Romano Pontifice susceptum a debita tibi [the Bishop of Florence] reverentia subtrahatur." The answer:

> . . . quod, etsi decens sit, ut illis, quantum convenit, a te inter alios tibi subditos deferatur, quos benignitas Apostolica collatione ipsius ordinis honoravit, per eam tamen ab obedientia, quam alias tibi debent, minime absolvuntur.[106]

The text indicates that the main purpose of the inquiry was concern for the subdeacon's failure to give proper reverence and obedience to his ordinary. It was almost in passing that the

---

103 *Loc. cit.*

104 Boich, *Commentaria,* I, *de M. et O.,* ad c. 15; Hostiensis, *Commentaria,* I, *de M. et O.,* n. 2, ad c. 15, s.v. *majoritas multiplex est;* Benedictus XIV, *De Synodo Dioecesana,* Lib. III, c. X, §VIII.

105 *Commentaria,* I, *de M. et O.,* ad cap. 7, note s.v. *Romano Pontifice.*

106 C. 7, X, *de M. et O.*—Potthast, n. 2738.

Pontiff honored the principle in his original reply that anyone ordained by him was to be given special preference over other clerics. This resultant superior rank was only one of the prerogatives permitted to clerics ordained by the Pope as found in the legislation of this period. Others included the necessary permission of the Pontiff to advance to higher Orders anyone who had received any lesser Order from him; it was also required that a greater number of witnesses be heard prior to the conviction or condemnation of anyone ordained by the Pope. In the list of Gonzalez-Tellez the third prerogative is the one of greatest interest in this discussion: among other ministers of the same grade, a cleric ordained by the Pope should have preference.[107]

With typical thoroughness, Leurenius dealt in greater detail than other authors with the question affecting those "*qui ratione dignitatis ordinantis praeferendi ab aliis.*"[108] The reason, as explained by Leurenius, was not that the cleric received anything more from such an ordination, than he would have received if he had been ordained by any lesser prelate,[109] but rather that the Pope, in ordaining him, judged him particularly worthy, as the letter *Per tuas* pointed out.[110] By giving deference to the one ordained, an honor and reverence was actually being shown to the dignity of the ordaining prelate.[111]

Leurenius, like Pirhing, limited this prerogative solely to ordination by the Roman Pontiff: that is, solely to ordination, and solely to the pope as the ordaining prelate. They did not permit it to be used as a criterion at any other time.[112]

The gloss to the letter *Per tuas* applied this rule to all who had

107 *Commentaria,* I, *de M. et O.,* ad c. 7, note s.v. *quantum convenit.*

108 *Forum Ecclesiasticum,* I, *de M. et O.,* q. DCCCCVII.

109 E.g., a cardinal, archbishop, or bishop.

110 "...quos benignitas apostolica collatione ipsius ordinis honoravit..."—c. 7, X, *de M. et O.*

111 Leurenius, *loc. cit.;* Pirhing, *Ius Canonicum,* I, *de M. et O.,* Sect. I, § I, n. VI, *notandum* 1.

112 *Loc. cit.* Contra: Schmalzgrueber, I (pt. 2), lib. I, *de M. et O.,* §I, n. 3: ". . . attendi deberet ad dignitatem vel praecedentiam ordinantis aut certum gradum conferentis. Hinc 1. qui a summo pont. e.g ordinatus est . . ." This seemed to permit the norm to be used in regard to other prelates than the Roman Pontiff, whom Schmalzgrueber merely cited as an example.

received special privileges from the Roman Pontiff, comparing this to the rule in Roman law, which attributed the first place in the catalogue of municipal judges to the one who had obtained the dignity from higher authority.[113] Hostiensis understood this canon as referring to the sacrament of Orders, and as giving precedence to one ordained by an unspecified superior over all of the same Order.[114]

Although the use of the rank of the ordaining prelate would have been permissible under the principles just mentioned, Leurenius and Pirhing did not permit the use of this criterion of the ordaining prelate in these circumstances: for instance, if a priest was ordained by a cardinal, he did not have precedence over another ordained by any lesser prelate. The basis for their strict interpretation was the very text of the letter *Per tuas,* which mentioned ordination by the pope alone, but not by anyone else.

Again, the restrictive phrase, *ceteris paribus,* had to be employed for the proper interpretation of this basis, as it had also to be used for all secondary criteria. Leurenius specified that the two persons concerned had both to exist in the same Order and be of the same dignity; accordingly he did not permit a deacon ordained by the pope to have precedence over a priest ordained not by the pope, even though the priest was a junior by ordination.[115] Here, again, it was easy to see how the cleric in higher Orders was to have precedence. If the ordaining prelate was anyone other than the pope, only the priority of ordination was to be used as a criterion, all other things being equal.[116]

---

113 "Et merito est illis deferendum. Ceteris non concurrentibus ratio privilegii habenda est . . . quia lex dicit, quod primo scribenda sunt nomina eorum, qui dignitates judicio principis sunt consecuti."—*glossa ordinaria* ad c. 7, X, *de M. et O.*, s.v. *subdiaconatus,* (an example is given, i.e. the privilege of exempt bishops to have a more honorable place in the synod).

"In albo decurionum in municipio nomina ante scribi oportet eorum, qui dignitates principis iudicio consecuti sunt . . ."—D (3,2), 2—*Corpus Iuris Civilis, Digesta Iustiniani Augusti* (recog. Theodorus Mommsen; Berolini, 1928).

114 *Commentaria,* I, *de M. et O.*, cap. 15, n. 2; cf. Lawrence P. Graves, *Precedence* (Unpublished licentiate dissertation, The Catholic University of America Canon Law Studies, 1947), pp. 30-31 .

115 *Loc. cit.*

116 Pirhing, *loc. cit.*

ARTICLE 6. SUPERIOR RANK AND PRECEDENCE FROM CUSTOM

Very frequently the authors on matters of precedence conditioned the criteria or principles for determining a superior rank with the clause, ". . . unless there be a contrary custom." Typical of such conditions was that of Pope Benedict XIV: ". . . quamvis revera difficile sit, in hac praecedentiae materia, certam regulam definire; cum potissimum inhaerendum sit consuetudini, quae pro locorum diversitate diversa est."[117] Post-Tridentine commentators were merely following the example set for them by the pre-Tridentine decretalists, such as Hostiensis. In his *Summa Aurea* he had written: "Praeterea dicta permutatio fit de consuetudine praelatorum approbante. . . . Consuetudo autem ecclesiae in hoc servanda est."[118]

In view of the difficulties connected with custom, it is understandable that many controversies should have arisen over the rights of precedence based thereon. The relatively numerous Rotal decisions concerned with custom bear this out. These seem to have been the main source of norms for commentators such as Sabelli,[119] and for such studies as those of Pallottini[120] and Ferraris (1687-1763).[121]

Sabelli stated in his *Summa:* "Praecedentia competit ex pluribus causis . . . [here he named more than fifteen sources, many of which were declared unacceptable by later decrees of the Congregations] . . . et huiusmodi, in quibus maxime consuetudo debet attendi."[122]

117 *De Synodo Diocesana,* Lib. III, c. X, § IX.

118 Lib. I, *de M. et O.,* s.v. *in quibus consistat maioritas.* Cf. also *Commentaria,* I, *de M. et O.,* ad c. 1, s.v. *habeatur.*

119 *Summa Diversorum Tractatuum,* s.v. *praecedentia* § XXXII.

120 Salvator Pallottini, *Collectio omnium conclusionum et resolutionum quae in causis propositis apud Sacram Congregationem Cardinalium, Sancti Concilii Tridentini Interpretum prodierunt ab ejus institutione anno MDLXIV ad annum MDCCCLX, distinctis titulis alphabetico ordine per materias digesta* (18 vols., Romae, 1868-1895), s.v. *praecedentia* (hereafter cited as Pallottini).

121 L. Ferraris, *Prompta Bibliotheca, Canonica, Iuridica, Moralis, Theologica, necnon Ascetica, Polemica, Rubricistica, Historica* (9 vols., Romae, 1885-1899), VI, s.v. *praecedentia seu praeeminentia* (hereafter cited as Ferraris).

122 *Op. cit.,* s.v. *praecedentia,* n. 1.

Two of the Rota decisions of the XVII century mentioned in similar terminology that custom was the most powerful criterion for the determining of the rights of precedence.[123] A third decision repeated this principle, and added that to be valid the custom had to be reasonable: ". . . nam dum non est rationabilis . . . uti corruptela radicitus extirpanda . . ."[124]

This quotation introduced one of the primary requirements of a custom if it was to have the force of law in matters of precedence: it had to be a reasonable custom. Hostiensis had stated in his pre-Tridentine commentary that any custom which gave preference to a junior over his senior in time, or one which put an inferior before his superior, without any special reason, such as higher dignity or office, was an unreasonable custom . . . *impraescriptibilis et ecclesiis onerosa* . . . and therefore invalid.[125]

Manrique also mentioned that reasonableness was a requirement for a custom to be valid, but he approached the question with a sense of the practical by adding ". . . et dico arbitrarium esse quando dicatur rationabilis . . . quod illa dicitur quae iuri non repugnat et est praeter legem."[126] Manrique conceded that there must be some degree of reasonableness about the custom, but he preferred to leave to the judge the right to determine just what degree was necessary for the validity of the custom.[127] Manrique did give some idea of what he would have recognized

---

123 S. R. Rota, *Lucana,* 24 ian. 1628—*Sacrae Romanae Rotae Decisiones Recentiores* (25 vols., ed. Farinaccio, Rubeo, et Compagno; Venetiis, 1697), V (tom. 2), *argumentum ad decis.* 483 (hereafter cited as *S.R.R. Decis. Recent.*); S. R. Rota, *Terraconen.,* 13 ian. 1698—*Sacrae Romanae Rotae Decisiones coram Ansaldo* (8 vols., Romae, 1711-1777), I, decis. XXV, n. 12. Cf. S. R. Rota, *Placentina,* 27 iunii 1633—*S.R.R. Decis. Recent.* VI, decis, 224, *summarium,* n. 1.

124 S. R. Rota, *Vercellen.,* 9 maii 1644—*Decisiones Sacrae Romanae Rotae coram Otthobono* (Romae, 1657), decis. IV, *Argumentum.* Cf. S. R. C., 5 martii 1644—*Fontes,* n. 5434: *D.* n. 857; S. R. C., *Lunen-Sarzanen.,* 14 ian. 1640—*Fontes,* n. 5382: *D.* n. 695.

125 *Commentaria* Lib. I, *de M. et O.,* ad c. 1, s.v. *ut ipse prior.* Cf. Boich, *Commentaria,* Lib. I, *de M. et O.,* ad c. 15.

126 *De Praecedentiis,* q. XVIII, *de consuetudinis potentia in hac materia,* n. 12.

127 *Ibid.,* n. 13.

as a reasonable custom, however. The custom was of this character if it determined the precedence of ecclesiastics who were equals in rank by reason of dignity, Orders and time of ordination.[128]

A somewhat clearer notion of what could be considered a reasonable custom can be derived from a reading of the Rota decisions in regard to this matter.[129]

At first it might seem that if a custom was contrary to the law it was unreasonable, but this definitely was not true of the principles of precedence. As Sabelli stated in his *Summaria Tractatuum:*

> Quod consuetudo etiam iuri repugnans in his materiis [praecedentiis] totum efficiat. . . . Ubi nonnulla in contrarium circa consuetudinem iuri contrarium, quae potius dicitur corruptela; ideo intellige quando consuetudo est aliqua rationabili causa fulcita, alias non est attendenda.[130]

Just as the determination of the reasonableness of the custom was not ruled with any really definite guiding principles, so the length of time needed to give a custom of this kind full force of law at first appeared to be quite variable, according to the sources consulted. There were differences ranging from one single act (. . . *qui est in possessione per unicum actum acquisita* . . .)[131] through ten years, [132] twenty years, [133] even thirty[134] and forty years.[135]

---

128 *Ibid.*, n. 4.

129 S. R. Rota, *Calaguritana*, 14 martii 1668—*S.R.R. Decis. Recent.*, XV, decis. 212, *summarium* n. 12; S. R. Rota, *Hildesimen.*, 28 iunii 1699—*ibid.*, XVI, decis. 168, *summarium* n. 6; S. R. Rota, *Burgen.*, 8 febr. 1677—*ibid.*, XIX (tom. 2), decis. 469, *summarium*, n. 60; S. R. Rotae, *Hispalen. Process. super secundo dubio—Sacrae Romanae Rotae Decisiones coram Ansaldo*, II, decis. CLXV, *summarium* n. 25; S. R. Rotae, *Colonien.*, 1 iunii 1695—*S.R.R. Decis. Nuper.* IV, decis. 440, *summarium*, n. 23.

130 S. R. Rota, *Calaguritana, ut supra;* decis. IV, n. 35, and decis. 229, n. 2—*S.R.R. Decisiones coram Otthobono.*

131 Pallottini, s.v. *praecedentia*, XV, n. 103.

132 Ferraris, s.v. *praecedentia*, n. 87: S. R. Rota, *Colonien.*, 22 iunii 1701—*S.R.R. Decis. Nuper.*, VII, decis. 162, *summarium*, n. 14; S. R. Rota, *Conchen.*, 16 iun. 1677—*S.R.R. Decis. Recent.*, XIX (tom. 1), decis. 99, *summarium*, n. 12: S. R. Rota, *Romana*, 18 maii 1620—*S.R.R. Decis. Recent.*, IV (tom. 2), decis. 214, n. 2.

It seems that the length of the postulated time was determined by the type of custom being induced. If the custom was in conformity with the law, no time period was required, . . . *sed sufficit per duos actus sic consuetum fuisse. . . .*[136] This was particularly true of customs that went beyond the law. But if the custom was contrary to the law, it needed to be observed forty years according to canon law, although civil law required an observance of but ten years.[137]

One of the earlier indications of the variants in time was given in a decision of the Rota in 1749:

> . . . imo amplius hac in re, si sola tricenaria, aut quadragenaria observantia non infimae potestatis est, amplissimae certae authoritatis erit, quae non emergit ex longiori vetustissimo tempore supra hominum memoriam.[138]

In another instance there was a decision to favor a longer period of time, so that "Consuetudo quadragenaria servanda est etiam in iis quae habent iuris resistentiam."[139]

Two other sources made a further transition to a longer period of time, from forty years to the centenary or immemorial custom of one hundred years or more: "Quod procedit tum si trigenta vel quadraginta annorum, tum et maxime si centenaria vel immemorabilis et consuetudo."[140]

Some form of proof had to be offered to show that certain custom had existed for the required number of years. The mere allegations of the party who stood to gain new rank, and those

---

133 S. R. Rota, *Caesaraugustana,* 4 iulii 1664—*S.R.R. Decis. Recent.*, XIV, decis. 226, *summarium,* n. 7.

134 S. R. Rota, *Capuana,* 13 iuni, 1749—*Sacrae Romanae Rotae Decisiones coram Clemente* (Romae, 1781), decis. 101, n. 6.

135 S. R. Rota, *Pampilonen.,* 3 febr. 1700—*S.R.R. Decis. Nuper., VI,* decis. 245.

136 Manrique, *De Praecedentiis,* q. 18, n. 5.

137 *Loc. cit.*

138 S. R. Rota, *Capuana,* 13 iunii, 1749—*Decisiones Sacrae Romanae Rotae coram Clemente,* decis. 101, n. 6.

139 S. R. Rota, *Pampilonen.,* 3 febr. 1700, *ut supra.*

140 Ferraris, s.v. *praecedentia,* n. 92; S. R. Rota, *Burgen.*, 24 ian. 1721—*Sacrae Romanae Rotae Decisiones coram de Herrera* (Romae, 1731), decis. 154, *summarium,* n. 16.

of his opponent to the contrary, could not be accepted on their face value.[141] The most valuable and certain proof for the existence of a custom was that which came from many witnesses of every type with testimony to this effect which was as complete as possible: they had all seen this particular pattern of precedence, to which they testified, being followed every year; further, they had heard from their elders, who had told them of the same pattern's being followed.

These were the principles given in a Rota decision which rejected an earlier norm of accepting testimony from those who could testify only from their personal experience in the matter, without any recollection of having heard anything about it from their ancestors; it added on the other hand that, ". . . in hac mutua consensione ex decessorum et viventium testium reddito iudicio, constantique apud omnes diffusa fama, plena stat immemorabilis probatio."[142] The same decision, in its various summary headings gave additional criteria: witnesses of doubtful credibility and judicial officers should not be questioned; and the testimony of witnesses given from personal knowledge and without being asked should be held as very valuable.[143]

An earlier decision gave reasons and criteria with a familiar ring to the present-day canonist: "Testes nobiles ac publicae civitatis officiales de facto proprio deponentes plenam faciunt probationem, et iis omnino est deferendum . . . non vero testibus consanguineis."[144]

The greatest importance was placed on the testimony of the ordinary of the place also in this post-Tridentine period: "Neminem autem latere potest ordinarii testimonium circa consuetudinem ecclesiae suae quam maxime esse faciendum."[145]

---

141 Manrique, *De Praecedentiis,* q. 18, n. 3.

142 S. R. Rota, *Capuan.,* 13 iunii, 1749—*S.R.R. Decisiones coram Clemente,* decis. 101, n. 1.

143 *Ibid., summaria,* nn. 3-4.

144 S. R. Rota, *Syracusana,* 3 dec. 1731—*Sacrae Romanae Rotae Decisiones coram Rezzonico* (Pope Clement XII) (3 tomes, Romae, 1759-1762, I, decis. 29, *summaria,* nn. 9-10; cf. Code of Canon Law, cc. 1755, § 2, 2°; 1757, § 2, 3°; 1791, § 1.

145 S. R. Rota, *Firmana,* 20 ian. 1826—*Sacrae Romanae Rotae Decisiones coram Marco et Catalan* (2 vols., Romae, 1829), II, decis. 290, n. 22; cf. *S. R. Rotae Decisiones coram Ansaldo,* IV, decis. 401, n. 14.

The one outstanding treatment of custom as a criterion for superior rank in this post-Tridentine period was furnished by Manrique. He listed seven rules or principles one was to follow in determining the validity of a custom in matters of precedence:

1) the custom must be truly proper to the person or the group desiring superior rank; such person or group must have had an active part in the induction of this custom;

2) the custom must have been observed for the required length of time, less for customs according to or beyond the law, more for customs contrary to the law;

3) the custom must be reasonable (which Manrique thought was quite an arbitrary matter, best left to the judge in the individual case);

4) if the custom induced superior rank for a group of people, such as a chapter, a majority of the chapter must have taken an active part in inducing it with a will or intention of introducing a new right for themselves. Since custom is an unwritten law, the superior must deliberately consent, and have the power to authorize and confirm a custom;

5) those with the authority to consent to or confirm the custom must have had knowledge of this custom so that they (. . . *qui praejudicium sentire possint* . . .) could be said to have had the opportunity to confirm or abolish the custom;

6) there must have been a sufficient number of acts for the judge to determine that over a certain period of time a custom had truly been established;

7) the practice must have been continuous, for even one contrary prescription would break its continuity, and thus the process of inducing a custom would be broken.[146]

A final notion on the force of custom in matters of precedence concerned the *Caeremoniale Episcoporum* issued by Pope Clement VIII in 1600.[147] This papal constitution in promulgating the new

146 Manrique, *De Praecedentiis,* q.18, *de consuetudinis potentia in hac materia,* nn. 16-23.

147 Const. *Cum novissime,* 14 iulii 1600—Josephus Catalani, *Commentarium in Caeremoniale Episcoporum* (2 vols., Parisiis, 1860), I, *Constitutiones Pontificiae* n. 1, pp. xix-xx; *Bull Lux.,* III, p. 110, n. LXIX.

ceremonial mentioned the force that this official liturgical book would have in these words: ". . . non obstantibus praemissis . . . ac constitutionibus . . . statutis et consuetudinibus ceterisque contrariis quibuscumque." Later revisions promulgated by Pope Innocent X (1644-1655)[148] and Benedict XIII (1724-1730)[149] restated the force of these official texts in almost identical words:

> . . . non obstantibus praemissis ac apostolicis etiam in universalibus provincialibus et synodalibus conciliis editis generalibus, vel specialibus constitutionibus . . . necnon . . . statutis et consuetudinibus privilegiis quoque indultis . . . quomodolibet concessis, confirmatis, et innovatis.[150]

It did not seem unusual, therefore, for the Rota in 1700 to rule that a specific case of an immemorial custom contrary to the *Ceremoniale* could not be maintained: ". . . censeatur reprobata per constitutionem Clementis VIII abrogantem cum decreto irritanti quamcumque consuetudinem in contrarium."[151] But a year later this decision was reversed for the following reasons:

> . . . Constitutio vero Clementis VIII derogat quidem omnibus aliis consuetudinibus *sed immemorabilem praeservat* . . . quia consuetudo retinendi sedes laicorum in presbyterio non est directe contra caeremonialis dispositionem, dum illud expresse id non prohibet, sed solum statuit decere principibus habere sedes plus, et minus ornatas pro cuiusquam dignitate et gradu . . . ex hoc autem cum inferri nequeat prohibitio per actum negativum, sed ea solum eliciatur per modum affirmativum, implicitam negationem tantummodo habentem inde sequitur tantam non esse eiusdem caeremonialis resistentiam, ut per immemorabilem consuetudinem non possit laicus acquirere ius retinendi scamnum in presbyterio candemque consuetudinem per consequens non censeri per dictam constitutionem abrogatam cum haec eas

148 Const., *Quanquam alias,* 30 iulii 1650—Catalani, *op. cit.,* n. II, pp. xx-xxi; *Bull. Rom. Taur.,* XV, p. 662, n. CXXXVIII where the opening words are *"Etsi alias."*

149 Const. *Licet alias,* 7 martii 1727—Catalani, *op. cit.,* n. III, pp. xxi-xxii; *Bull. Lux.,* XIII, p. 278, n. CXXIX.

150 Innocentius X, const. *Quanquam alias—Loc. cit.*

151 S. R. Rota, *Pampilonen.,* 3 febr. 1700—*S. R. R. Decis. Nuper.,* VI, decis. 245, n. 28.

> tantum consuetudines damnet quae expresse, ac directe adversantur dispositis in dicto caeremoniali.[152]

Even after Benedict XIV's edition of the *Ceremonial* (1741) immemorial customs contrary to the *Ceremonial* could remain if they were laudable and reasonable. It is stated in the *Praelogium* to the 1860 edition of Catalani's *Commentarium* on the authentic edition of Clement VIII, corrected by Innocent X, with additions by Benedict XIV:

> Laudabiles atque probatas Ecclesiarum consuetudines antiquas scilicet et immemorabiles a nostro ceremoniali non tolli, ex compluribus memoratae S.R.C. decretis Doctores omnes uno ore affirmant[153] innuitque non uno loco novum hoc nostrum ceremoniale ubi iam varia caeremoniarum capita consuetudine ecclesiarum relinquuntur; et licet summus pontifex in nova sua Constitutione pro observatione Caeremonialis Episcoporum ab eodem emendati inter alia consuetudines Caeremoniali ipsi contrarias damnet, intelligendum puto eum locum de consuetudine quae sunt irrationabilis non vero de laudabilibus ac probatis, quas servari nos Romae vidimus, vel dum ipse zelantissimus Pontifex viveret,[154]

This is borne out by a decree of 1880 which treated of such immemorial customs contrary to the *Caermoniale:*

> Censeri praeservatas solummodo consuetudines immemorabiles, ceteroquin laudabiles, licet Caeremoniali contrarias, eo quod Pontificis Constitutio dum omnes generatim contrarias tollunt consuetudines, de immemorabilibus expressam mentionem non faciunt.[155]

It seems reasonable to conclude from these facts alone that any custom contrary to the prescriptions of the *Caeremoniale Episcoporum* in any of its various editions was to be reprobated unless it came under the classification of immemorial and laudable. However, this explanation failed to mention a decree from

---

152 S. R. Rota, *Pampilonen.*, 7 martii 1701—*ibid.*, VII, decis. 53 (Italics supplied by writer.)

153 The index to the edition of the *Decreta Authentica* of the S.R.C. begun in 1898 lists at least eleven decrees to this effect over a period of time extending from 1603 to 1826.

154 *Commentarium in Caeremoniale Episcoporum*, I, p. xv, § XIV.

155 S. C. Concilii, 14 aug. 1880, ad VI—*Acta Sanctae Sedis* (41 vols., Romae, 1865-1908), XIV, 142 (hereafter cited as *ASS*); cf. footnote n. 1, *ibid.*

the Congregation of Sacred Rites in 1826, which required that recourse be had to the same Congregation in each particular case for a judgment on the laudability of a particular custom. In explaining this requirement the Congregation stated:

> S.R.C. dum servandum iubet Caeremoniale Episcoporum haud intendi adprobare, vel reprobare peculiares Ecclesiarum consuetudines, sed sibi reservat eorundem examen in casibus particularibus, ut cognoscere possit num rationabiles et laudabiles sint, vel potius habendae ut corruptelae et abusus, ac tales propterea sint ut reprobari et eliminari omnino debeant . . . id privatorum iudicio non est relinquendum multae quippe consuetudines quae laudabiles privato aliquorum iudicio videri possunt tales revera non sunt.[156]

The simple procedure after this decree seems to have been this: if any custom contrary to the *Ceremoniale* existed, the ordinary had a choice of abolishing it and bringing it into conformity with the *Ceremoniale,* or of submitting it to the Congregation of Sacred Rites for a decision as to its laudability.

After this brief survey, the reader will surely agree with Leurenius' reaction to all the detailed confusion in regard to custom in matters of precedence:

> Consuetudinem esse . . . quasi impossibilem . . . eo quod ad ejus probationem necesse sit probare omne id quod ad eius constitutionem requiritur: nimirum num a majore parte communitatis ex animo eam inducendi sit inducta, an per tempus legitimum continuoque usu fuerit observata; quod ipsum probare perquam difficile est, praesertim cum mores populi valde sint mutabiles ac variabiles. . . .[157]

Article 7. Precedence in Councils and Synods

Throughout the history of the Church, the holding of a council or a synod has, of its very nature, brought together a great number of the clergy into one place. On these occasions, perhaps more than at any other time, it was necessary to determine proper rank and order of precedence if there were to be orderly proceedings.

---

156 S.R.C., *Alexandrina,* 10 maii 1826, Adnotationes ad dubium II—*D.* n. 2646.

157 *Forum Ecclesiasticum,* I, q. CCCXCIII.

Some of the first notions of precedence among the clergy came out of such circumstances, and many of the principles established in the beginning continued to be followed up to the time of the promulgation of the Code of Canon Law in 1917.

For instance, in 325 the I General Council of Nicaea specified that deacons were not to sit in the midst of priests at councils and similar gatherings.[158] In 599 Pope Gregory I insisted that bishops take their proper places, whether sitting in council or signing the decrees of the council.[159] A little later (663) the IV Provincial Council of Toledo required that bishops in synod should occupy seats arranged in a corona with the priests sitting in back of them, and the deacons standing in sight of the bishops.[160] This principle of seating the participants in a circle is found in the *Caeremoniale Episcoporum* to this day:

> Sedes Metropolitani collocabitur apud altare . . . et ante faciem ipsius, sedilia episcoporum per gyrum, deinde conduplicatis sedilibus post episcopos, ceteri proximores vel remotiores pro graduum diversitate. . . .[161]

Other principles governing the precedence of the participants in a council or a synod may here be mentioned: the metropolitan of the province was to preside;[162] other bishops from the province who attended the council took their proper places according to the time of their ordination (consecration);[163] a procurator or proxy for one of the absent bishops could represent someone of higher rank and obtain a higher rank for himself from the fact of his representation.[164] It was on these preliminary

---

158 Canon 18, cited as c. 14, D. 93—Mansi, I, 19.

159 C. 5, D. 17—*MPL,* LXXVII, 1055; Jaffé, n. 1265.

160 Canon 4—Mansi, X, 617; Bruns, I, 222, 223.

161 Lib. I, cap. XXXI, n.8.

162 Letter of Pope Gregory I to the Bishop of Autun, cited as c. 5, D. 17—Ep. IX, 108, *MPL,* LXXVII, 1055.

163 *Loc. cit.*

164 Canon 7, Council in Trullo, cited as c. 26, D. 93—Mansi, XI, 943; *glossa ordinaria ad hoc;* cf. list of signers of the I General Council of Nicaea—C. H. Turner, *Ecclesiae Occidentalis Monumenta Iuris Antiquissima, Canonum et Conciliorum Graecorum Interpretationes Latinae* (2 vols. in 9, Oxonii: 1899-1939), Vol. I, pars I, (1899), n. 36 col. IV, V; Hostiensis, *Summa Aurea,* I, *de officio archidiacono,* s.v. *majoritas in ecclesia dicitur quadruplex.*

norms of rank that the commentators after the Council of Trent based their notions of precedence in councils; and with such norms the councils regulated the precedence of their attending clergy.

The places occupied in the council and the order followed in the signing of the acts came to be considered as general norms for determining precedence outside the council as well. This is known definitely in regard to deriving precedence from the order of signing the documents, as may be witnessed in Rotal decisions;[165] it can only be deduced from the appearance of a prohibition against the practice in the *Acta* of some of the councils, however, that some tried to establish a general norm for precedence also from their appointed place in the seating arrangement of the council.[166] The celebrated treatise of Benedict XIV, *De Synodo Dioecesana,* gave some details of synodal precedence, particularly in the tenth chapter of the third book, entitled "De ordine sedendi in Synodo."[167]

In determining proper places, Benedict XIV noted in this work that there was at least one difference in the problems of precedence in general councils compared with those in particular councils: namely, there were cardinals for whom a place had to be established.[168] He cited as a precedent for the high rank given to cardinals the I General Council of Lyons under Pope Innocent IV in 1245. At this council cardinals had precedence over bishops,

---

165 S. R. Rota, *Placentina,* 1 febr. 1623—*Decis. Recent.,* VI, 615, decis. 322; S. R. Rota, *Nullius seu Montis Cassinen.,* 22 iunii 1711—*Sacrae Romanae Rotae Decisiones coram Molines* (5 vols., ed. Corazza; Romae, 1728) V, 627, decis. 1316; cf. also Franciscus Bassi, *Bibliotheca Iuris Canonico-Civilis Practica (seu Repertorium),* (4 vols.; Mutinae, 1758), s.v. *praecedentia,* n. 2 (hereafter cited *Repertorium*).

166 Conc. Trident., sess. II, "Decretum de modo vivendi et aliis in concilio servandis," § *Insuper; Concilium Provinciale Remensis* (1849), tit. I, cap. ii—*Coll. Lac.,* IV, 104; *Concilium Provinciale Senonensis* (1850), "De modo vivendi in concilio,"—*Ibid.,* col. 874, c; *Concilium Provinciale Rothomagensis* (1850), tit. praev., cap. ii—*Ibid.,* col. 547-48; *Concilium Provinciale Albiensis* (1850), *Prima Congregatio Publica,* § 3—*Ibid.,* col. 448.

167 Benedictus XIV, *De Synodo Dioecesana* lib. III, cap. X.

168 *Ibid.,* n. 1.

even though they themselves were not consecrated.[169] Similar examples were cited from other councils, such as the Council of Rome in 1059 under Nicholas II[170] as well as the II General Council of Lyons in 1274 and the Council of Florence (1438-45).[171]

For the purpose of the diocesan synod, Benedict XIV acknowledged the difficulty of properly determining precedence according to the proper norms, since allowances had to be made for customs of different places and groups. His suggestion was that the bishop at the opening of the synod promulgate a decree establishing a certain order for sitting as well as for the signing of the acts, in imitation of the example of St. Charles Borromeo in the V Provincial Council of Milan (1579).[172] In this particular instance, a decree was issued which was similar to that issued at the Council of Trent, "De modo vivendi et aliis in concilio servandis," cited above. This decree stated that no one was to have any claim to future rights of precedence in view of his place as assigned during this particular council.[173]

One example of this provision for precedence in a provincial council can be found in the acts of the Provincial Council of Esztergom, held in 1858. It will be given here in its entirety to serve as a pattern of what Benedict XIV must have meant. It is one of the best examples of several attempts along these lines which could be found.

> Omnes ad concilium rite convocati . . . convenerunt . . . et ingressi sunt ecclesiam S. Stephani, occupantes quisque locum suum, prout subpraefectus e mandato eminentissimi metropolitae per affixam schedam designavit: [the outline which follows was translated and arranged by the present writer]

---

169 "Ad dexteram et in eminentioribus locis sederunt episcopi cardinales, ex altera vero presbyteri cardinales, archiepiscopi et episcopi post eos."—Jean Hardouin, *Acta Conciliorum et Epistolae Decretales ac Constitutiones Summorum Pontificum* (12 vols., Parisiis, 1714-1715), VII, 378.

170 Hardouin, *op. cit.*, VI (pt. 1), 1066.

171 Benedict cited Raynaldus' work *"ad eundem annum* [1274], *num. 3"* for the reference to Lyons.

172 *Acta Ecclesiae Mediolanensis* (Lugduni, 1683), Part I, 278.

173 *De Synodo Dioecesana,* lib. III, c. X, § IX.

1) At a table in the middle of the sanctuary:
   a) the suffragan bishops of the province according to the date of their promotion;
   b) the two titular bishops of the suffragan diocese of Esztergom;
   c) the Archabbot of St. Martin's;
   d) the Vicar Capitular of Nitria;
2) At the first table at the Gospel side:
   a) the abbots and
   b) the *praepositi,* both according to the date of their election to their offices;
3) At a second table on the Epistle side:
   a) the procurators of the metropolitan cathedral chapter, and
   b) the procurators of the suffragan cathedral chapters, both groups arranged among themselves in the same order as that of their respective bishops;
4) Two other tables in the sanctuary and the nave:
   a) the other procurators of the cathedral chapters;
   b) the procurators of collegiate chapters;
   c) the secular *praepositi;*
   d) the theologians chosen from among the canons;
   e) the procurator of the theological faculty of the University;
   f) the prior regent of the vacant abbacy of the Cistercians;
   g) the provincial *praepositi* of the Jesuits;
   h) the prior provincial of the Servants of Mary;
   i) the provincial ministers of the Order of St. Francis and the Brothers of Mercy of St. John of God; and, finally,
   j) the theologians.[174]

It may be noted that the bishops were required to sit according to the date of their promotion, rather than according to the date of their consecration, as had been the practice for centuries before. But shortly before its conclusion the Council of Trent declared that the precedence of bishops was to be derived from the date

174 *Acta Concilii Provincialis Strigoniensis 1858, Congregatio Generalis—Coll. Lac.,* V, 98.

of their promotion. This became the only correct norm; but some commentators continued to use the other norm of consecration for some time after the Council of Trent, as was noted in sections three and four above. One instance of a correct use of the date of consecration as a norm for determining superior rank was given by the Sacred Congregation of the Council in regard to a doubt about the norms of precedence for a provincial council as set forth by the Council of Trent. This norm could be used for the determining of the senior suffragan, who was to be empowered to call such a provincial council when the metropolitan was legitimately hindered.[175]

Reference was made above to a warning, issued at the opening of the Council of Trent, which forbad anyone to claim a new basis for superior rank from the fact that he had enjoyed such in the Council itself.[176] A special decree was incorporated in the twenty-fifth session on the same matter.[177] There had been some controversy among two of the archbishops, the one claiming the rank of primate, the other denying this claim.[178] This prompted Pope Pius IX to issue a more detailed instruction[179] about precedence as it was to be observed in the last sessions:

> Itaque, ad tollendam omnem controversiam materiarum quae inter praelatos ad celebrationem sacri oecumenici et generalis concilii in civitate Tridentina pro tempore congregatos, super eorum praecedentia forte iam sunt exortae et in dies oriri possunt . . . volumus . . . ac mandamus. . . .

---

175 S. C. Concilii, *in dubio ad cap.* 2, sess. XXIV, *de ref.,* cited by Pallottini, s.v. *praecedentia,* n. 84.

176 Sessio II, "Decretum de modo vivendi et aliis in concilio servandis," § *Insuper.*

177 Sessio XXV, *de ref., (continuatio sessionis die IV decembris),* "Decretum de loco oratorum."

178 *Concilium Tridentinum, Diariorum, Actorum, Epistularum, Tractatuum, Nova Collectio* (13 vols. ed. a Societate Goerresiana; Friburgi Bresgoviae: B. Herder, 1901-1950), VIII, *Concilii Tridentini Actorum Pars Quinta* (ed. Stephanus Ehses; 1919), n. 232, "Altercatio inter primates et archiepiscopos circa praecedentiam in Concilio Tridentino" (hereafter cited as *Collectio Goerresiana de Tridentino*).

179 The earlier papal pronouncement was the bull, *Sicut ea,* 31 dec. 1561—*Collectio Goerresiana de Tridentino, VIII,* n. 204.

Thereupon follow these norms:

1) All prelates, e.g., patriarchs, archbishops and bishops, in all public acts whatsoever, should enter, sit and take their places according to their grade and the order of their promotion to their churches. As a result, he who was appointed earlier to a church was to be first in his order;

2) No consideration was to be given to any primatial dignity, true or pretended;

3) These were to supersede any norms given earlier. [180] According to a footnote to the third point, these special provisions constituted the reason for the repetition of the earlier warning in the twenty-fifth session cited above.

When Pope Pius IX (1846-1878) issued the norms of precedence for the Vatican Council (1869-70), he may have had in mind the confusion caused by the primates at the Council of Trent, for he listed the participants of the Council in this order:

1) cardinal bishops, priests, and deacons;

2) patriarchs;

3) primates, according to the order of their promotion to the rank of primate. "Id autem pro hac vice tantum indulgemus, atque ita, ut ex hac Nostra concessione nullum ius vel ipsis Primatibus datum, vel aliis imminutum, censeri debeat;"

4) archbishops, according to their promotion to the archiepiscopal rank;

5) bishops, likewise according to the date of their promotion;

6) abbots *nullius dioeceseos;*

7) abbots general, moderators general of Orders with solemn vows even though they are called vicars general, as long as in actual fact they have all the rights and privileges of supreme moderators for their whole Order.[181]

Despite this special provision for the primates, there were some archbishops whose claim to the title of primate had been

---

180 Pius IV, brief, *Nuper,* confirming the bull, *Sicut ea,* of December 31, 1561, issued February 14, 1562, and read at the session held on February 26, 1562—*Collectio Goerresiana de Tridentino,* VIII, n. 232.

181 Pius IX, litt, ap. *Multiplices,* 27 nov. 1869—*Fontes,* n. 553, § IV; *Coll. Lac.,* VII, 19-20, n. IV.

overlooked, with the result that they were assigned to places among the other archbishops. These aggrieved primates were from the archdioceses of Bar (Antivari) Malines, and Salerno. In their petition, they sought to prove their claim by pointing out documents wherein they had been referred to as primates. After investigation, it was decided that the petition was justified, and they were granted the right to be seated among the other primates, but only for the occasion of the council, and with the usual condition: ". . . quin exinde ullum ius datum, vel aliis imminutum censeatur ad formam litt. ap. *Multiplices.*"[182] With these three added to those who already had assigned to them places among the primates for the Vatican Council, there were twelve primates altogether. The other nine were the archbishops of Armagh, Braga, Gniezno and Poznán, Lyons, Salzburg, São Salvador da Bahia, Esztergom, Tarragona, and Toledo, Spain.[183] As one might suspect, the precedence given primates in both the Councils of Trent and of the Vatican did in actual practice set up a new norm of precedence for them, despite the contrary prescription added to the precedence norms established in both councils.[184]

Three provincial councils of the XIX century provided further detailed norms for precedence in a council by specifying the proper places for theologians and canonists. They were to be in a body, within which their individual precedence was to be derived from that of their respective bishops, who in turn were arranged in the order of their promotion to the episcopacy.[185]

The Provincial Council of Cologne (1860) established precedence for a visiting bishop. The Prince-Bishop of Breslau was given the first place of honor after the presiding archbishop,

182 *Ex Actis Concilii Vaticani—ASS,* V (1869), 343; *Coll. Lac.* VII, 726, b *in Congregatione* XXV.

183 Joachim Nabuco, *Ius Pontificalium, Introductio in Caeremoniale Episcoporum* (Parisiis: Desclée et Socii, 1956), note 32, p. 48 (hereafter cited as *Ius Pontificalium*).

184 *Loc. cit.*

185 *Ex Actis in Congregatione Prima Privata Concilii Provincialis Turnonensis 1849—Coll. Lac.,* IV, 286-87; *Acta Congregationis Generalis Concilii Provincialis Burdigalensis 1850—Ibid.,* IV, 616; *Ex Actis in Congregatione Prima Privata Concilii Provincialis Auscitanae 1851—Ibid.,* IV, 1212, n. 5.

and before the suffragan bishops.[186] It is presumed that the reason for this rank was not a special courtesy to his status as visiting bishop, but a deference to his rank as Prince-Bishop.

The notion of a procurator or proxy at the council was more important historically than would appear at first. At an early period recognition was given to the fact that a procurator, proxy, or substitute, was entitled to share in the rank of the person whom he represented. Gratian had included such a principle in his *Concordia Discordantium Canonum:*

> Praecipimus, ne diaconus (quamvis etiam in dignitate hoc est in offitio quolibet ecclesiastico sit), ante presbiterum sedeat, nisi cum locum habuerit proprii patriarchae aut metropolitani pro aliquo capitulo; tunc enim sicut illius locum tenens honorabitur . . .[187]

Although this particular decree dates back only to the year 692, Gonzalez-Tellez stated in his commentary that this special rank had been acknowledged for papal legates (papal proxies) during at least one earlier council, as may be noted in the order of signatures on the acts and decrees of the Council of Ephesus (431). Here the papal legate signed after the patriarch and before all other metropolitans and bishops.[188]

Hynes, in his study of the historical development of the cardinalitial rank, gives as the second reason for the growing importance of this office in the Church the fact that cardinals were frequently sent as legates to councils. On these occasions, although they might be only priests or deacons, they preceded the bishops in signing the decrees.[189] Here, somewhat similar to the case of the primates mentioned above, a privilege intended to be enjoyed only for a single occasion, viz., when acting as a procurator, came to be acknowledged in jurisprudence as something attached to this dignity in a more or less permanent fashion.

---

186 *Acta Congregationum Generalium et Sessionum Concilii Provincialis Coloniensis 1860—Coll. Lac.* V, 248, § *Placuit.*

187 C. 26, D. 93, citing can. 7, VII Synod of Constantinople—Mansi, XI, 943.

188 *Commentaria Perpetua,* I, *de M. et O.*, 841, n. 9.

189 Harry Hynes, *The Privileges of Cardinals,* The Catholic University of America Canon Law Studies, n. 217 (Washington, D. C.: The Catholic University of America Press, 1945), p. 33.

Of historical interest to American canonists in particular are the findings in regard to precedence as it was observed in the Plenary Councils held in Baltimore. The I Plenary Council (1852) noted in the first solemn session that everyone sat *iuxta ordinem* for the opening Mass.[190] In checking the list of the archbishops and bishops in attendance at this Mass[191] one readily notes that the date of promotion to the rank of archbishop or bishop was followed accurately with one exception. The bishop of Nesqually (later Seattle), Augustine Blanchet, seemed to be out of place on the basis of the date of promotion alone. Promoted to the rank of bishop in 1864, he was preceded in this list by four other bishops promoted in 1847 and 1848.[192]

There was also confusion in regard to the precedence of the theologians which the bishops had in attendance at the council. In procession as well as in council, these theologians according to the general practice in Europe at that time were supposed to follow the order in which their respective bishops went in procession or sat in council. Although this was evidently the goal of all three plenary councils, it was achieved only in the last one. It was merely a matter of inversion of names in the lists in the other two councils, probably through an oversight.[193]

---

190 *Concilium Plenarium Totius Americae Septentrionalis Foederatae Baltimori Habitum Anno 1852* (Baltimori, 1853), p. 13.

191 *Ibid.*, p. 14. This list is identical with that giving the signatures affixed to the decrees, pp. 50-52, and another, on page 67, listing all those present at the council.

192 The Right Reverend A. Rappe (1847), the Right Reverend John Timon (1847), the Right Reverend John Spalding (1848), and the Right Reverend James Vandevelde (1848).

193 *Ibid.*, pp. 17-18. For instance the bishops in the I Plenary Council are listed in one order: Pittsburgh, Little Rock, and Albany. Their theologians are listed in another order: Pittsburgh, Albany and Little Rock. A second inversion is found at the end of the lists, where the bishops are listed in this order: the Bishop of Richmond, the Vicars Apostolic of New Mexico and of the Indian Territory East of the Rocky Mountains, the Bishop of Philadelphia. Their theologians follow another order: for the Bishop of Richmond, for the Vicars Apostolic of the Indian Territory and New Mexico, for the Bishop of Philadelphia. Cf. also *Concilii Plenarii Baltimorensis II, Acta et Decreta* (ed. altera, Baltimorae, 1894), pp. xviii-xx *vs.* pp. xxiii-xxv; cf. also *Acta et Decreta Concilii Plenarii Baltimorensis Tertii* (Baltimorae, 1886), pp. xliv-xlv *vs.* pp. xlvii-xlix.

The preliminary meeting of the III Plenary Council stated in § III,[194] that the order of the processions, as well as that of the sessions and the various meetings, followed the directions of a booklet entitled *Praxis Synodalis*,[195] *Pars* I, cc. ii, iii, iv, and all of *Pars* II. Chapter iv is entitled *"Ordo Praecedentiae"*, and is primarily intended for the provincial council. In this section the precedence of bishops is based on the date of their promotion, which the III Plenary Council followed carefully.[196]

It has been seen in rather brief fashion that the councils from the Council of Trent to the Code, general, plenary and provincial, made rather successful efforts at following the norms for proper precedence among those in attendance. Several of the councils followed the example of the Council of Trent in declaring that no precedence was to be changed for anyone when he had occupied a place in the council not in keeping with his proper rank. In establishing a definite precedence that was to serve only for the council, as was done in the case of the Vatican Council, a practical problem was being approached in a practical way. The larger the group of persons for whom precedence must be determined, the more difficult it is to be absolutely correct in determining the precedence of each individual. For the sake of efficiency and to achieve the necessary peace and order within the council, a compromise of sorts had to be agreed upon. It was this type of compromise that Benedict XIV suggested in his *De Synodo Dioecesana*,[197] and which the Code empowers the bishops to make for their synods and councils today, with due regard

194 "Quoad Methodum Conciliarem quae sequuntur approbata sunt"—*Op. cit.*, p. xxxvi.

195 *Praxis Synodalis, Manuale Synodi Diocesanae* [*sic*] *ac Provincialis Celebrandae* (New York, 1883).

196 In the preface to *Praxis Synodalis*, the compiler stated that he relied heavily on two earlier works for his material: Gavantus, *Praxis Celebrandae Synodi Dioecesanae* and Benedict XIV, *De Synodo Dioecesana*. In adding the norms for provincial councils, he borrowed from the councils of the Provinces of Vienna, Prague and Cologne in the years 1858-60. With *Praxis Synodalis* newly printed the year before, the III Plenary Council had a handy norm for ready reference, which it manifestly put to good use.

197 Lib. III, cap. X, n. IX.

for the express provisions of the law.[198] This particular facet of the problem of precedence, the bishop's right to determine it for his subjects in his diocese, will be discussed in further detail in the commentary on canon 106. However appropriate a more detailed discussion of the norms of precedence in synod or council might be in this historical section, it will be postponed to its proper place in the commentary on the Code, for much of it still has practical value.

---

198 Canon 106, 6°

PART II

Canonical Commentary

CHAPTER IV

GENERAL PRINCIPLES OF PRECEDENCE IN THE CODE OF CANON LAW

ARTICLE 1. PRELIMINARY NOTIONS OF PRECEDENCE

Precedence is a general term denoting the right of one person to outrank another in any place or situation where some orderly procedure is being followed. There is practically no limit to the variety of occasions on which precedence may be properly followed, although in practice there seems to be an even greater variety of circumstances in which it is not.

To some, precedence is a useless complication of the confusion already reigning in a given case. The principles of precedence, after centuries of experience, are the Church's wise solution for ending the confusion. The norms of precedence were never intended to add to the confusion, or in any way to complicate it.

Some are confused with the word itself. The term indeed reflects an anomaly until the criteria for precedence are duly understood. The ordinary meaning of the verb, to precede, is to be, go, or come before someone else, as in rank or dignity. This ordinarily connotes a higher place of honor; very often it indicates a place in front of others.

In canonical precedence, however, the front or place of honor varies according to the circumstances. Very often, as in processions, the place of honor is at the end, or after everyone else. In some processions, such as those honoring the Blessed Sacrament, the place of honor is given to the Blessed Sacrament itself; but this is not necessarily at the end of the procession. This is clear from the liturgical norms of precedence for prelates in this particular case: they are directed to go behind the Blessed Sacrament, in a descending order of preeminence. In this circumstance, the closer one is to the Blessed Sacrament, the more honorable the position; the farther away, the less honorable.[1]

---

[1] Adrian Fortescue, *The Ceremonies of the Roman Rite Described* (8. ed. rev. by J. B. O'Connell; Westminster, Maryland: Newman Press), p. 346; in the 10. ed; 1958, p. 318.

On at least one occasion, the more honorable position is at the head of the procession, as when the members of the choir come in procession without a cross or vested celebrant. In this case the more dignified walk before the others.[2] At other times, as in the signing of documents, to have precedence will actually mean that a person signs first or at least before others. In stating, then, that some person precedes someone else, the legislator means merely that this person is given a more honorable position, as reflected under the attendant circumstances. If the place of honor, then, is at the end of the procession, to have precedence over someone else would in fact mean to follow that person. Therefore, care must be taken not to confuse the meaning of the word "precedence" in any of its grammatical forms by limiting it to the meaning given above: to go, be, or come before.

Canonical precedence is nothing more than an enlargement on the principles of everyday courtesy put into legal form. It is doubtful if a polite person would be labelled as undemocratic for his deference to his superiors. On the other hand, if the superior insisted that this deference be shown him, some such charge may have more foundation.

The rules of precedence can best be looked upon as norms whereby the individual can recognize to whom he should give deference and a more honorable position in recognition of rank or dignity, as a matter of courtesy and respect.

When this becomes the common outlook on matters of precedence, everyone will know his proper place in regard to his superiors, and in taking that place will be performing a twofold virtuous act of respect for superiors, and humility in regard to self. Those of lesser rank or dignity, in turn, observing the proper norms, will give their respect and honor to their superiors. In this way no one will have to expose himself to the charge that he lacks humility or is undemocratic in insisting on his proper precedence, which is referred to in the Code as a right, *ius praecedentiae*.[3] It is a right, however, which should be more observed by inferiors toward their superiors in rank and dignity, than insisted on by superiors in regard to those of lower station.

---

2 *Op. cit.*, 8 ed. p. 27; *op. cit.*, 10 ed. p. 46.

3 Canon 106, 2°.

On the other hand, the individual has no right to refuse his proper rank or station according to the norms of precedence. If an ecclesiastical person is entitled to a certain position he should take it, at least to avoid the confusion that will ensue all along the line if he does not. If he is not entitled to a certain position and assumes it anyway, or is allowed to assume it, an abuse is introduced against which it is the right and at times becomes the duty of any cleric to protest.[4]

Article 2. Competent Authority in Matters of Precedence

The Code of Canon Law has provided the members of the Church with a very complete set of norms to determine precedence among its members, especially the clergy. But as is the case with other norms found in the Code, the legislator could not possibly include a norm for every detailed situation, even if it had occurred to him. This will call for intelligent application of the general principles if possible. Where this is not feasible, recourse may be had to the Sacred Congregation which is competent in a given case.

It has been noted in the historical study how at various times in the history of the Church several different Congregations enjoyed this competence, but along lines that were not too clearly specified. The Code, following largely the reorganizational constitution, *Sapienti consilio,* issued by Pope St. Pius X on June 29, 1908,[5] now presents, clearly defined, the competence of these various Congregations.

By virtue of canon 250, §3, the Sacred Congregation of the Council is the primary competent Congregation which can decide "*. . . de controversiis circa praecedentiam . . .*" However, this same canon makes allowance for the fact that other Congregations have limited competence in this matter also.

The Sacred Congregation for Religious has exclusive competence in matters affecting the discipline of all religious of the Latin rite, regardless of sex, whether they take solemn or simple

---

4 Peter A. Baart, *Legal Formulary, A Collection of Forms to be Used in the Exercise of Voluntary and Contentious Jurisdiction* (New York, 1898), n. 131.

5 *Fontes,* n. 682.

vows, or live in common without vows. Even Third Orders Secular come within the competence of this Congregation. Therefore, in any controversy regarding precedence which involves any religious, this Congregation acquires competence because of the religious.[6] There are some restrictions however. In missionary countries which do not have a fully constituted hierarchy as yet, the religious in their capacity as missioners are subject to the Sacred Congregation for the Propagation of the Faith. Problems of precedence which might arise among such religious would accordingly be solved by this Congregation.[7] Controversies regarding precedence which arise within societies of ecclesiastics founded exclusively for the missions would also be solved by this Congregation for the Propagation of the Faith.[8] The *Annuario Pontificio* for 1959 lists one exception: the Pious Society of the Missionaries of St. Charles, whose constitution was approved as recently as 1948, is subject to the Sacred Consistorial Congregation.[9]

Religious of Oriental rites are also excepted from the general competence of the Sacred Congregation for Religious, and placed within the competence of the Sacred Congregation of the Oriental Church.[10]In some countries, this Congregation enjoys full and

---

6 Canon 251.

7 Canons 251 and 252, §§ 3, 4.

8 Canon 252, § 3. These would include the following, listed according to the date of their first pontifical approbation (simple approbation or decree of praise): the Consolata Society for Foreign Missions (I.M.C.), the Congregation of the Missionaries of Mariannhill (C.M.M.), the Paris Foreign Mission Society (M.E.P.), the Pontifical Missionary Institute of Sts. Peter and Paul (P.I.M.E.), the White Fathers (P.A. or W.F.), the Society of the African Missions (S.M.A.), the St. Joseph's Society for Foreign Missions (M.H.F. — the Mill Hill Fathers), the Catholic Foreign Mission Society of America (M.M. — the Maryknoll Missioners), St. Columban's Foreign Mission Society. —*Annuario Pontificio per l'Anno 1959* (Citta del Vaticana: Tipografia Poliglotta Vaticana, 1959), pp. 922-936. The *Annuario* lists only pontifically approved religious institutes.

9 Page 922.

10 Canon 257, § 1. According to the *Annuario Pontificio* for 1959, the following would come within the competence of this Congregation: Ordo Mechitaristarum, O.S.B. (Armenians); Ordo Antonianus (Maronites and Chaldeans); Ordo Basilianus (Melchites); Tertius Ordo Carmelitarum Discalceatorum (Malabars). — pp. 876, 886, 889-91, 921.

exclusive competence over even the members, the hierarchy, and the institutions of the Latin rite.[11]

The Sacred Congregation of Ceremonies is the only competent Congregation to settle difficulties of precedence affecting cardinals and diplomatic representatives accredited to the Holy See.[12]

Whenever there are any controversies, then, in regard to precedence, these are the competent authorities for the solution of such difficulties. One other authority is provided for explicitly by the Code in canon 106, 6°, which authorizes the local ordinary to settle such problems of precedence in the more urgent cases. Since the canon itself states that this power can be exercised by the ordinary of the place ". . . *etiam inter exemptos quatenus ii collegialiter cum aliis procedant* . . ." it seems quite certain that *a fortiori* he can use this power to settle controversies about precedence among non-exempt religious as well. This is a practical norm provided by the Code for emergencies. It is one more indication that the supreme legislator expected the norms of precedence to be working principles available for use. There was no intention of allowing for their non-observance merely because there was some misunderstanding and too little time to have recourse to the Holy See for a solution.

---

11 Egypt, the Peninsula of Sinai, Eritrea and Northern Ethiopia, Southern Albania, Bulgaria, Cyprus, Greece along with Western Thrace, the Dodecanese Islands, Iran, Iraq, Lebanon, Palestine, Syria, Transjordan, Asiatic Turkey, and European Turkey (Eastern Thrace). — Pius XI, *Motu Proprio,* 25 martii 1938 — *Acta Apostolicae Sedis, Commentarium Officiale* (Romae, 1909-1929; Civitate Vaticana, 1929—) XXX (1938), 154 (hereafter cited as *AAS*).

". . . in the above-mentioned regions this Sacred Congregation possesses—not only for the faithful of the Oriental rite but also for the faithful of the Latin rite, and for their hierarchy, works, institutes and pious associations—all the faculties which the other Sacred Congregations possess for the faithful of the Latin rite outside these territories. . . ." — translation of the above, § II, in *The Canon Law Digest* (Vols. I-III [ed. T. L. Bouscaren], Vol. IV [ed. T. L. Bouscaren and J. I. O'Connor] (Milwaukee: Bruce Publishing Co., 1934-58), II, 111.

12 Canon 254. Although the Sacred Congregation of Rites originally was competent in matters of precedence, the Code removed precedence from its competence completely. — Canon 253, § 1.

Article 3. The Procedure to be Followed in the Treatment of Precedence

In treating the canonical norms for precedence, the writer thought it best to treat first the general principles as found in canon 106, 1° to 4°. At that point a study of canon 491 will be inserted, inasmuch as that canon provides norms for determining the different species of moral persons. Thereupon follows a study of the norms for determining the precedence among moral persons of the same species. Finally, the remaining general norms of canon 106 are treated.

In the next article, the special norms alluded to in canon 106 will be applied. Wherever it was considered useful, a schematic outline of the notions discussed in a given division is presented at the end of the division for ready reference.

Article 4. No. 106

Canon 106: *Circa praecedentiam inter varias personas seu physicas seu morales, serventur normae quae sequuntur, salvis normis specialibus quae suis in locis traduntur.*

SECTION 1—INTRODUCTORY NOTIONS

In this canon, for the first time in the history of the Church, the legislator has provided the members of his Church with adequate general principles arranged in an orderly fashion.[13] Prior to the Code, precedence was regulated by almost innumerable decisions from the Roman Curia, local practice and customs. So completely was this matter treated in the Code that the Sacred Congregation of the Council[14] in 1919 declared the principle of canon 22[15] to be applicable to the laws of precedence.[16]

---

[13] Gommarus Michiels, *Principia Generalia de Personis in Ecclesia, Commentarius Libri II Codicis Canonici, Canones Praeliminares (87-106)* (2.ed.; Romae: Desclée et Socii, 1955), p. 683 (hereafter cited as *De Personis).*

[14] This is the Congregation ordinarily competent in matters of precedence. Cf. canon 250, § 3.

[15] "Lex posterior. a competenti auctoritate lata, obrogat priori si . . . totam de integro ordinet legis prioris materiam. . . ." — c. 1, *de constitutionibus,* I, 2, in VI°.

[16] S. C. C., *resolutio, Cunen. et Utinen.,* 17 maii 1919 — *AAS,* XI (1919), 349ff.

SECTION 2—PRESENT STATUS OF PRE-CODE NORMS OF PRECEDENCE

It does not seem to be completely clear either to what extent or in what way this principle of canon 22 is applicable to the new legislation on precedence. Both the dioceses represented in the resolution offered by the Sacred Congregation of the Council in 1919 had offered problems concerning the precedence of their vicars general. It seems, at least as a first impression, that the Congregation was referring only to a complete reorganization of the precedence of the vicar general. This is apparently the same conclusion that was reached by Cicognani in his commentary on canon 22:

> In such cases [of the readjustment of a certain institute, affair, argument of law or of some juridic matter], though the legislator does not expressly declare himself, still it is otherwise sufficiently clear that he intends to readjust the entire subject matter of the former law or juridical institute. In this manner, for example, the Code recast the laws on precedence with respect to the vicar general (can. 370).[17]

Other commentators leave little if any doubt that they consider not only the norms of precedence of the vicar general completely organized, but all norms of precedence. Beste, in his commentary on canon 22, says:

> Sic Codex *generatim* totum ius anterius intra limites canonum 1-6 de integro ordinat et systematice proponit, nisi aliud expresse caveatur circa aliquod punctum, et *speciatim materiam de praecedentia in canone 106 et locis parallelis.*[18]

Michicls, in a footnotc to his discussion of canon 22, con cludes likewise that the whole matter of precedence has been so thoroughly revised that it abrogates any previous law on the matter.[19]

---

17 *Canon Law,* p. 631.

18 Udalricus Beste, *Introductio in Codicem* (4.ed.; Collegeville, Minnesota: St. John's Abbey Press, 1956), p. 91. Italics supplied by writer. Cf. canon 6: "Codex vigentem huc usque disciplinam *plerumque* retinet, licet opportunas immutationes afferat."

19 "Ita expresse S.C. Concilii 17 maii 1919 (*AAS,* XI [1919], 352), ubi tota materia praecedentiae dicitur in canone 106 de integro ordinata." —

The journal *Periodica* reprinted the essence of the resolution of the Congregation of the Council and the conclusions drawn from it. Pertinent to this discussion is a statement under paragraph n. 3: ". . . ius de praecedentia ex integro ordinatur; non est ergo ad ius vetus appellandum."[20]

Bouscaren's *Digest* lists a mere reference to this same resolution of the Congregation under canons 6 and 22, with the note that the Code's laws on precedence are all affected by the principle of canon 22, which abrogates all earlier legislation if it is completely readjusted by a later legislator.[21] Under canon 370, which treats of the precedence of the vicar general in paragraph one, Bouscaren gives a lengthier resume of the resolution without stating anything about the abrogation of prior legislation, even for the vicar general's precedence, except indirectly.[22]

The Congregation's own conclusions to the resolution read in part as follows:

> Codicem autem immutasse de facto ius antea in hac parte vigens, res est manifesta; immo leges de praecedentia in Codice contentae sunt et apparent ex illis legibus quae "totam de integro ordinant legis prioris materiam" (canon 22) et ideo ad normam canonis 6, 1°, quaslibet leges sive particulares sive contrarias omnino abrogant. Enimvero in Codice primum (canon 106) inveniuntur normae generales, perspicuae illae ac omnino rationabiles hanc materiam ordinantes, quae singulis locis variis muneribus applicantur, utpote in canone 370 officio vicarii generalis. Frustra quid simile perquires in toto corpore iuris. . . . Merito itaque Codex totam ex integro hanc materiam ordinavit non modo praecedentiam definiens quoad singula munera, sed etiam principia

---

Michiels, *Normae Generales Juris Canonici* (2 vols., 2.ed.; Parisiis-Tornaci-Romae: Desclée et Socii, 1949), I, 658, note 2.

20 *Periodica de Re Morali, Canonica, Liturgica, (Periodica de Religiosis et Missionariis,* Brugis, 1905-1919; *Periodica de Re Canonica et Morali, utilia praesertim Religiosis et Missionariis,* Brugis, 1920-1927; *Periodica de Re Morali, Canonica, Liturgica,* Brugis, 1927-1936; Romae, 1937 —),X (1922), 66 (hereafter cited as *Periodica*).

21 *The Canon Law Digest,* I, 52 and 58.

22 "Rights of precedence, therefore, may be changed by the law without interfering with vested rights." — *Ibid., pp.* 215-16.

> generalia statuens unde illae singulae sanctiones aestimarentur. . . .[23]

With this resolution and the conclusions of the Congregation in mind, the reader may wonder as he sees each norm of precedence in the Code compared with its pre-Code counterpart, just why these norms should have abrogated the former rules of precedence. Perhaps with some notion of the principles of canon 6, 1°, which abrogates all laws contrary to the Code if no specific exception is made for them, the reader may think that a contradictory quality is likewise necessary for the principles of canon 22 to abrogate prior legislation. When it is seen how closely the earlier legislation often matches that of the Code, it may seem difficult to apply canon 22.

Michiels attempts an explanation by stating three conditions under which the principles of canon 22 operate: (1) for later legislation to be considered a new law, it is enough if the later law is only a partial rearrangement or a summary of the old; (2) "*ut de integro ordinet* . . ." it is sufficient if an orderly codification has been made for the purpose of giving unity to the legislation on a particular juridical institute or notion, even if part of the old law is repeated in the new arrangement; (3) ". . . *tota materia* . . ." may be the whole institute, as the Congregation of the Council declared to be true of precedence; or it may be only a part of the whole institute, or body of laws revised; this part, however, is objectively a complete entity in itself, which had already been arranged more or less completely by the earlier law, and is now merely inserted bodily into the new arrangement.

When any one of these three conditions has been fulfilled in one of the ways mentioned, the earlier law is automatically abrogated by a later law, even though the former law is not contrary to the new legislation. This must be true, first of all, from the context of the principle of canon 22 as it is found in the Code. If the principle of this canon as found in one of Boniface VIII's decretals[24] were to affect contrary laws only, it

---

23 S. C. C., *resolutio, Cunen. et Utinen.*, 17 maii 1919 — *AAS*, XI (1919), 352-53.

24 C. 1, *de constitutionibus*, I, 2, in VI°.

would be repetitious to incorporate it into the Code, for laws contrary to the Code are abrogated by the provisions of canon 6, 1°. Secondly, this interpretation of the principle of canon 22 must be true, because by this new and complete ordering the legislator has sufficiently demonstrated that his complete mind and will are contained simply in the later law. Therefore, canonists should seek out the intention of the law-giver only in this later, revised form of the law.

It is not required that the total complexus of some question be reordered, according to the teaching of Michiels; neither is it necessary for the new law to have more provisions than the old law. There is even less need to have all new provisions. The mere fact that some old provisions are repeated in the new law can be a sign of a complete rearrangement of the whole matter. But this conclusion must be drawn from the tenor of the new law and from various circumstances: did the legislator merely intend to reorder certain matters by this law, or did he intend that other provisions of the same material retain their legal force while only determining some particular point and giving new legal force to it alone?[25]

It would seem, at first, that no single answer could be given in regard to the laws of precedence for several reasons. The field they cover is so broad that one simple answer as to their abrogation could not possibly be made by any commentator. Some of the Code's principles on precedence are taken bodily out of the old law, such as the norms governing moral persons of the same species and grade,[26] and the prohibition against any distinction in the rights of precedence because of different rites.[27] Other principles, such as that concerning the vicar forane

---

25 Michiels, *Normae Generales,* I, 658.

26 Canon 105, 5°, according to Holböck, *Tractatus de Jurisprudentia Sacrae Romanae Rotae* (Graz: In Officina Libraria "Styria", 1957), p. 24, citing *Decisiones Sacrae Romanae Rotae* (40 vols., Romae, 1912 —), VII, decision 36, nn.12ff., pp. 403ff.; XVIII, decision 20, nn. 5ff., pp. 160ff.: this canon completely incorporates the old law about quasi-possession of precedence which was originally found in Gregory XIII, const. *Exposcit,* 15 iul. 1583 — *Fontes,* n. 151: *Bull. Luxem.,* II, 501.

27 Canon 106, 4°, taken from Benedict XIV, const. *Etsi pastoralis,* 26 maii 1742, § IX, n. XVII — *Fontes* n. 328: *Bull. Luxem.* XVI, 94.

(canon 450), are completely new in their present form, though such an office existed before the Code and its holder enjoyed some form of precedence.[28]

In view of the resolution of the Sacred Congregation of the Council, and the rather common opinion adopted by the authors, it seems safe to conclude with them that the rules of precedence have been so thoroughly revised that they alone represent the mind of the lawgiver. Some indication of this reorganization will be given in the various sections. The new law, then, replaces the old. But the former legislation, when a similar institute and similar norms existed, may safely be studied for a better understanding of the present norms in their historical light.

SECTION 3—*Maioritas* VS. *Praecedentia* IN THE CODE OF CANON LAW

Pre-Code norms of precedence and their commentators were concerned primarily with the *maioritas* (superior rank) of a person from which the right of precedence flowed as a consequence. The Code is more directly concerned with the rights of precedence themselves, and only indirectly hints that whoever has precedence must for some reason also enjoy a higher rank *(maioritas)*.

The word *maioritas* itself, moreover, is not used in any of the canons dealing with precedence. But in comparing these two notions of superior rank and its consequent right of precedence as they are now understood, Michiels states that *maioritas* primarily describes the relationship of superior to inferior, from which a right to precedence is derived; therefore, it is primarily concerned with the notion of authority in some form. On the other hand, the notion of *praecedentia* in the Code is concerned, besides, with sources other than authority from which one can derive a right to precedence, such as the dignity of the office (even though there may be less or no authority connected with it). Nevertheless, precedence in Code law substantially corresponds

---

28 Note the absence of any footnotes to this canon in Gasparii's edition of the Code. This serves as an indication that new principles were introduced that find no counterpart in the old law.

to a wider notion of the *maioritas* treated in the decretals (Gregory IX, Liber I, *de maioritate et obedientia,* 33).[29]

Coronata puts it more simply in stating that *maioritas* is the relation of superior to inferior, while *praecedentia* is simply the right of one person to go before another.[30] He adds that sometimes (e.g. canon 106, 2°) both *maioritas* (superior rank) and precedence will be held cumulatively by the same person. This form of precedence will occur among people who are bound together by the relationship of superior and subject. However, canon 106, 3°, provides ample proof for the fact that even when this relationship of authority sometimes does not exist ". . . *inter diversas personas ecclesiasticas quarum nulla habeat in aliis auctoritatem* . . ." one person may have a right to precede another for a different reason.

Michiels has one of the more detailed definitions of precedence as it is known today:

> Ius ad externam praeeminentiam honoris majoremve reverentiam in publicis conventibus aut manifestationibus, alicui prae aliis competens ratione excellentiae majoris.[31]

SECTION 4—THE NATURE OF CANONS 106 AND 491

Adopting a practical approach, Michiels implies that canon 106 is merely a supplementary norm for the special norms given in other canons. He bases his claim on the words of the opening sentence of canon 106 which states ". . . *salvis normis specialibus quae suis in locis traduntur* . . ."[32] He admits that in many instances these special norms are nothing more than authentic applications of the norms of canon 106 to specific persons or

---

29 Michiels, *De Personis,* p. 682, note 2.

30 M. Conte a Coronata, *Institutiones Iuris Canonici ad usum utriusque cleri et scholarum* (5 vols., Taurini-Romae: Marietti. Vol. I, *Normae generales, de Clericis, de Religiosis, de Laicis,* 4 ed., 1950), I, n. 155 (hereafter cited as Coronata, *Institutiones*).

31 *De Personis,* p. 682.

32 ". . . praeprimis attendendae sunt normae speciales . . . tam si discrepent a normis generalibus in canon 106 propositis quam si iisdem sint conformes . . ." — *De Personis,* p. 684.

situations. Canon 370, for instance, merely applies the rule of canon 106, 1°, to the vicar general; he ". . . *qui alius personam gerit* . . .", derives his precedence from the fact that he is the ordinary's *alter ego*. There will be times, however, when these special norms will depart from the general principles of canon 106. Even canon 370, although it conforms basically to the general principles of canon 106, 1°, immediately makes an exception and denies the vicar general precedence over a member of the diocesan clergy who is a consecrated bishop, if the vicar general himself is not. A special provision made for the ordinary in his own diocese by canon 347 is not consistent with canon 106, 3°. For this general principle would give precedence to any archbishop, even though only a titular one, over the local ordinary who is not of archiepiscopal rank. The special norm of canon 347, however, gives precedence to the local ordinary over everyone else within the limits of his diocese except cardinals, papal legates, and the proper metropolitan. Michiels would have recourse to the general principles of canon 106 only when no one of several such special norms[33] was available for some particular case.[34]

The present writer will concede that in practice this may be the more efficient procedure for determining the precedence of individuals. It does not seem logical, however, to imply that the general norms are only supplementary, or to give greater attention to the exceptions or applications of the general rule than to the rule itself. The very choice of the phrase, ". . . *salvis normis specialibus* . . .", indicates that anything else is merely secondary. It further points out that canon 106 is to be considered the primary rule to follow, unless the legislator has provided a secondary and more particular rule for a specific person or situation.

---

33 Cardinals created *in petto*, c. 233, § 2; precedence among the cardinals in a certain order, c. 236, § 2; cardinal dean, c. 237, § 1; cardinals in general, c. 239, §1, 21°; papal legates, c. 269, § 2; patriarchs, primates, archbishops, c. 280; ordinary in his own diocese, c. 347; vicar general, c. 370; cathedral chapter, c. 408 (omitted from this study); vicar forane, c. 450; pastor of the cathedral, other pastors and vicars, c. 478; secular vs. religious and religious among themselves, c. 491; associations of the faithful, c. 701 (omitted from this study); lay patron, c. 1455 (omitted from this study).

34 *De Personis*, p. 685.

SECTION 5—THE KINDS OF PERSONS IN THE CHURCH

Canon 106 in its introductory sentence mentions ". . . *varias personas seu physicas seu morales*. . . ." Who are the persons under discussion here?

Juridically, a person is a subject capable of enjoying rights and obligations.[35] Canonically, a person is a subject capable of enjoying rights and obligations in the Church of Christ. Every baptized person in virtue of his baptism is a citizen of the Church with all the rights and obligations of a Christian, unless there exists an obstacle which impedes the bond of ecclesiastical union, or a censure imposed by the Church.[36]

In checking Gasparri's index to the Code under the word "*praecedentia*", one will note how wide an application is made of this principle that anyone baptized in the Church is considered a person in it. The norms of precedence are listed there for nearly all in the Church, from cardinals down to certain classes of laymen.

A. Moral Persons in the Church

However, there is in the Church, besides the physical or individual persons described above, another type of persons which is mentioned in canon 106: the moral persons ". . . *publica auctoritate constitutae quae distinguuntur in personas morales collegiales et non-collegiales*. . . ."[37] The Catholic Church itself and the Apostolic See evince the full stature of moral persons constituted by divine right; all others are to be considered as subordinate moral persons constituted by the authority of the Church. As such, they derive their personality either explicitly from the provisions of law, or from a special concession of the competent ecclesiastical superior. This superior can constitute a subordinate moral person for a religious or a charitable purpose by issuing a formal decree.[38]

What is a moral person in the Church? The Code does not give a proper definition that is complete. However, a comparison

---

[35] Wernz-Vidal, *Ius Canonicum*, II, n. 1.

[36] Canon 87.

[37] Canon 99.

[38] Canon 100, § 1.

and combination of canons 99, 100,§1, and 87 will give a rather full picture, as Michiels demonstrates in giving this description:

> Persona moralis, scilicet, est *illud omne in Ecclesia a persona physica distinctum* (canon 99), *quod in finem religiosum vel caritativum* (canon 100,§1) *publica auctoritate constitutum est* (canon 99) *in subjectum capax iurium et obligationum* (canon 99 coll. canon 87).[39]

According to the foregoing definition, a moral person constituted by civil authority and recognized by the Church would be included among ecclesiastical moral persons.

More often the juridical personality intended by the Code is that which conforms to canons 99 and 100, because it has been constituted by the public authority of the Church, and not by that of the State.[40]

B. The Kinds of Moral Persons in the Church

A moral person will be a religious moral person if it has God and the fostering of relations with Him as its goal. If men are the object of its concern, considered as beings destined to a supernatural end, towards which the moral person seeks to help them through spiritual and temporal means, then it is a charitable moral person.[41] If the primary and ultimate purpose of a recreational organization is the supernatural care of souls insofar as it intends to protect youths against worldly temptations, it is a religious juridic person, participating in a definite way in the general reason for which the Church was founded.[42]

These ecclesiastical moral persons as understood in canon 106 may be divided in other ways. They may, for instance, be either collegiate, that is corporate, or they may be non-collegiate, or institutional.[43] It will suffice here to give a general notion of these various kinds of moral persons to facilitate a recognition of them as such.

---

39 *De Personis*, p. 347.

40 *Ibid.*, p. 355.

41 Stephanus Sipos, *Enrichiridion Iuris Canonici*, ed. Ladislaus Gálos (6. rev. ed.; Romae: Orbis Catholicus—Herder, 1954), p. 79.

42 John Abbo and Jerome Hannan, *The Sacred Canons* (2 vols., rev. ed.; St. Louis: B. Herder Book Co., 1957), I, 144.

43 Canon 99; Michiels, *De Personis*, p. 355.

The collegiate moral person is an association of physical persons, enjoying a personality distinct from that of the members. This would be exemplified in a religious congregation, a chapter, or a confraternity.[44] Such a moral person, at the time of becoming established, must consist of at least three physical persons, as is stated in canon 100, §2.

The non-collegiate moral person in the canonical sense of the term is an aggregation of specified things or goods, such as those which make up a seminary, a hospital, a church, or a benefice.[45] This type of moral person is separated from the ownership and control of other persons and dedicated to some religious or charitable purpose.[46] By implication, of course, there is required the co-operation of physical persons who administer the non-collegiate moral persons, or for whose benefit the moral person exists. Insofar as these persons represent the non-collegiate moral body, they can act for it.

Whether a moral person is collegiate or non-collegiate, it has all the rights of physical persons except those which of their very nature are proper only for physical persons. Therefore, they can acquire goods, obtain privileges, and have the right of precedence.[47]

Canon 106 makes no distinction about the types of moral persons concerned in matters of precedence. The fact that a non-collegiate person has the rights of physical persons where possible leaves the way open for it also to enjoy precedence through its administrator as though he were a type of proxy. Collegiate moral persons, on the other hand, could enjoy precedence either personally, or through their proxy. Since a moral person *per se* (inherently) cannot act of itself, whatever is said of its precedence must be applied to those who act in its name.

Those who so act are sometimes individuals; at other times it is a group which acts as a collegiate person, although it is not such in fact; sometimes, this group acts as a true collegiate person forming a true college. When those who represent a moral person

---

44 Abbo-Hannan, *The Sacred Canons* I, 144.

45 *Loc. cit.;* cf. Canon 99.

46 Bouscaren-Ellis, *Canon Law,* p. 86.

47 Sipos, *Enchirdion Iuris Canonici,* p. 79.

act as a collegiate group, they have the precedence of the collegiate person, even though the person itself is not collegiate, or the persons representing it do not actually belong to it.[48]

The phrase ". . . *serventur normae quae sequuntur, salvis normis specialibus* . . ." indicates the general norm for the use of canon 106: use these norms unless there is some more specific norm provided. Where will these more specific norms be found?

The norms of precedence found in the rules and constitutions approved for any college or moral person, particularly the religious orders and congregations, third orders secular, confraternities, pious unions, cathedral and collegiate chapters, as well as other societies in the Church, will provide the exceptions to canon 106. At least the lawgiver extends to them that privilege, if they want to use it. This is quite evident from the wording of canon 106, 5°, which leaves the determination of internal precedence entirely to particular law, and in fact points to the universal law merely as the third possible criterion for determining this internal precedence.

Custom has always been one of the norms which regulated precedence. The lawgiver specifically acknowledges this fact in regard to precedence in canon 106, 5°, for the internal precedence of members of a moral person, as well as in canon 106, 6°, where the ordinary of the place is given power to determine the precedence of his subjects.

---

48 Coronata, *Institutiones,* I, n. 159.

CHAPTER V

THE PRECEDENCE OF PHYSICAL PERSONS IN THE CHURCH

ARTICLE 1. PRELIMINARY NOTIONS ABOUT PROXIES

Canon 106, 1°: *Qui alius personam gerit, ex eadem obtinet praecedentiam; sed qui in conciliis aliisque similibus conventibus procuratorio nomine intersunt, sedent post illos eiusdem gradus qui intersunt proprio.*

The *"procurator"* of canon 106 is best understood as "proxy"; the English "procurator" carries with it the connotation of an agent of business or finance. Here the Code is interested in the substitute or representative with authority to act for another.[1] Frequently this authorization is found in a written document presented by the proxy in the name of the person he represents, the principal.[2] An additional courtesy is a second document sent by the principal directly to the person who presides over the assembly which he himself is hindered from attending personally.

---

1 The proxy *(procurator)* is a personal representative. When he takes the place of a plaintiff or defendant in litigation he is more properly styled a *procurator ad litem.* Without this specification the term denotes a personal representative in any affair in which the law permits someone to act through a representative. It is a recognized principle in canon law that one may do those things through another which one can do in person.

An agent *(negotiorum gestor)* is likewise a personal representative of the principal, but he differs from the *procurator ad litem,* because the agency may extend to a great variety of affairs and need not be as formal as the appointment of a proxy in a trial. The *procurator ad litem* may not act in court for his principal until after he has deposited with the court the formal document of appointment as proxy for the lawsuit (canon 1659). — Stanislaus Woywod and Callistus Smith, *A Practical Commentary on the Code of Canon Law* (2 vols., 7. printing; New York: Joseph F. Wagner, 1943), II, n. 1631 (hereafter cited as *Commentary*).

2 "Possessio beneficii etiam per procuratorem speciale mandatum habentem capi potest." — Canon 1445; "Procurator ne prius a iudice admittatur quam speciale mandatum ad lites scriptum, etiam in calce ipsius citationis mandantis subscriptione munitum, et locum, diem, mensem et annum referens, apud tribunal deposuerit." — Canon 1659.

The pre-Code norm of precedence for the proxy is summed up best in Gratian's *Concordia Discordantium Canonum:*

> Praecipimus ne diaconus (quamvis etiam in dignitate, hoc est in officio ecclesiastico, sit) ante presbyterum sedeat, nisi cum *locum habuerit proprii patriarchae aut metropolitani* sui pro aliquo capitulo. Tunc enim *sicut illius tenens honorabitur.* . . .[3]

A twofold difference can be found in the comparing of this former law with the present. The right of the proxy was limited "*pro aliquo capitulo* . . ." or some sort of meeting. The Code law does not limit the use of a proxy or his right to precedence simply to meetings or councils; a proxy may also be sent to other types of gatherings of a liturgical, ceremonial or social nature. There is, however, a similarity with the Code law insofar as a special condition is made for meetings or councils, for therein the Code grants only a limited form of precedence, after all those of the same rank that the principal would have enjoyed if he had been present personally.

The second difference is the unlimited type of precedence given the proxy in the old law ". . . *sicut illius locum tenens honorabitur.* . . ." This full enjoyment of the principal's right to precedence is granted to proxies by the Code only when they are not in a council or some similar gathering.

This seems to be enough reorganization of the old law even when considered apart from the other Code norms of precedence to justify the conclusion that, according to the principle of canon 22, it would abrogate the earlier law on the precedence of proxies.

SECTION 1—PROXIES OUTSIDE A COUNCIL

In this part of canon 106 there are two principles. The one is a limiting norm, the other is a very broad principle: whoever takes the place of someone else, enjoys the same precedence as the person whom he represents. This very general law has several particular applications that are rather evident.

It is on the basis of this principle, for instance, that the Roman Pontiff has his precedence above all others in the Church as the Vicar of Christ. Other vicars taking their precedence from the

---

[3] C. 26, D. 96, citing canon 7 of the Council in Trullo (692) — Bruns, I, 39.

persons they represent are the vicar general (canon 370, §1), who is the episcopal ordinary's *alter ego,* and the vicar capitular (diocesan administrator during the vacancy of the See). To the latter falls the task of representing the cathedral chapter (or in the United States, the diocesan consultors) in the administration of the diocese vacated by the death of the episcopal ordinary. Although there is a special canon giving the specific norms for the precedence of papal legates (canon 269, §2), their right is based on the fact that they are the *alter ego* of the Roman Pontiff.[4]

Another specific example of a proxy who takes his precedence from the person he represents is cited by Coronata: the delegate whom the ordinary is permitted to send to assist at the election of a Superioress-General or Abbess of a monastery of nuns (canon 506, §2), or the Mother-General of a congregation of women religious (§4).[5]

Since there is a limitation made specifically for the proxy in councils and similar meetings, it may be concluded that on other occasions there is no such limitation, unless the saving clause of the opening sentence of this canon comes into effect: ". . . *salvis normis specialibus quae suis in locis traduntur. . . .*" Otherwise the proxy enjoys exactly the same precedence as the person whom he represents. Michiels asserts this specifically with the clause: ". . . *etiamsi ratione qualitatum personalium nulla aut minore gaudeat praeeminentia. . . .*"[6] The substitute is considered to have the same personality and dignity as the person whose place he takes regardless of his personal status, or of the great difference existing between his personal rank and that of his principal. Gratian found a very pointed example of a subdeacon being the proxy for the pope at a council.[7] The papal legate today, even though he enjoys no jurisdiction, precedes all ordinaries with the one exception or special norm provided by the law itself: he would not precede a cardinal.[8]

---

4 Canon 266.

5 *Institutiones,* I, n. 158.

6 *De Personis,* p. 685.

7 C. 1, D. 94.

8 Canon 269, § 2. However, if he were a cardinal himself, the legate would precede even the cardinals, contrary to the norms of this canon. — Canon 239, § 1, 21°.

There is practically no limit to the number of other applications this rule for proxies may have. Ordinarily one would imagine that it would be most useful among persons of higher rank in the Church, such as cardinals, patriarchs, archbishops, bishops, abbots or major religious superiors. There are many occasions when one of these might feel that circumstances call for his presence at a given place or time. It is easy to see how at times it may be quite impossible for him to be present personally. On such occasions he may want to send a substitute to show his interest or good will, or in appreciation for an invitation. In some circumstances proper social protocol may demand it. In that case a proxy may be appointed by means of a special mandate given him to prove his mission. At the same time a notice should be sent, out of courtesy, to the person in charge of the function. Such notice would state the inability of the principal to be present, and his desire to have his proxy represent him. Provided the occasion is not a council or some similar type of meeting, the proxy, no matter what his personal rank, will enjoy the same precedence that his principal would have enjoyed had he been present. A simple priest, for instance, could represent his ordinary at an episcopal consecration, at a funeral, or at some other function where precedence should be observed. If he did, he would take the exact place of his ordinary among the bishops according to the ordinary's date of promotion in consistory. The same exceptions that would have to be made for the determining of the ordinary's precedence would apply to the determination of the proxy's own. The provision of canon 347, which safeguards the precedence of the ordinary of the place in his own territory, would still remain effective.

Were the affair taking place in some other province than that to which the proxy belongs, his own precedence as a proxy for his own archbishop would likewise be limited by the prescriptions of canon 347; otherwise he would go among the archbishops, and again, according to the date of his archiepiscopal ordinary's promotion in consistory. At a later time it will be pointed out how special attention may have to be paid to the Archbishop of Baltimore in the determining of his precedence among other archbishops and their proxies in this country in view of his primacy of place, which gives him special precedence on certain occasions.

What is to be said if the local ordinary is hindered from attending some such affair in his own diocese at which protocol would seem to require his presence either personally or through a representative? The problem would be less complicated if the vicar general would be appointed as the proxy, since the law already provides for his precedence over all the other clergy of the diocese, except those who are consecrated the while he himself is not.[9] The situation could also be simplified if one of the auxiliary bishops (the senior, if more than one) were appointed as proxy. He would then enjoy the precedence given by way of exception to the ordinary in his own diocese over all others except cardinals, papal legates, and his own metropolitan (canon 347). What is to be said, however, if the ordinary passes over the auxiliary bishop and appoints his vicar general (who is not a bishop) or someone less than a vicar general as his proxy? The law makes no distinction outside of councils; therefore it is presumed that unlike the exception of canon 370, when the vicar general is not a bishop, none are to be made, even in these extreme cases. It is quite likely, however, that the ordinary will be aware of the possible confusion resulting from the appointment of a lesser cleric, and accordingly will appoint the highest ranking cleric in the diocese as his proxy. To avoid conflict, it will sometimes be better for one or the other ecclesiastic to absent himself from some functions.[10]

In practice, the precedence of the proxy is determined for all occasions, except councils and similar meetings, within the perspective of the precedence of the principal if he were present personally, with careful attention paid to the special norms, such as those in canon 347. With that perspective duly established the precedence of the proxy has likewise become determined.

SECTION 2—PROXIES IN A COUNCIL

The law places a limitation on proxies in the second part of

9 Canon 370, § 1.

10 Joachim Nabuco, *Pontificalis Romani Expositio iuridico-practica* (3 vols., Petròpolis, Brazil: Vozes, 1945), I, n. 29.

canon 106, 1°: in councils and similar meetings a proxy yields precedence to those other attendants who are equal in rank with his principal. It will prove helpful to discuss first the persons who, as principals, are entitled to send a proxy to a council.

Canon 359, §1, states: "Iis qui ad synodum venire debent, si legitimo impedimento detineantur, non licet mittere procuratorem qui eorum nomine synodo intersit." From this it is clear that there can be a question of conciliar representatives only at provincial, plenary, national and general councils of the Church.[11]

The Code states that those who with a deliberative vote must attend these councils[12] must attend either personally, or prove their excuse and send a proxy in their place.[13]

A. The General Council

It is not directly within the scope of this study to go into a detailed investigation of who is included in the category of those who are to be called to the council, and who have a deliberative vote in it; but it will be useful at least to enumerate the various participants. Those who must attend a general council in virtue of canon 223, §1, are the following:

a) cardinals, even though they are not bishops;
b) patriarchs;
c) primates;
d) archbishops;[14]
e) residential bishops;[15]
f) abbots *nullius;*
g) prelates *nullius;*

---

11 "A plenary council denotes a meeting of the ordinaries of *several ecclesiastical provinces* under the presidency of a delegate of the Holy See. . . . A national council denotes a plenary council attended by the ordinaries of *all the ecclesiastical provinces* of a whole nation." — Abbo-Hannan, *The Sacred Canons,* I, 328 [Italics supplied].

12 General council, c. 223, § 1; plenary councils, c. 282, § 1; provincial councils, cc. 282, § 1; 285; 286, § 1.

13 Canons 224, § 1; 287, § 1.

14 Canon 282, § 1, in referring to the plenary council, and by direction of canon 286, § 1, to provincial councils, uses the term "metropolitan."

15 They need not be consecrated, as long as they have canonically taken possession of their dioceses. — Sipos, *Enchiridion Iuris Canonici,* p. 157.

h) abbots primate;
i) abbot superiors of monastic congregations;
j) supreme moderators of exempt clerical institutes only.

Although titular bishops may in consequence of canon 223, §2, be invited to attend a general council, and despite the fact that they will have a deliberative vote if they do attend, they are implicitly excluded by canon 224, §1, from sending a proxy if they are unable to accept the invitation, for that canon specifically binds only those participants in the council who are obliged to attend by reason of canon 223, §1.[16]

B. *The Plenary Council*

The list of those "... *qui assistere debent cum suffragio deliberativo* ..."[17] at a plenary council differs enough to be given separately:

a) papal legate [as president and proxy for the Roman Pontiff];
b) metropolitans;
c) residential bishops;[18]
d) apostolic administrators;
e) abbots *nullius;*
f) prelates *nullius;*
g) vicars apostolic;
h) prefects apostolic;
i) vicars capitular (in the United States, the administrators of the vacant diocese).[19]

In comparing this enumeration with that of a general council, one will note that, of all the ordinaries listed in canon 198, only

16 Sipos, *op. cit., p.* 158, note 10.

17 A. Vermeersch and I. Creusen, *Epitome Iuris Canonici* (3 vols.; 7. ed., Mechliniae-Romae: H. Dessain, 1949-56), I, n. 396: "... *omnes et soli Ordinarii locorum, vicario generali excepto* ... "; cf. c. 198, § 1.

18 Even those who are not yet consecrated must attend if they have taken canonical possession of their diocese. — Elias Olarte Poblete, *The Plenary Council,* The Catholic University of America Canon Law Studies, n. 372 (Washington, D. C.: The Catholic University of America Press, 1958), p. 34.

19 Canon 282, § 1.

the superiors of exempt institutes or abbots of monastic congregations are excepted from attending plenary councils.[20]

It is not clear whether titular bishops who are resident in the territory are obliged to attend by force of the law or as a result of the invitation from the papal legate according to his specific instructions. The canon states: ". . . si vocentur, adesse debent habentque suffragium deliberativum nisi . . . aliud expresse caveatur."[21] According to canon 287, §1, this condition seems to qualify them to send a proxy if they are legitimately hindered.[22] At least one author argues that if titular bishops are called to the council, it is merely a privilege given to them personally, which they cannot delegate to another.[23]

C. The Provincial Council

A third enumeration will be justified by sufficient differences in the listing of those who are not only obliged to attend a provincial council, but who also have a deliberative vote therein. Canon 286 gives the general norm referring first to the various ordinaries mentioned in canon 284. Once these have chosen "one of the neighboring metropolitans"[24] and have had that choice confirmed *semel pro semper,* they have to attend the councils of that chosen metropolitan. This group includes, in the order given in canon 285:

a) residential bishops who are not subject to any metropolitan;

b) abbots *nullius;*

c) prelates *nullius;*

d) archbishops who have no suffragans (in the United States, the Archbishop of Washington is immediately subject to the

---

20 However, they are listed at the end of the procession after the consultors of the cardinal-legate and the bishops in the *Ordo in Concilio Plenario Servandus* (Vaticana: Typis Polyglottis, 1946), p. 11.

21 Canon 282, § 2.

22 "Qui . . . interesse debent cum voto deliberativo . . ."

23 Coronata, *Institutiones,* I, n. 426.

24 Murphy's translation of *"aliquem viciniorem metropolitam."* — Francis J. Murphy, *Legislative Powers of the Provincial Council,* The Catholic University of America Canon Law Studies, n. 257 (Washington, D. C.: The Catholic University of America Press, 1947), p. 98.

Holy See and has no suffragans.—*Annuario Pontificio* (1959), (p. 516).

Then, in addition to these ordinaries, the following must also attend, in accordance with canon 286, §1:

e) all suffragans of the province;

f) all those obliged to attend the plenary council as listed above according to canon 282, §1;[25]

g) cathedral chapters (in the United States, the diocesan consultors) of each diocese whose ordinary must attend, must themselves be invited; once invited, the consultors of each diocese must send two deputies to the council, even though they will have only a consultative vote.[26] Canon 286, §3, speaks of these deputies of the diocesan consultors as *designati,* whereas the other canons treated above used the term found in canon 106, 1°, *procuratores.* A Vatican publication of 1946, indicating the precedence in plenary councils, lists in fifth place, *procuratores capitulares.*[27] It seems justifiable then to link the obligation to send *designati* with this reference to *procuratores* and to conclude that the cathedral chapters (or diocesan consultors) are included in the group that is obliged to send proxies to provincial councils, even though such representatives do not have a deliberative vote.[28]

The status of titular bishops at provincial councils is somewhat similar to their status at plenary councils. Canon 286, §2, like canon 282, §2, states that, if they are invited, they have a deliberative vote ". . . *nisi aliud . . . caveatur.*" However, there seems to be no obligation on their part to accept this invitation

---

25 The papal legate who must attend the plenary council will naturally be excluded, as may be seen in a comparison between canons 281 and 282, §1. Canon 281 mentions that the Roman Pontiff will send to a *plenary* council his own legate as the presiding officer. Canon 282, § 1, states that, besides the papal legate, others are obliged to attend. — Murphy, *op. cit.,* p. 92. By the very nature of the case, there will not be more than one metropolitan present for a provincial council; he will preside in accordance with canon 284.

26 "*Mittant*" of canon 286, § 3, is taken to imply an obligation, according to Wernz-Vidal *(Ius Canonicum,* II, n. 537*)*, Coronata (*Institutiones,* I, n. 412.) and Augustine (*Commentary,* II, p. 175); Vermeersch-Crusen, however, to the contrary.—*Epitome,* I, n. 398, 3°.

27 *Ordo in Concilio Plenario Servandus,* p. 11.

28 Canon 286, § 3.

to the provincial council in the same way they are apparently obliged to attend a plenary council, once they are invited to the latter.[29]

Who, then, may and must send proxies to the provincial council when they are hindered from attending in person? Canon 287, §1, answers the question in principle: "Qui Concilio plenario aut provinciali interesse debent cum voto deliberativo, si iusto impedimento detineantur. . . ." This qualification applies to the following:

a) bishops who are not subject to any metropolitan, but who have chosen once for all a neighboring metropolitan, approved by the Holy See, whose provincial council they will attend;[30]

b) abbots and prelates *nullius* of the same description and under similar circumstances;[30]

c) archbishops who have no suffragans, in similar circumstances;[30]

d) all the suffragan bishops of the province;[31]

e) cathedral chapters (groups of diocesan consultors) of each diocese whose ordinary must attend in accordance with canon 286, §1. Each such group must send two representatives of the body;[32]

f) major superiors of exempt clerical religious communities;[33]

g) superiors of monastic congregations who have actual residence in the province;[33]

---

29 In regard to titular bishops at plenary councils, canon 282, § 2, states: "*. . . si . . . vocentur, adesse debent . . .*" *There is nothing similar to this* in canon 286, § 2, concerning their attendance at provincial councils according to Vermeersch-Creusen (*Epitome,* I, n. 398, 2°). There is greater doubt about their right to send a proxy to the provincial council, since canon 287, in stating who must send proxies, makes two requirements: (1) obligatory attendance of the principal at the council, which Sipos (*Enchiridion Iuris Canonici,* p. 188) maintains is not required of titular bishops; (2) his legitimate impediment from attending. These two requirements do not seem to be fulfilled in the case of the titular bishops. Coronata (*Institutiones,* I, n. 320) explicitly denies the titular bishop the right of a proxy.

30 Canon 285.

31 Canon 286, § 1.

32 Canon 286, § 3.

33 Canon 286, § 4. Some authors maintain that the titular bishops who have domicile or quasi-domicile in the province must also attend, and may there-

h) apostolic administrators of diocese;[34]
i) vicars and prefects apostolic;[34]
j) vicars capitular (diocesan administrators)[34]

SECTION 3—THE KINDS OF PROXIES

The Code itself provides for two kinds of proxies at councils. In canon 224, §2, it is suggested that one of the fathers at the general council may be selected as the proxy for an absent father. He would nevertheless enjoy but one deliberative vote at most. The same provision is made for this kind of proxy in plenary or provincial councils, by force of canon 287, §2, with the same limitation to a single deliberative vote.

The second kind of representative, as delineated by the Code law itself, receives mention in canon 282, §1, which states that metropolitans and residential bishops ". . . *sui loco, mittere possunt coadiutorem vel auxiliarem. . . .*" Here the text seems to state clearly that these possible proxies (though they are not so named by the law itself) enjoy a deliberative vote (in the plenary council with which this canon is concerned, or also in the provincial council, because of the reference in canon 286 to this same canon). This particular provision of law caused some confusion to at least one commentator.

Augustine (1872-1943) concluded from this that no substitutes were to be admitted to plenary councils except coadjutors or auxiliary bishops.[35] It is difficult for the present writer to reconcile such an interpretation of canon 282, §1, with canon 287, §1, for the latter requires anyone who is under obligation to attend the council but who is legitimately impeded from doing so to send a proxy. Many of those metropolitans or residential bishops who are obliged to attend but who are legitimately impeded may not have coadjutors or auxiliary bishops. Such bishops would be held to the impossible, and the two canons would be almost totally contradictory. It seems that the difficulty can best be solved as follows.

---

fore send a proxy. The present writer is not of this opinion, however, for the reasons shown above.

34 Canon 282, § 1, as indicated in canon 286, § 1.

35 *Commentary*, II, 38.

Canon 287, §1, provides that the representative has only a consultative vote. But canon 282, §1, gives a deliberative vote to the coadjutor or the auxiliary bishop sent as proxy. If the ordinary selects one of these two, his proxy will have a deliberative vote; otherwise he will have only a consultative vote through his representative.[36]

It seems quite clear that the ordinary has a choice, however; for although canon 287, §1, obliges him to send a proxy, canon 282, §1, merely states that he *may* send his coadjutor or auxiliary (". . . *qui sui loco, mittere possunt coadiutorem vel auxiliarem.* . . ."). The example given by Regatillo is the case of a priest attending a plenary council in the name of his archbishop, which would violate the law as Augustine understood it.[37]

Thus the Code specifically names as possible representatives either one of the fathers of the council, or the coadjutor or auxiliary of a metropolitan or residential bishop. May anyone else be designated as a proxy? Since canon 287, §2, states: "*Procurator, si fuerit unus ex patribus* . . .", and canon 282, §1, provides that the metropolitans or residential bishops *may* send their coadjutors or auxiliaries, it is quite evident that the proxies need not belong to either of these two groups.

SECTION 4—THE QUALIFICATIONS OF PROXIES

The Code itself lists specific qualifications or requirements only for someone who is to be a representative for a litigant (*procurator ad litim,* canon 1657). In his study on the plenary council, Poblete states that such persons should be "*habiles, doctores, et discreti.*"[38]

In general the persons selected as substitutes must be suited to the work of giving advice to the conciliar body, and must likewise be well informed about the situation in their diocese. They must be well recommended for their prudence, and should

---

36 Coronata, *Institutiones,* I, n. 369 bis, note 5.

37 Eduardus F. Regatillo, *Interpretatio et Iuris-prudentia Codicis Iuris Canonici* (3. ed.; Santander: Sal Terrae, 1953) *sub can.* 106, *Anotationes.*

38 *The Plenary Council,* p. 37, citing S. C. Conc., *Tarraconen.,* 4 dec. 1638—*Fontes,* n. 2596.

be doctors in canon law or theology, or at least well-versed in these matters.[39]

Both Poblete[40] and Murphy[41] suggest that, when the proof of the impediment is sent to the president of the council in a written document, the name of the substitute should be mentioned at the same time.[42] In addition, both require that the proxy himself be given a written document attesting to his mandate from his principal.[43]

It cannot be demanded that all the judicial details required by canon 1659 are necessary for some other non-judicial proxy, but these norms can certainly serve as a safe guide. For they list the ordinary characteristics identifying any authentic document: the signature of the principal, the place, date, and official seal of the principal. In addition, a brief statement excusing personal attendance and naming the proxy will complete the mandate.[44]

SECTION 5—THE PRECEDENCE OF A PROXY IN A COUNCIL

The Code gives a special norm for the precedence of proxies at council: ". . . sedent post illos eiusdem gradus qui intersunt proprio."[45] It will be necessary to consult the commentary on the third numerical division of this canon to understand this norm completely. In that later part, the differences between *gradus* and *ordo* will be discussed at length. It is sufficient here to mention the norm as it applies specifically to the proxy.

The practical approach to a solution of the proxy's rights of precedence would first determine the precedence of the principal according to canon 106 and the other special norms that may be

---

39 Canon 1657 requires that the *procurator ad litem* (the proxy of the defendant or plaintiff at a trial) should be at least twenty-one years of age, and of good reputation. A non-Catholic is admitted only by way of exception and in case of necessity. — Woywod-Smith, *Commentary,* II, n. 1631.

40 *Op. cit.*, p. 37.

41 *Legislative Powers of the Provincial Council,* p. 99.

42 This is merely a matter of courtesy.

43 Cf. also A. Blat, *Commentarium Textus Codicis Iuris Canonici* (5 vols. in 6; Romae, 1919-1927), II, 257.

44 Cf. also canon 1445.

45 Canon 106, 1°.

necessary. For example, it may be supposed that, the principal is a residential archbishop. He has furnished proof of his impediment to the president of the council, and has given a mandate to a proxy who will represent him.

First, the precedence of the archbishop must be determined. If the archbishop had been in attendance at the council personally, he would have enjoyed precedence with all the other archbishops over all bishops, and the lesser clergy. The principal would likewise have been preceded by primates, patriarchs, and cardinals. His rank or *gradus* would have been that of an archbishop. His proxy will enjoy the same rank or *gradus.*

Within that rank, however, the archbishop would have taken his position in relation to the other archbishops of the same *gradus* or rank, according to the time of his preconization, or the date of the consistory announcing his elevation to the rank of archbishop. The archbishops announced in an earlier consistory would have had precedence over the principal, and therefore would have followed him in a procession. The principal, on the other hand, would have precedence over all archbishops promoted in consistory at some later date.

It is this second facet of the archbishop's precedence (proper precedence within the *gradus* or rank according to promotion) which is denied the proxy: he will take his place ". . . *Post illos eiusdem gradus qui intersunt proprio.*" Therefore, the substitutes come after all the other archbishops who are present personally at the council.[46]

One would use the same procedure to determine the rights of precedence for the proxy of any member of the council entitled to send a proxy, in accordance with the norms outlined above, whether he be cardinal, primate, bishop, or some other father of

46 "In concilio generali vel plenario, procurator archiepiscopi locum sumit post archiepiscopos omnes, qui adstant nomine proprio, sed ante episcopos, licet mandans archiepiscopus iure gaudeat praecedendi super plures archiepiscopos praesentes ratione antiquitatis promotionis." — Beste, *Introductio in Codicem,* sub can. 106, 1°.

"Sacerdos qui procuratorium mandatum habet a cardinali sedet immediate post omnes cardinales, sed ante patriarchas, archiepiscopos, etc. . . ." — Michiels, *De Personis,* p. 685.

the council. It matters not what the personal qualities of the proxy might be.[47] No specific norms are established by law; some general norms have been suggested above. Ordinarily, it would seem that a layman would not be capable of fulfilling the requirements which at least prudence would seem to demand. Basically, however, there seems to be no principle of law against having a layman as proxy if he has the capability that matches his obligations at the council.

If a reason is sought for the exceptional precedence of proxies at a council, Michiels, in the company of others, states that the representation of the proxy at the business of the council is not a complete representation, ". . . *sed solum dimidiata*."[48] Another possible reason has been voiced by Murphy in a different context. However, it may be equally applicable here: "The present law does not favor the practice of sending proxies. This is evidenced not only in the requirement set forth in the canon 287, §1, that a just impediment must be proved, but also in the fact that procurators as such lack a [deliberative] vote, under the general comprehension of the law, unless the law specifically confers it upon them."[49]

SECTION 6–PRECEDENCE AMONG SEVERAL PROXIES IN THE SAME *GRADUS*

One final principle may be added in the event that more than one proxy attends a council or any other meeting of a similar nature. The proxies' rights of precedence within their own *gradus* or group can hardly be determined satisfactorily by the date of their own appointments to that *gradus* which is the general norm of canon 106, 3°. Even if it might be possible, it would not be altogether proper to show suitable honor to the proxies solely in virtue of their personal qualities, when they are present simply by reason of their principals. Having been put into a separate *gradus* by reason of their mandates as proxies,

---

47 Michiels, *ibid.*, p. 685.

48 *De Personis*, p. 685; Ojetti, *Commentarium*, II, 205; Wernz-Vidal, *De Personis*, n. 46, ad 1; Maroto, *Institutiones Iuris Canonici ad Norman Novi Codicis* (Vol. I, 3.ed.; Matriti, 1921), I, n. 478, note 3 (hereafter cited as *Institutiones*).

49 *Legislative Powers of the Provincial Council*, p. 101.

the representatives proceed to determine their own precedence according to that which their principals would have enjoyed in relation to each other, had they been present personally. This, in turn, would have been determined by the date of their promotion to their *gradus* or rank, whether it be primate, archbishop or titular bishop. Therefore the pattern of precedence which would have been found among those present in their own name is duplicated at the bottom of each rank among the proxies after this fashion:

a) cardinal bishops, according to the date they were named to their suburbicarian sees (or the *gradus* of cardinal bishop);[50]

b) proxies of cardinal bishops according to the same principle;

c) cardinal priests, and then cardinal deacons, in their proper order, according to the date they were named to the College of Cardinals;[51]

d) proxies, first of cardinal priests, then of cardinal deacons, within both groups according to the date the principals were appointed to the Sacred College;

e) patriarchs according to canon 106, 3°;

f) proxies of patriarchs in the same order;

g) primates according to canon 106, 3°;

h) proxies of primates in the same order;

i) and so on down the line of the hierarchy.[52]

---

50 Hynes, *The Privileges of Cardinals,* p. 35; cf. canon 106, 3°. This norm can be deduced from the order in which the cardinal bishops are listed in the *Annuario Pontificio* for 1959, pp. 39-47, and is stated in footnote 1, p. 39.

51 From canon 236, § 2, it seems quite certain that the two orders of cardinals, priests and deacons, are for many purposes considered less distinct from each other as far as precedence is concerned, since for both it is based on the date of their nomination to the college, but within their proper order. To the contrary, the cardinal bishops have the date of their elevation to the suburdicarian sees as their singular determining principle. There seems less justification for breaking the group of cardinal priests and cardinal deacons into two parts in order to place the proxies of the cardinal priests before the cardinal deacons who are present personally. *Sed contra:* Michiels, *De Personis* p. 685.

52 "Si vero adsint plures aliorum procuratores mutua eorum praecedentia determinanda est ex praecedentia qua in illis conciliis [vel aliis coetibus quibuscumque] respective gaudent personae a procuratoribus representatae." — Michiels, *De Personis,* p. 685, footnote 1.

In summary, then, a proxy derives his precedence from his principal *(mandans)* absolutely, unless there is a question of precedence in a council, or some special norm.[53] The proxy in council is required for those who must be present and who have a deliberative vote, according to the lists of canons 223, §1, 282, §1, and 286, §1. The law itself makes no special qualifications nor demands any formal appointment, though in practice some standard must be met in regard to both.[54]

A proxy is required only for those who are obliged to attend the council and have a deliberative vote therein. A proxy sent by someone apart from all obligation to do so would necessarily be taking the place of a principal who did not have a deliberative vote.[55] At an ecumenical council, he could represent only a theologian or a canonist, or some titular bishop under special circumstances in which he would not have a deliberative vote.[56] At a plenary or provincial council, such a proxy could represent titular bishops under similar special circumstances, all other clergy not listed in canon 282, §§1,2,[57] the diocesan consultors, the major superiors of exempt clerical religious institutes, and the superiors of monastic congregations.[58]

However practical or impractical it might be in the individual instances cited above, a proxy could apparently be sent as a mark of courtesy, although none of the persons mentioned is required to send one. The proxy's precedence in this case would be determined by the general principles of canon 106, 1°, for councils and similar gatherings, since the Code itself makes no distinction between proxies who are required by the law, and those who are sent out of courtesy.

SECTION 7—*Similibus Conventibus* OF CANON 106, 1°

What are the *similes conventus* of which this canon speaks? The canon itself alludes to the deliberative nature of the

53 Papal legates in canon 269, §2.

54 Cf. canons 1445, 1659.

55 Canons 224, § 1, and 287, § 1.

56 Canon 223, §§ 2, 3.

57 Canon 282, §§ 2, 3.

58 Canon 286, §§ 2, 3, 4.

gathering in stating the norms for the precedence of proxies "... *in conciliis et similibus conventibus*. ..." To be similar to a council, a meeting would have to have something of the nature of a council about it. Omitting specific references to the nature of the council, the following might be offered as a definition: "... *congregatio legitima* ... *quae* ... *de negotiis* ... *Ecclesiae deliberet et decernat*."[59]

The word *conventus* appears thirteen times in the Code.[60] Twice it is used in the meaning of a religious convent.[61] The other eleven times it is used in indication of a meeting of a deliberative nature, as opposed to a liturgical, ceremonial, or social function. In three of these canons the word is used in designation of the meeting of the bishops of the province. This quinquennial meeting is given three specific tasks: to determine the agenda of the next provincial council;[62] in the absence of a provincial council, to determine the taxes and stipends for the province;[63] to establish uniform judicial fees throughout the province.[64]

Canon 131, §1, uses the word *conventus* for the deanery meetings, and explains that they are also called *collationes seu conferentias,* indicating the deliberative nature of these gatherings. Canon 448, §1, uses the word again to refer to these deanery meetings.

In canon 1871, the word is used three times in reference to the meeting of the college of judges to discuss the facts of a case at trial and the reasons for their opinions. In canon 411, the word is used in designation of a business meeting of the chapter of canons.

There seems to be no doubt that the meaning of the word *conventus* in canon 106, 1°, indicates a meeting having the nature of business and purpose of a council. This strict interpre-

59 Vermeersch-Creusen, *Epitome,* I, n. 341.

60 Arcturus Lauer, *Index Verborum Codicis Iuris Canonici* (Civitate Vaticana: Typis Polyglottis, 1931), s.v. *conventus.*

61 Canons 622, § 3, and 2394, 3°.

62 Canon 292, § 2.

63 Canon 1507, § 1.

64 Canon 1909, § 1.

tation is important insofar as it limits the application of the restrictive rule for the precedence of proxies to councils and similar gatherings. Therefore, only at such gatherings will the proxy take precedence after all those of the same grade as his principal. At other types of gatherings of a liturgical, ceremonial, or social nature, the proxy will derive his precedence from exactly that of his principal, without any diminution of honor.

Article 2. Precedence Based on Authority

Canon 106, 2°: *Cui est auctoritas in personas sive physicas sive morales, eidem ius est praecedentiae supra illas.*

In this numerical division of canon 106 there is found the first principle of precedence that is based on a personal qualification. This differs from the principles of the preceding numerical division which determines the precedence of a proxy according to the qualification of the principal; but this second division of canon 106 is quite in conformity with the original notions of precedence as a derived right of authority, or *maioritas,* in the strict sense; for originally the two major sources of precedence were sacramental Orders and jurisdiction.[65]

Orders were often listed first in a series of sources for precedence; but second in the list most often was dignity, jurisdiction, or prelacy. These terms were used more or less interchangeably, and generally implied some sort of authority. Canon 106, 2°, does not reflect a new principle, then, but merely puts into succinct form some similar notions which were prevalent before the Code, although possibly not on such a wide and general basis as they are now. For in the Code the notion of authority is the primary basis; Order becomes a secondary criterion for determin-

---

[65] C. 15, X *de M. et O.,* I, 33, established the principle that whoever was in a higher sacramental order should have precedence over those who were in lower Orders. The one exception repeated from commentator to commentator was that of the archdeacon; although he was lower in Orders than the archpriest, nevertheless he took precedence over the latter because he had greater jurisdiction. Cf. Hostiensis, *Summa Aurea,* lib. I, *de M. et O.,* n. 1, s.v. *in quibus consistat obedientia;* also Boich, *In Quinque Decretalium Libros Commentaria,* lib. I, *de M. et O.,* ad c. 15.

ing the mutual precedence of two or more persons who have no authority over each other.

Canon 108, §2, makes two basic distinctions between those who rule and those who are ruled, and further between a jurisdictional hierarchy of divine institution (the pope and the bishops) and another of ecclesiastical institution, which includes all other grades of jurisdictional authority (§3).[66] Sipos (1875-1949) further divided the hierarchy of ecclesiastical origin into supra-episcopal, quasi-episcopal, and infra-episcopal grades without stating exactly whom he classified in each.[67] This information seems to be supplied by Abbo-Hannan in their list of offices which are of ecclesiastical institution: the metropolitan (supra-episcopal), apostolic administrator (quasi-episcopal), and the vicar general (infra-episcopal).[68]

SECTION 1—THE NATURE OF THE AUTHORITY IN CANON 106, 2°

What is meant by authority in this second numerical division of canon 106? If it is not jurisdiction, what other forms of authority form a basis for precedence?

The rather general consensus of commentators on this matter is that any kind of authority which is recognized in the Church will give the person who has that authority the right to precede his subjects. That authority may be public or private, jurisdictional, domestic, or dominative (in regard to religious), ordinary or delegated, proper or vicarious, judicial or non-judicial, legislative or administrative.

Michicls admits ". . . *qualiscumquc auctoritas* . . ." and specifically gives the examples of public or true jurisdiction, whether ordinary or delegated, and of private authority. The latter would derive from the contract of marriage, or from the

---

66 There are as many grades in the hierarchy of jurisdiction as there are positions in the Church which are specifically different. These include the Roman Pontiff, patriarchs, primates, metropolitans (archbishops), bishops, vicars and prefects apostolic, and prelates regular and secular. — Coronata, *Institutiones,* I, n. 169.

67 *Enchiridion Iuris Canonici,* p. 87.

68 *The Sacred Canons,* I, 209.

contract between employer and employee; private authority could likewise be domestic, as between parents and children, or it might be the power of the religious superior over his religious subjects.[69]

Beste acknowledges precedence based on "... *quaecumquc superioritas* ..." and names jurisdictional, dominative and domestic authority as examples.[70]

Regatillo gives as a source of precedence from authority, "... *quaevis potestas imperii: sive iurisdictionis ... sive administrativa ... sive dominativa* ..."[71] Jone approaches the discussion from a negative angle: "*Auctoritas de qua hoc loco sermo occurrit non necessario est potestas iurisdictionis.* ..."[72]

Coronata simply cites Michiels in admitting every possible form of authority as a basis for precedence; Coronata gives a somewhat more detailed description of the authority of a religious superior, however. He acknowledges that some public and some private power are given to such a superior in a religious society, without any participation in jurisdiction.[74]

Sipos admitted either jurisdictional or dominative power, as falling under authority without making any distinctions or giving any specific examples.[75]

Nearly every one of the authors cited above limits the application of the principle of authority to the territory in which that authority may be exercised *(intra ambitum)*.[76]

Beste states his interpretation in a way that limits the precedence of the superior over his subject to the territory in which the superior can validly exercise his authority, and chooses, the favorite

69 "Non solummodo publica fundata in vera iurisdictione sive ordinaria sive delegata, sed etiamvero privata in partione, societate herili vel domestica, societate religiosa etc. fundata." — *De Personis*, p. 686.

70 *Introductio in Codicem, sub canone* 106, 2°.

71 *Institutiones Iuris Canonici* (2 vols., 5. ed., Santander: Sal Terrae, 1956), I, n. 218.

73 *Commentarium in Codicem Iuris Canonici* (3 vols.; Paderborn: Officia Libraria F. Shoeningh, 1950-55), *sub canone* 106, 2°; cf. Ojetti, *Commentarium*, II, 205.

74 *Institutiones*, I, n. 156.

75 *Enchiridion Iuris Canonici*, p. 83.

76 Michiels, Beste, Coronata, *locis citatis*.

example of the commentators, the vicar general. By virtue of canon 370, §1, he has precedence over the diocesan clergy, with a special exception made for the case in which one of them is a bishop and he himself is not. Outside the diocese the precedence of the vicar general over other diocesan clerics of his own diocese is not so certain. Although some forms of authority may be exercised only within the proper territory, voluntary jurisdiction may be exercised outside that proper territory as well.[77] Since the authority of the vicar general connotes a voluntary jurisdiction,[78] it can be used in his own favor, while outside the diocese, and in reference to a subject who is absent from the territory. On this basis, Regatillo would permit the vicar general, on the basis of his authority, to take precedence over his fellow diocesan clergy even outside the diocese. His example is the auxiliary bishop, who as vicar general would take precedence outside the diocese over the second auxiliary bishop, despite the fact that the second auxiliary is the senior by promotion to the episcopacy.[79]

The argument favoring the claim of the vicar general to his authority as a basis for precedence is ruled out by the norms of precedence for bishops. It has been stated that (according to canon 106, 3°) whoever is of the same grade or rank as another, has relative precedence according to the date of promotion to that grade. In Regatillo's example, both persons are of the episcopal grade or rank. According to the general norm, the one first promoted to this rank should have precedence. For bishops, this is the promotion announced in consistory, not the consecration or appointment to a specific church or diocese.[80] An exception to this general rule is made by canon 347 for the ordinary of the place in his own diocese. There seems to be no

77 Canon 201, § 3.

78 Sipos, *Enchiridion Iuris Canonici*, p. 224; canon 1573, § 1, implies this by requiring a special *officialis* with judicial power to be appointed in each diocese. Such judicial power cannot be used for one's own benefit (voluntary); but that power which includes legislative and executive (non-judicial), and is called voluntary, can be used on one's own behalf. — Abbo-Hannan, *The Sacred Canons*, I, 257-58.

79 *Institutiones*, I, n. 218.

80 PCI, 10 nov. 1925 — *AAS*, XVII (1925), 582.

justification for any other, particularly not in the case of the vicar general who is bishop. Admittedly, if this same problem arose in the proper diocese, there would be no question about the precedence of that bishop who was also the vicar general. Outside his own diocese, the ordinary is considered merely as a bishop. His precedence is determined solely by the date of his promotion. In this way it would be possible for the Auxiliary to precede his ordinary.[81]

SECTION 2–THE KINDS OF AUTHORITY IN THE CHURCH

The Code itself specifically names some of the kinds of authority or power in the Church, and refers also to the divisions of these types of authority.[82] Canon 118 mentions a two-fold general division into the power of Orders and the power of jurisdiction. Authors commonly speak of the power of jurisdiction in the Church as being public or private. Coronata defines public power indirectly by defining jurisdiction as ". . . *potestas publica a Christo ecclesiae concessa regendi fideles in ordine ad vitam aeternam.*"[83] The Code itself, in canon 197, §1, proceeds to give a division of the power of jurisdiction into two classes: that which is attached to an office by law (ordinary), and that which is given to a person by commitment (delegated).

A. Ordinary Jurisdiction in the Church

For ordinary power it is required that it be attached to an office by law (canon 197, §1). Canon 145, §1, gives the principle that "office" is to be understood in the strict sense unless the contrary appears from the context. This strict notion of an office defines it as a function established with a permanent character by either divine or ecclesiastical law, to be conferred according to the norms of the sacred canons, and entailing some participation in the ecclesiastical power of Orders or of jurisdiction.

---

81 Cf. "A List of Cardinals, Archbishops, and Bishops in the United States in the Order of their Seniority, " *The Official Catholic Directory* (New York: P. J. Kennedy and Sons, 1912—); cf. *infra* on rank, pp. 131 ff.

82 Canons 118, 196, 197, 948, 1312, § 1, 2214.

83 *Institutiones,* I, n. 276.

This function *(munus)* must be one which looks to a supernatural goal and purpose determined by ecclesiastical or divine law.[84] The permanent relation between the office and the power attached to it may be seen from the fact that the office is not restricted to time, person or place. If the incumbent loses the office, it merely becomes vacant: it does not cease to exist. The powers attached to it are there, no matter who the incumbent is or what his qualifications are.

The ecclesiastical law by which an office can be established may be the universal law, or the particular law, whether general or special in character. It may even be a law which has originated from custom, statute, prescription or privilege.[85] Canons 147-172 establish the legal manner of obtaining these offices: it may be by free conferral, by institution, by confirmation, by admission, or by election and its acceptance.[86]

Canon 145, §1, adds that the incumbent of an office in the strict sense enjoys some ecclesiastical power of Orders or of jurisdiction. Canon 197, §1, states that this jurisdiction will be ordinary, if it is attached by law to an office.[87] The power of Orders which is attached to an office must be distinct from that which is conferred by ordination (which is attached to the person, in contrast).[88] Examples of this type of the power of Orders attached to an office would be found in canon 294, §2, and in canon 310.

This ordinary jurisdiction can be further divided into that which is proper to the incumbent, or simply vicarious.[89] The former is strictly attached to the office, but it is exercised by the office-holder in his own forum and in his own name.[90] Vicarious ordinary power, on the other hand, is also attached to an office, but it is exercised in the name of another.[91]

---

84 Sipos, *Enchiridion Iuris Canonici,* p. 115.

85 Coronata, *Institutiones,* I, n. 278.

86 Canon 148, § 1; cf. canons 1448-1471.

87 Vermeersch-Creusen, *Epitome Iuris Canonici,* II, n. 742, maintain that delegated jurisdiction suffices for the content of an office.

88 Bouscaren-Ellis, *Canon Law,* p. 122.

89 Canon 197, § 2.

90 Coronata, *Institutiones,* I, n. 279.

91 Wernz-Vidal, *Ius Canonicum,* II, n. 366.

Any office-holder in the Church referred to by the name "vicar" obviously has this kind of power: the vicar general, acting in the name of his bishop-ordinary, and in his proper forum in administrative matters; the vicar capitular (or diocesan administrator where the consultors replace the cathedral chapter); vicars apostolic who act in the name of the Roman Pontiff. The vicarious nature of the power attached to other offices is not always so obvious: the local ordinary uses vicarious ordinary power when he dispenses from the general law in virtue of canon 81;[92] so does the apostolic administrator who is acting in the name of the Roman Pontiff; likewise the Roman Congregations, Tribunals, and Curial Offices, as well as the curial offices of the bishop and of religious orders—all of these use a vicarious ordinary power.[93] Abbo-Hannan add to this list the vicarious ordinary power of apostolic delegates and vicars forane,[94] while Bouscaren-Ellis include that of the vicar econome of canon 473, whose power is ordinary because it is attached to his office, but vicarious because it is exercised in the name of another.[95]

It can be seen, then, that ordinary power, which is either proper or vicarious, must have two essential conditions fulfilled: it must be attached to an office in the strict sense of the term; further, it must be attached to that office by the law itself. One may thus sum up these notions:

> Ordinary jurisdiction is thus that which, in virtue of law or custom the incumbent of an ecclesiastical office acquires automatically from the office, not by privilege or any other act of his superior subsequent to and distinct from the acquisition of the office itself, no matter whether his tenure is permanent or temporary [such as that of an apostolic delegate (canon 268, §2), vicars general (canon 366, §2), vicars capitular (canon 443, §2), or vicars substitute for an absent pastor (canon 465, §§4,5)].[96]

---

92 Coronata, *Institutiones,* I, n. 279.

93 *Loc. cit.*

94 *The Sacred Canons,* I, 254.

95 Bouscaren-Ellis, *Canon Law,* p. 135.

96 Abbo-Hannan, *The Sacred Canons,* I, 253-54, and footnote 11.

Since ordinary jurisdiction is obtained with the acquisition of an office, all who have power by virtue of an office can be called "ordinaries" in a wide sense. In law, however, the name "ordinary" has a special signification. An ordinary can only be one of the ordinaries listed in canon 198, §1. These include the following:

a) the Roman Pontiff;

b) all residential bishops;[97]

c) abbots or prelates *nullius* (canons 319, 323);

d) the vicar general of a residential bishop (canon 366), or of an abbot or prelate *nullius* (canon 323, §1);

e) the apostolic administrator (canons 312, 313, 315);

f) the vicar and the prefect apostolic (canon 292);

g) the successors of any of the foregoing by way of provision of the law or in consequence of a ruling contained in approved religious constitutions: cathedral chapters (diocesan consultors), or also abbatial or prelatial chapters before the election of the vicar capitular (diocesan administrator); the vicar capitular; the pro-vicar or pro-prefect in a vicariate or prefecture apostolic;

h) major superiors (canon 488, 8°) in exempt clerical religious institutes, but only for their subjects (therefore, not major superiors of non-exempt clerics, or of exempt lay religious).

To these must be added another:

i) ecclesiastical superior of an independent mission.[98]

In comparing the foregoing list of ordinaries-at-law with all those who would be found in a list of persons having ordinary power, either proper or vicarious, one would have to add the following (although *per se,* i. e., inherently they are not ordinaries, *per accidens* i. e., on occasion, they may have that title): cardinal legates, patriarchs, metropolitans, primates, coadjutor bishops, auxiliary bishops, abbots and prelates without territory,

---

97 Titular bishops or auxiliary bishops are called ordinaries in the sense of this canon only when they are the vicars general of their diocese, or hold some other office enumerated in this canon.

98 S. C. Prop. Fid., 31 aug. 1934—Private letter to the Apostolic Delegate of the East Indies—*Canon Law Digest,* III, 74-75.

officials and vice-officials of the curia, vicars forane, minor superiors, and pastors.[99]

B. Delegated Jurisdiction in the Church

The second kind of jurisdiction described in canon 197, §1, is delegated power, that which is given to a person rather than attached to an office; that which is given within limits, rather than permanently and universally. Delegated jurisdiction can be negatively defined as that which does not fulfill the two requirements of ordinary jurisdiction, viz. the permanent attachment to an office by law.

Delegated power may be divided into two classes: that which is delegated by the law itself[100] and that which is delegated by a superior in consideration of the office held[101] or of the special qualifications or the dignity of the person delegated *(industria personae).*

Delegation by the law gives a priest jurisdiction in the case of a danger of death (canon 882) to hear all confessions and absolve from all sins and censures. It is also the type of jurisdiction which by canon 883 is given to a priest to hear confessions on a sea-voyage.

Delegation *ab homine,* on the other hand, envisages the method by which a priest receives faculties from his ordinary to hear confessions in the diocese. As Bender explains it: any one who does not have an office in the strict sense of the term is acting with delegated jurisdiction, derived either *a iure* or *ab homine.*[102] However, the mere fact that he has an office does not necessarily mean that he always uses ordinary power. He may also be exercising delegated power, as would be the case

---

99 Coronata, *Institutiones,* I, n. 280.

100 Some say that this has been abrogated by the Code; e.g., N. Hilling, *Das Personenrecht des Codex Iuris Canonici* (Paderborn, 1924), pp. 88-89 and p. 89, note 1; Franciscus Roberti, *De Processibus* (2 vols.; Romae: apud Aedes Facultatis Iuridicae ad S. Apollinaris, 1926), I, n. 146.

101 Cf. canon 66, § 1, concerning the habitual faculties of bishops; canon 310, § 2, providing for the power of the pro-vicar or pro-prefect.

102 Ludovicus Bender, *Potestas Ordinaria et Delegata* (Roma: Desclée et Socii, 1957), p. 17.

of an ordinary using his quinquennial faculties, or of a priest using the powers delineated in canons 1044 and 1098, 2°.[103]

When the jurisdiction is granted by means of a special act of the superior it is said to be delegated. Such *ab homine* derived delegation can come from the Holy See, as it is stated in canon 199, §2, from some authority lower than the Roman Pontiff, as it is noted in canon 199, §§2,3, or from one already delegated by a higher authority, as it is mentioned in canon 199, §§4,5.

According to its extension, delegated power can be considered as intended for all cases (canon 199, §2; canon 200, §2), for a special case or number of cases only, or for a specified length of time. This type of delegated power may be either judicial or non-judicial, for either the internal or the external forum.

C. Private Power in the Church

Public power, or jurisdiction, is defined as that power which is necessary to bring a public society to its proper goal. Some such power is necessary in a private society as well. The nature of this authority will be determined by the nature of the society in which it is used. The domestic society of the family requires that the children be entirely subject to the authority of their parents, according to the natural law, in everything which is necessary for their education. Within narrower limits the wife is subject to her husband's authority on the basis of their marriage contract.

Anyone joining a social group must submit himself to the authority which directs that group towards its goal. When a personal authority is brought to bear directly on the will of the subjects who are entirely dependent on the superiors, this private power may be called dominative, the term used in canon 1312, §1. Others prefer to call it domestic power.[104]

Regatillo defines dominative power as the power which superiors have over the will of others in an imperfect society of private persons striving after a private good.[105] This dominative

---

103 Coronata, *Institutiones* I, n. 286, 3°, and note 2.

104 J. Creusen, *Religious Men and Women in the Code,* (5. ed. rev. by Adam Ellis; Milwaukee: Bruce Publishing Co., 1953), n. 46.

105 *Institutiones,* I, 74.

power is found particularly in religious superiors.[106] Sometimes such superiors enjoy only this type of private or dominative power; at other times it is joined to jurisdiction, as in the case of superiors in exempt clerical religious institutes.[107] In addition to superiors, general chapters and some provincial chapters have dominative power over the religious of their communities.

What is the source of this power in religious superiors? It has been seen that ordinary jurisdiction originates with the office held; delegated jurisdiction comes from a superior. But private or dominative power may come from several sources. The private power of parents over their children (domestic power) comes from the fact of their parenthood. The power of the master over the servant, or of the employer over the employee, comes from a contract. But the dominative power of religious superiors, depending on the nature of the religious community, comes from the vows of religious profession, or from a promise (in the societies whose members live in common without vows, such as the Oratorians, Vincentians, or Sulpicians).[108]

Dominative power differs from jurisdiction or public power in that it does not include true legislative, judicial, or coercive power. A major difference lies also in the fact that, although women cannot acquire jurisdiction in the Church, they can acquire dominative power, as superiors of their communities.

In a wide sense, one can speak of public and private dominative power. It can be said to be formally public when it is used for the ruling of a juridic society, such as a religious community. But the dominative power which is used for the ruling of a private society, such as the family, pious associations of the faithful, or a confraternity, is private.[109]

Though each superior has dominative power, every religious community is under a twofold power; both jurisdiction and private power. All religious are subject to the public or jurisdictional power of the Roman Pontiff. In exempt clerical religious

---

106 Canon 1312, § 1.

107 Canon 501, § 1.

108 Coronata, *Institutiones,* I, n. 527. cf. E. Roelker, *Precepts* (Paterson: St. Anthony's Guild Press, 1955), p. 53.

109 Coronata, *Institutiones,* I, n. 527.

institutes this power is communicated to the religious superiors. Religious communities of diocesan approval are subject not only to their religious superiors, but also to the full jurisdiction of the ordinary of the place; unless they are placed beyond his authority, religious of diocesan approval are likewise subject to their proper pastor. In the present law, even exempt religious are subjects of the ordinary in some things;[110] members of non-exempt institutes approved by the Holy See are subject to the local ordinary as clerics or as members of the faithful; as religious, they depend entirely upon their religious superiors.[111]

Of particular interest in matters of precedence is the dominative power of religious superiors over their subjects, for this will serve as a basis for their precedence over them likewise, in accordance with canon 106, 2°. Briefly, then, a discussion of the various classes of superiors in religious communities will be given.

These superiors vary as the communities themselves vary in their organization. However, the Code, in giving a list of the major superiors in canon 488, 8°, makes no distinction. They are enumerated as follows:

a) the abbot primate;[112]

b) the abbot superior of a monastic congregation;[112]

c) the abbot of an independent *(sui iuris)* monastery, even if it belongs to a monastic congregation (headed by an abbot superior or president);[113]

---

110 Canon 500.

111 Creusen, *op. cit.*, n. 53.

112 These two, although they are listed as major superiors in the law, do not have all the power and jurisdiction which the law of the Code shares with major superiors; rather their powers are determined by their proper constitutions and particular decrees of the Holy See.—Canon 501, § 3; cf. also canons 655 and 1594.

113 What is said here of abbots of independent monasteries is true also of superiors of independent houses, by whatever name they are called. The same is true of abbesses and superioresses of independent houses, although they naturally are not included under the name of ordinaries—Larraona, "Commentarium Codicis"—*Commentarium pro Religiosis* (Romae, 1920-34), IV (1923), 40-44 (hereafter this commentary on the Code in volume IV of the *Commentarium* will be referred to as Larraona, CpR, IV (1923), with the proper page and footnote references).

d) the supreme moderator;[114]

e) the provincial superior;

f) the vicars of all of these[115] as well as all those who possess authority equal to that of a provincial superior.[116]

In clerical institutes which are exempt, the major superiors are considered ordinaries for their subjects according to canon 198, §1. It is not required, however, for a major superior to have lesser superiors subject to him. The superior of an independent house or of a religious community having but one house is also called a major superior. [117]

There is a hierarchy among religious which is not too apparent from the foregoing list. It will help first to make a general classification into the following divisions:

a) supreme superiors are those who are in charge of an entire religious community. These are called by several titles, most of which are characterized with the word "general," such as abbot general, administrator general, minister general, procurator general. Others which are obvious include the Rector major, and supreme moderator.

b) Other major superiors are in charge of a province, of a monastic congregation, or of a house which is *sui iuris* or independent. In this class are the provincial superiors, abbots president of the Benedictine Congregations, and the ruling abbots *(de regimine)* of local independent houses.

c) Subordinate superiors are those who are in charge of houses which are not independent, such as conventual priories.[118]

---

114 He has the power over all provinces, houses, and members of his religious community. This does not include abbots primate and the superiors of monastic congregations—Larraona, *CpR,* IV (1923), 44.

115 Not all vicars are major superiors. Only those who actually have the power can claim the name. This must be determined from particular law.—Larraona, *CpR,* IV (1923), 45.

116 These include the provincial commissars, visitators, custodians, vice-provincials, quasi-provincials, vicars of the missions, and superiors regular of the missions, provided they possess at least a vicarious ordinary power.—Larraona, *CpR,* IV (1923), note 305, p. 45, and note 314, p. 46.

117 Coronata, *Institutiones,* I, n. 537.

118 Coronata, *Institutiones,* I, n. 506. All superiors of exempt clerical institutes are *praelati,* even the minor local superiors, if they possess ordinary

Sipos, approaching the matter from a different point of view, divided these superiors on the basis of the hierarchical organization within the religious institute. In the hierarchical religious institute, there are several religious houses and several distinct grades of superiors, all joined together under and subordinate to one superior, forming one universal and strictly juridical society with a centralized authority. Such unions, all constituting part of one and the same religious community, are called provinces (canon 488, 6°). In religious institutes which are set up on a non-hierarchical basis, several independent monasteries are also joined together under the same superior and with an authority that comes, in some, from the constitution of the confederation. The bond here is a moral one rather than a juridic one. These are the monastic congregations mentioned in canon 488, 2°.[119]

The non-hierarchical religious communities have the following superiors:

* a) the abbot primate, who presides over the whole religious community, but without full jurisdiction, according to canon 501, §3. The sole example of this superior is the head of the Confederation of Black Benedictines;[120]

* b) the abbot superior or president of a monastic congregation, who could, of course, be the abbot of an independent monastery at the same time;[121]

---

jurisdiction in the external forum.—Larraona, *CpR,* IV (1923), notes 335 and 337, p. 76.

119 For instance, the Cistercian Order has thirty-one independent houses, which form eight congregations (The *Annuario Pontificio*—1959, p. 887, lists nine such congregations of Cistercians).—Sipos, *Enchiridion Iuris Canonici,* p. 273. Coing one step higher in organization, the Benedictine Confederation unites fifteen congregations into one confederation.

120 The Confederation of Black Benedictines was approved by Leo XIII, in a brief, *Summum semper,* July 12, 1893.—*Leonis XIII Pontificis Maximi Acta,* Vol. XIII (Romae: ex Typographia Vaticana, 1894), 207. The Abbot Primate is also the Abbot of St. Anselm's in Rome. This is the abbot primate referred to in canons 223, § 1, 4°; 501, § 3; 510. The Abbot General of the Hungarian Congregation of the Benedictines has merely an honorary title of primate.—Larraona, *CpR,* IV (1923), note 270, p. 40.

121 The abbot superior is also called an abbot president, abbot general, or archabbot. The abbots general of the Congregations of Beuron, Brazil, and

* c) the ruling abbot *(de regimine)* of an independent monastery.[122]

Those religious institutes which are organized hierarchically have these superiors:

* a) the supreme moderator, who presides over the whole community: all provinces, houses and members, according to the proper constitutions (canon 502);[123]

* b) the provincial superior, with power within his province;

c) the local superior for each house.[124]

Of the aforementioned superiors, in either hierarchical or non-hierarchical institutes, all marked with an asterisk (*) are major superiors. To be added to these for the completion of the list of major superiors mentioned in canon 488, 8°, are the vicars of these superiors, and all others who enjoy the powers

---

Cassino are always called archabbots. However, in the American Cassinese Congregation, it is not the superior general of the Congregation, but the Abbot of the Monastery of St. Vincent de Paul, the mother abbey of the Congregation in America, who is the archabbot. The supreme abbot of the Bavarian and Swiss Congregations is the abbot president. For the Cassinese Congregation of the Primitive Observance, the supreme abbot is the abbot general. The abbot general of the Congregation of Solesmes is called the superior general.—Larraona, *CpR,* IV (1923), note 273, p. 40.

122 A prior conventual is the elected superior of an independent monastery which has not yet been raised to the rank of an abbey. Larraona includes him among the major superiors.— *CpR,* IV (1923), 41.

123 This superior may be called by various names, as was suggested above, p. 120.

124 Local superiors may be either major or minor superiors. Such local minor superiors are the directors of schools, of hospitals and of other pious houses, provided they are also the superiors of the religious under them in regard to their religious discipline.—Coronata, *Institutiones,* I, n. 538. In contrast, local major superiors are superiors of independent houses, or superiors of religious institutes that have only one house.—*Ibidem,* footnote 6, p. 642. In neither case is there any reference here to the superiors of houses which are strictly filial (not possessing their own property, or not considered as a distinct community). Such superiors are only delegates of the superior of the motherhouse to which they are attached.—S. C. de Rel., resp. 1 febr. 1924—*AAS,* XVI (1924), 95. A pious house is a religious moral person dedicated to pious works, such as an orphanage, a hospital, a college, or some other school. A religious house (canon 448, 5°) is a dwelling or center for men or women religious or for the members of societies who live in common without vows.—Sipos, *Enchiridion Iuris Canonici,* p. 587.

equivalent to the powers possessed by provincials *(ad instar provincialium)*.[125]

The Cardinal Protector enjoys no authority or jurisdiction in any religious community or over any of its members, unless this is specified in particular cases.[126]

Within the individual religious institutes there is a certain hierarchy among the various superiors of all ranks. By the very nature of the differences that exist between orders and congregations, no one single rule for the internal precedence of these religious superiors can be delineated. Each constitution will have to be consulted for these details. However, Larraona[127] went into great detail to study the precedence of these officials in general. Abundant footnotes present the variations from group to group. A synopsis of this study will be found in Chapter VIII of this study.

Article 3. The Determination of Precedence in the Absence of the Critereon of Authority

Canon 106, 3°: *Inter diversas personas ecclesiasticas quarum nulla habeat in alias auctoritatem: qui ad gradum potiorem pertinent, praecedunt eis qui sunt inferioris gradus; inter eiusdem gradus personas sed non eiusdem ordinis, qui altiorem ordinem tenet, praecedit iis qui in inferiore sunt positi; si denique ad eundem gradum pertineant eundemque ordinem habeant, praecedit qui prius est promotus ad gradum; si eodem tempore promoti sint, senior ordinatione, nisi iunior ordinatus fuerit a Romano Pontifice; et si eodem tempore ordinem receperint, senior aetate.*

It has been seen how it is fitting and reasonable for the superior to have precedence over his subjects by reason of his authority over them. But there will be many occasions when the various persons present for a function, although they may well be superiors for someone, will have no form of authority over each other. In this case, it is necessary to turn to some norm other than that of authority as it is found in canon 106, 2°.

125 The entire explanation above on hierarchical and non-hierarchical religious institutes is essentially that of Sipos, *Enchiridion Iuris Canonici*, pp. 273-74, except when specific reference is made to others.

126 Canon 499, § 2.

127 "Commentarium Codicis," *Commentarium pro Religiosis*, IV (1923), 168-73; 210-18; 273-80; 331-35; 360-67.

Canon 106, 3°, provides a gradated series of norms. When one fails, another in a hierarchical list will determine proper precedence. In the order of their importance, these are the norms, in brief, which are to be followed when the notion of authority is not applicable:

a) he precedes who has the higher grade or rank;

b) when this fails in the case wherein both have the same rank, he precedes who is in the higher order;

c) in succession, recourse is then to be had to the priority of promotion to the given rank;

d) then to the priority of promotion to an order;

e) Exception: if two people are of the same rank and in the same order, and were both promoted to the rank at the same time, he who was ordained by the Roman Pontiff takes precedence over the other who was not ordained by him, even though the latter may have been ordained earlier;

f) if rank and order, and the dates of promotion to both are equal, the final criterion is age.

SECTION 1—THE DIFFERENT ECCLESIASTICAL PERSONS AFFECTED BY CANON 106, 3°

Canon 106 in its introductory number stated that the principles contained in the canon were for various kinds of persons, physical as well as moral. The second number made the same explicit statement about the persons in authority. Number 3 makes no such distinction. At first sight, one is tempted to say that since the Code does not distinguish here, and in view of the general norm in the introductory numerical division no distinction should be made: this number should apply to physical and moral persons equally. The final solution to the difficulty of determining the extension of this third number of canon 106 will be reflected differently as the notions of *gradus* and *ordo* are differently interpreted.

If an attempt is made to include moral persons in the provisions of the third number of canon 106, the following arguments seem to favor such a conclusion. In comparing the general provision for both physical and moral persons made in the introductory preamble with the particular norms found therein for moral persons, one discovers a *lacuna:* specific norms are provided for moral persons of the same species and grade in the fifth number, but what principles are to be applied if the moral persons are not of the same grade and species? If these moral persons are religious communities, then one may invoke the norms of canon 491 in order to determine the hierarchy of the various moral persons which are religious institutes. That leaves non-religious moral persons of different species and grade without any norms to determine their precedence. However, the legislator clearly implies in the fifth number that there will be different grades or ranks of moral persons. Therefore, some norms must be available for them.

Michiels maintains that there is no special norm for determining the rank and species in an orderly hierarchical series of moral persons. Only the nature of the various moral persons and the various texts of the Code can yield a norm. He gives the common examples of three kinds of collegiate persons.[128] They could be composed of secular clerics, who as a body, would have precedence over religious clerics in a body, according to canon 491, §2.The religious, in turn, would have precedence over a body of lay people by force of canon 491, §1. Within the secular body, precedence could be determined by the normal rules of canon 106, 1° (proxy), 2° (superior and subject), 3° (rank, order, age), 4° (no distinction between Oriental and Latin rite clerics), and 7° (members of the papal household). Within the religious group, a division would be made into the species of religious institutes, according to canon 491, §1. Within each species and grade, the rules for moral persons of the same species and grade would be followed as they are given in canon 106, 5° (quasi-possession of the right of precedence or priority of establishment in a given place). Within each of these individual groups, in turn,

---

128 Michiels maintains that the term *persona moralis* here would have to be understood in the wide sense to include all colleges and ecclesiastical institutions, even if they lack juridic personality in the strict sense; for such "moral persons" frequently appear at public manifestations where precedence is observed, and one must find some norm to determine the rights of precedence for them as well as for the others.—*De Personis,* p. 693.

canon 106, 2°, and the triple norm of canon 106, 5°, for determining the precedence of members within a given college would be applicable (according to their proper and legitimate constitutions, by legitimate custom, or finally, according to the universal law of the Code).

Within the third group, the lay people, the only specific norms available are those which pertain to the pious associations of the faithful mentioned in canon 701 (whereby Third Orders precede archconfraternities, who in turn precede confraternities, and so on). Michiels maintains, however, that the principle of authority in number two of canon 106 might be applied; for the remainder of the group, the rule of prior enrollment and greater age might be invoked.[129]

Close examination will show that Michiels has used some of the norms of number 3 in drawing up this combination of principles for moral persons of different grade and species, despite his earlier statement that this number referred only to clerics, in view of canon 118, for only clerics may exercise the power of orders or of ecclesiastical jurisdiction. As will be seen in the study of the precedence of religious within a community, the norm of number three is often applied, so that whoever was first promoted to the rank which he holds in the community has precedence over someone who came into this rank later. This is equally true among superiors and subjects. The norm proposed for lay people according the date of their enrollment and age is likewise an application of the *"prius promotus ad gradum."* Canon 701 itself determines the various grades of laymen specifically in four particular instances. Number three would have to be used, however, for a determining of the relative precedence of those associations which are mentioned as *"aliae piae uniones"* in canon 701, §1,5°.

It seems to be a safe conclusion that whenever no specific norms are available for determining the precedence of moral persons of different species and grade, whether clerical, religious or lay, the norms of canon 106, 3°, *mutatis mutandis,* could and should be used. However, it depends on the interpretation of *gradus* and

129 *De Personis,* p. 693.

ordo. If *gradus* is to be understood as jurisdictional rank, and *ordo* as sacramental orders, moral persons made up of the laity cannot be included in the norms of this paragraph. This will be taken up in the next section.

SECTION 2—*Gradus* AND *Ordo* IN CANON 106, 3°

Few authors have gone into so detailed a study of this problem of the meaning of *gradus* and *ordo* as Michiels, whose presentation is given here in substance. By way of introduction, one may say that the precise meaning of these words in this canon is not provided by the legislator himself, and that as a consequence of this the commentators differ widely in their interpretations on these two points.

Gradus in the Code generally indicates a position or office of divine or ecclesiastical origin, which may pertain either to the hierarchy of Orders or to that of jurisdiction.[130] The word *gradus* in various grammatical forms appears in the Code seventy-nine times in fifty-four canons.[131] All but eleven of these canons use the word in reference to the degrees of consanguinity or affinity, the instances of judicial procedure, academic degrees, or the heroic degree of sanctity in the canonization requirements.[132]

Three of these uses occur in canon 106, 1°, 3° and 5°, where, presumably, all three uses point to the same thing.[133] Canon 108 uses the term *gradus* to indicate that not all clerics are in the same category *(in eodem gradu):* one is subordinated to another. The same canon in another paragraph indicates the division of the hierarchy into that of Orders and another of jurisdiction, indicating that some of both groups are of divine origin, and that ". . . *alii quoque gradus* . . ." are of ecclesiastical origin. No distinction is made; the canon seems to refer to both jurisdictional and sacramental *gradus* indiscriminately with the same word *gradus.*

In canon 109, on the other hand, the legislator is very careful

---

130 *De Personis,* p. 688.

131 Lauer, *Index Verborum Codicis Iuris Canonici,* pp. 250-51.

132 The eleven are: cc. 106, 108, 109, 119, 236, 393, 405, 876, 1224, 1263, 2332.

133 Coronata, *Institutiones,* I, n. 157; cf. can. 18.

to speak specifically of a "*gradus potestatis ordinis*" and a "*gradus iurisdictionis.*" Here the word *gradus* clearly refers to both Orders and jurisdiction.

Canon 119 directs the faithful to give proper reverence to the clergy ". . . *pro diversis eorum gradibus et muneribus.* . . ."

An interesting departure from the terminology generally used in relation to the cardinals is found in canon 236, §4, where there is mention of a cardinal bishop reaching the *gradus decani.* This stands as an indication of the fact that, although the entire college of cardinals itself is commonly considered a *gradus,* there are other *gradus* within this *gradus.* Also of interest is the fact that in connection with this *gradus decani* there is no special Order or jurisdiction which is not shared by the other cardinal bishops. For canon 237, §1, states: ". . . Decanus . . . antiquior promotione ad aliquam sedem suburbicariam, cui tamen nulla est in ceteros cardinales iurisdictio, sed ipse primus habetur inter aequales." This is just one more indication that the word *gradus* need not be used only in connection with the notion of jurisdiction.

Canon 393, §1, uses the word *gradus* to refer to the kinds of lesser benefices within a collegiate chapter, whereas canon 405, §1, uses the word to refer to everyone in the chapter. Canon 876 applies the term to both secular and religious priests ". . . *cuiusvis gradus aut officii.* . . ."

There can hardly be any connection with jurisdiction, when canon 1224, 2°, uses the word *gradus* in speaking of the prohibition of a religious ". . . *cuiuslibet gradus aut dignitatis* . . ." to choose the church and cemetery for his own funeral and burial. Canon 1263 is definitely not speaking of *gradus* in connection with either jurisdiction or Orders in permitting a special place for the civil officials ". . . *pro eorum dignitate et gradu.* . . ."

Probably the widest application of the word *gradus* is found in canon 2332, which treats of the censure incurred by each and every person ". . . *cuiuscumque status, gradus, seu conditionis etiam regalis, episcopalis vel cardinalitiae.* . . ." for appealing to a universal council over the Pope.

that intention, as in canons 108 and 109, When he intended to indicate an instance of the judicial process, the academic degrees, or the degrees of relationship or sanctity, that too was specifically pointed out. On other occasions, when the word *gradus* is used without any limitation, it seems to have a much wider meaning, as in canons 119, 236, §4, 393, §1, 1224, 2°, 1264, and 2332. In these instances, it seems that the word vaguely indicates some sort of level or degree or division of persons according to norms which are not more clearly specified. It does not seem tenable or valid to restrict the meaning of the word *gradus* as applicable only to jurisdiction or Orders.

Ordo likewise has a twofold meaning in the Code. The strict sense, as it is given expression in canon 950, is the one regularly used. Accordingly the term includes the consecration of a bishop and all major and minor orders leading to and including the priesthood ". . . *nisi aliud ex natura rei vel ex contextu verborum eruatur.*" This final clause leaves the way open for a wider range of interpretations than does canon 948, which treats of *ordo* as that which distinguishes clerics and laymen, and which was instituted by Christ for the ruling of the faithful and the ministry of their worship. Sometimes it is used more loosely in indication of a series of persons ". . . *ad exemplar sacrorum ordinum in quibusdam collegiis. . . .*"[134] This is particularly true in canon 231, which describes the three "orders" of cardinals: bishops, priests, and deacons. This is the meaning likewise in canon 408, §2, which makes a similar division among the canons in chapters: priests, deacons, and subdeacons. Although these distinctions in orders were once based upon the sacramental Orders enjoyed by each rank of cardinal or canon, they serve simply as examples today ". . . *ex natura rei* . . ." as canon 950 allows.

Some authors[135] hold that both *ordo* and *gradus* in canon 106 refer to the same thing, a determinate state, condition or dignity

---

134 Michiels, *De Personis*, p. 688; Regatillo, *Institutiones*, I, n. 218.

135 Perathoner, *Kurze Einfuehrung in das neue kirchliche Gesetzbuch* (Brixen, 1919), I, 38; Maroto, *Institutiones*, I, n. 478; Albertus Toso, *Ad Codicem Iuris Canonici Commentaria Minora* (5 vols.; Romae, 1921-27), p. 57 (hereafter cited as *Commentaria Minora*).

which some person holds in the hierarchy of the Church, in one way or another. These authors would call the genus of these positions a *gradus,* and the species an *ordo.* The classical example of this interpretation is the college of cardinals, which they call a *gradus,* and three divisions within this college, which they call *ordines.*[136]

Others[137] maintain that the two terms are objectively different in their meanings. Michiels incorrectly infers further that these authors limit *gradus* to specific positions in the jurisdictional hierarchy and *ordo* to the hierarchy of Orders.[138] This explanation leaves no place for such dignities in the Church as cardinals (who do not necessarily have positions with jurisdiction), patriarchs in the Latin rite (of whom only one has jurisdiction and that not patriarchal) and primates (of whom only one has true primatial jurisdiction).

Michiels contends that the word *ordo* in canon 106 must be interpreted strictly according to canons 948-50, as a determined power of Orders conferred through a sacred rite. The very obvious opposition between the two words as they are used in this canon would seem to favor the adoption of this interpretation also,[139] with the exception of the college of cardinals and cathedral and collegiate chapters, which have an internal subdivision *"ad exemplar ordinum."*

On the supposition that this strict meaning of *ordo* must be intended by the legislator, it becomes quite clear that *gradus*

---

136 Against this interpretation of the word *ordo* is the second last statement of number 3 of this canon: "si eodem tempore promoti sint, senior ordinatione nisi iunior ordinatus fuerit a Romano Pontifice." This certainly refers to sacramental Orders; the legislator is presumed to use a word with the same meaning at least within a given paragraph! Cf. Coronata, *Institutiones,* I, n. 157; cc. 948-50; canon 18.

137 Vermeersch-Creusen, *Epitome,* I, n. 230, ad 3; Coronata, *ibid.,* ad b; Blat. *Commentarium, II,* 36; Hilling, *Das Personenrecht des Codex Iuris Canonici,* n. 37, ad 3; Ojetti, *Commentarium,* II, 206; Berutti, *Institutiones,* II, n. 25; Beste, *Introductio in Codicem,* p. 106; Eichmann-Moersdorf, *Lehrbuch des Kirchenrechts* (7. ed.; 3 vols; Paderborn: Verlag Ferdinand Schoeningh, 1953-1954), I, 249.

138 "Gradus non refertur ad hierarchiam jurisdictionis."—Vermeersch-Creusen, *Epitome,* I, n. 230, ad 3.

139 *De Personis,* p. 689. Cf. also Coronata, *Institutiones,* I, n. 157, a.

must mean something different, contrary to the opinion of the commentators of the first school mentioned above, who consider order as a species under the genus *gradus*.

A. Precedence and Higher Rank

Vermeersch (1858-1936)—Creusen maintain that *gradus* cannot refer to jurisdiction, since that notion is already adverted to in number 2 of this canon; nor can it be Orders, since number 3 specifically provides for that.[140] Sipos (1875-1949).[141] and Maroto (1875- 1937),[142] on the other hand, are equally certain that *gradus* is based essentially on the notion of jurisdiction.

Michiels, however lets *gradus* have a very vague and indeterminate meaning, as it actually has elsewhere in the Code when not specifically limited by some other term. In this way it would include almost any basis for precedence except direct authority over a subject and sacramental Orders. The conclusions of this section can be summed up in Michiel's description of *gradus:*

> . . . non solummodo considerari munera seu officia hierarchica stricte jurisdictionalia,[143] sed omnia munera, status,[144] conditiones, in iure accurate definita, sive stabilia sive temporaria, sive ab homine sive a iure constituta, determinatam secumferentia participationem cuiusvis auctoritatis (iurisdictionis aliusve potestatis) vel dignitatis, aut praeeminentiam tituli seu nominis, non attendendo ad efficientiam quam habere vel qua carere potest.[145]

The notion of jurisdiction is important when one considers the meaning of *gradus,* however; one who exercises jurisdiction

140 *Epitome,* I, n. 230, 3; cf. Jone, *Commentarium, sub canone* 106, 3°.

141 *Enchiridion Iuris Canonici,* p. 83.

142 *Institutiones,* I, n. 477.

143 Canon 145; cf. Coronata, *Institutiones,* I, n. 157, ad a; also I, n. 406, where *munus* is described as ". . . *cumulus iurium et obligationum.* . . ."

144 Clerical, religious, or lay. Cf. cc. 107, 948.

145 *De Personis,* p. 689. Cf. Aloisius Moretti, *Caeremoniale iuxta Ritum Romanum seu De Sacris Functionibus* (4 vols., Taurini: Marietti, 1936-39), I, n. 151 (hereafter cited as *De Sacris Functionibus*); Vermeersch-Creusen, *Epitome,* I, n. 230, ad 3; Toso (+1946), (*Commentaria Minora,* p. 57) extended the meaning of *gradus* to include authority in general; Blat (1870-1943) (*Commentarium,* II, 36) held that *gradus* was to be computed from jurisdiction, dignity or office.

is sometimes considered to have greater standing in the Church than one who does not, even though the first party does not have authority over the second person. To carry the idea one step farther, the person who has broader jurisdiction will be considered of higher rank than one with more restricted jurisdiction; this is true in the case of the pastor and his assistant, or in comparison between the ordinary and his auxiliary (aside from any special provisions in this case).

On the other hand, there are some positions in the Latin Church to which no jurisdiction is attached, such as the rank of cardinal, patriarch and primate; yet these members of the hierarchy, because of their particular dignity or preeminence of title, are considered to have a higher rank than bishops or archbishops, who may have broader powers of jurisdiction.

The power attached to a certain position need not be that of jurisdiction. The same principles would apply to this number 3 as were discussed under article two of this chapter: all forms of authority of any degree or kind could entitle the holder to a certain rank, in comparison with someone else who had no such authority or a lower form of it.

This implies a hierarchy of power in the Church, with one grade higher than the other. Between two equals, the one with ordinary power is considered to have greater rank than the one with only delegated power; whoever exercises proper ordinary power holds higher rank than one who exercises his ordinary power vicariously. One who holds power delegated *a iure* may be considered to have greater rank than one who holds power delegated *ab homine,* unless the latter power comes directly from the legislator who is above the law itself. Someone with power delegated by the Roman Pontiff would certainly outrank anyone delegated by the local ordinary; likewise, anyone with power delegated by the ordinary would outrank another with power delegated by his pastor.

Ordinarily one will not need to apply such rules in order to determine precedence, for in many cases by force of custom and through the provisions of the written law this hierarchy of authority, dignity and preeminence has been determined within the Church. It is based primarily on the degree of power, or on the resemblance thereto, as is the case with the titular Latin patriarchs, who, though they have no jurisdiction, resemble the jurisdictional patriarchs of the Oriental rites. This is what Michiels and Vermeersch-Creusen seem to mean in stating that no particular attention is to be paid to the effectiveness of the authority which serves as a basis determining rank.[146] Under this interpretation Jone includes tiular archbishops and bishops together with residential archbishops and bishops.[147]

For the universal Church the following is a schematic outline of the relative importance of the various ranks or grades in the hierarchy of the Church, based on one or more of the various principles enunciated in Michiels' description of *gradus:*

a) cardinal legates *a latere;*[148]

b) cardinal dean and sub-dean;[149]

c) cardinal bishops, priests and deacons;[150]

d) legates of the Roman Pontiff;[151]

---

146 *De Personis,* p. 689: *Epitome,* I, n. 230, ad 3.

147 *Commentarium,* I, *sub can.* 106. n. 3.

148 "Cardinalis autem Legatus a latere praecedit extra Urbem omnibus aliis."—canon 239, § 1, n. 21.

149 "Sacro Cardinalium Collegio praeest Decanus, idest antiquior promotione ad aliquam sedem suburbicariam, cui tamen nulla est in ceteros Cardinales iurisdictio, sed ipse primus habetur inter aequales. Vacante decanatu, ipso iure succedit Subdecanus. . . ."—canon 237, §§ 1, 2.

150 "Sacrum Collegium in tres ordines distribuitur: episcopalem . . . presbyteralem . . . diaconalem. . . ."—canon 231, § 1. ". . . inter eiusdem gradus personas sed non eiusdem ordinis, qui altiorem ordinem tenet, praecedit iis qui in inferiore sunt positi . . ."—canon 106, 3°. "Praecedendi omnibus Praelatis etiam Patriarchis, imo ipsis Legatis Pontificiis, nisi Legatus sit Cardinalis in proprio territorio residens . . ."—canon 239, § 1, 21°. "Cardinales creantur et publicantur a Romano Pontifice in Consistorio sicque creati et publicati obtinent ius ad electionem Romani Pontificis et privilegia de quibus in canon 239."—canon 233, § 1. "Cardinalis ex ordine diaconali, transiens per optionem ad ordinem presbyteralem, locum obtinet ante omnes illos Cardinales presbyteros, qui post ipsum ad sacrae purpurae honorem assumpti sunt." —canon 236, § 2.

151 "Legati . . . licet forte charactere episcopali careant, praecedunt tamen omnibus Ordinariis qui non sint cardinalitia dignitate insigniti."—canon 269, §§ 1, 2.

e) patriarchs;[152]

f) primates;[152]

h) metropolitans in their own province;[153]

i) bishops in their own diocese;[153]

j) archbishops (whether metropolitans or archbishops without suffragans)[154] and bishops outside their proper territories;

k) abbots and prelates *nullius;*[155]

---

152 Cf. *infra,* p. 263, note 45, for explanation of the precedence of patriarchs and primates over an ordinary in his own diocese.

"Patriarcha praecedit Primati, Primas Archiepiscopo, hic Episcopis, salvo praescripto can. 347."—canon 280.

153 "In suo territorio Episcopus praecedit omnibus Archiepiscopis et Episcopis, exceptis Cardinalibus, Legatis Pontificiis et proprio Metropolita; extra territorium serventur normae traditae in can. 106. "—canon 347. Logically, this same principle holds true for the metropolitan throughout his province also. Therefore, whenever both the metropolitan and the ordinary of the place are present in their proper province and diocese, they will have first and second places respectively over all other archbishops and bishops, except those named in canon 347 above. On the basis of canon 106, 2°, the ordinary of the place will have precedence over his auxiliaries or coadjutors within his proper territory. Apart from the exceptional cases for the metropolitan and ordinary above, all archbishops, residential or titular, and all bishops, residential or titular, determine their precedence outside their proper territories according to the date of their promotion to the rank of archbishop or bishop in consistory, and on this alone. If two are promoted on the same day, he who was named first has the right of precedence—PCI, 10 nov. 1925—*AAS,* XI (1925), 349. Cf. Beste, *Introductio in Codicem, sub canone* 106, 3°; Coronata, *Institutiones,* I, n. 401; H. A. Ayrinhac, *Constitution of the Church in the New Code of Canon Law* (New York: Longmans, and Co., 1930), n. 147, 2. Nabuco lists examples of higher rank: a metropolitan in his suffragan dioceses, an apostolic delegate or nuncio in the place to which he has been assigned, cardinals everywhere in the world, the ordinary of the place when a titular bishop performs an office in his presence.—*Pontificalis Expositio,* I, n. 29.

154 The Pontifical Commission was asked: "An ex Codice archiepiscopus metropolita, qua talis, extra suam provinciam praecedat archiepiscopo non metropolitae, seu episcopis suffraganeis carenti. Resp.: Negative."—*AAS* XXXIII (1941), 373.

155 " In iure nomine dioecesis venit quoque abbatia vel praelatura *nullius;* et nomine Episcopi, Abbas vel Praelatus *nullius,* nisi ex natura rei vel sermonis contextu aliud constet."—canon 215, § 2; cf. canon 347; canon 106, 3°. If either of these is named to a titular see and consecrated, he takes his precedence with the other bishops, residential and titular, and determines his

l) vicars and prefects apostolic;[156]

m) apostolic administrators;[157]

n) vicar capitular (diocesan administrator in the United States and other countries which do not have cathedral chapters—canon 423);[158]

o) vicar general;[159]

p) canons of the cathedral and collegiate chapters (in the United States, the diocesan consultors if they attend in a body as consultors);[159]

---

precedence according to the date of his promotion to the titular see in consistory.

156 "Vicarii et Praefecti Apostolici iisdem iuribus [praecedentiae) . . . in suo territorio gaudent, quae in propriis dioecesibus competunt Episcopis residentialibus, nisi quid Apostolica Sedes reservaverit."—canon 294, § 1; cf, also canon 347. Vicars apostolic are generally titular bishops.—*Annuario Pontificio* (1959), p. 774. When this is true, their precedence is determined according to the norms for bishops, just as the abbots and prelates *nullius* mentioned above in footnote n. 155, *supra*. Prefects apostolic are not generally raised to the episcopal dignity.—*Annuario Pontificio* (1959), p. 825. Whenever they are, they too follow the rules of precedence for bishops. Cf. "A List of Cardinals, Archbishops and Bishops in the United States in the Order of their Seniority," *The Official Catholic Directory*.

157 "Administrator Apostolicus permanenter constitutus iisdem iuribus [praecedentiae] et honoribus fruitur . . . ac Episcopus residentialis."—canon 315, § 1; cf. also canon 347. "Si ad tempus datus sit: Eadem iura [praecedentiae] . . . habet ac Vicarius Capitularis. . . ."—canon 315, § 2. Cf. next note. Since these administrators (apostolic) are usually titular bishops, they will determine their proper precedence according to their date of promotion in the consistory unless their letter of appointment provides differently. Cf. *Annuario Pontificio* (1959), pp. 766-68.

158 "Quae in canone 370 de Vicario Generali praescripta sunt, eadem de Vicario quoque Capitulari dicta intelligantur."—canon 439. "Praesente etiam Episcopo, Vicarius Generalis publice privatimque praecedentiae ius habet super omnibus dioecesis clericis, non exclusis dignitatibus et canonicis ecclesiae cathedralis [non excluso coetu consultorum in Statibus Foederatis Americae Septentrionalis] . . . nisi clericus charactere episcopali praefulgeat, et Vicarius Generalis eodem careat."—canon 370, § 1.

159 "Coetus consultorum dioecesanorum vices Capituli cathedralis, qua Episcopi senatus supplet; quare, quae canones ad gubernationem dioecesis, sive sede plena sive ea impedita aut vacante, Capitulo cathedrali tribuunt, ea de coetu quoque consultorum diocesanorum intelligenda sunt."—canon 427. In view of the second clause about the government of the diocese, authors generally did not acknowledge the right of precedence to the consultors in

q) rector of the seminary;[160]

r) vicars forane (rural deans);[161]

s) pastors, with the pastor of the cathedral preceding all others in the diocese;[162]

t) substitute and auxiliary vicars;[163]

---

the same way they recognized this right for the cathedral chapter. However, the new Oriental legislation has nearly the same canon which reads: "Collegii consultorum eparchalium vices *in omnibus* supplet Capitulum canonicorum ecclesiae cathedralis, ubi hoc constitutum est; quare quae canones ad gubernationem eparchiae, sive sede plena sive ea impedita aut vacante, consultoribus eparchalibus tribuunt, ea etiam de Capitulo cathedrali intelligenda sunt."—Pius XII, motu propr., *Cleri sanctitati,* 2 iunii 1957, canon 464—*AAS,* XLIX (1957), 433. The diocesan consultors are the more common body for the Oriental Church, just as they are for the United States. The Oriental legislation has merely put down explicitly what must be concluded for diocesan consultors in the United States from the norms for cathedral chapters in the Latin Code. It seems clear that the legislator would intend to have these two groups of diocesan consultors (Oriental and Latin) to have the same rights, inasmuch as he has given them the same obligations. In the Oriental legislation this group of consultors has been given the same precedence the cathedral chapter has in the Latin Code, canon 491, § 2: ". . . Capitulum vero cathedrale vel collegiale eisdem praecedit ubique locorum." Cf. Pius XII, motu propr., *Postquam apostolicis litteris,* 9 febr. 1952, canon 6, § 2.—*AAS,* XLIV (1952), 65. Since this norm in the Oriental legislation comes from the common legislator in identical matters, it seems to be interritual law, which is implied in canon 106, 4°, of the Latin Code, and canon 37 of *Cleri sanctitati:* "In praecedentia diversitas ritus non attenditur." If a group of diocesan consultors, one from the Latin rite and one from an Oriental rite, attend a function as a body, they should both have the same precedence. To give the Oriental consultors the precedence of the cathedral chapter, and to give the Latin consultors a lesser precedence would seem to violate the norm of canon 106, 4°. Some confirmation of this conclusion may be seen in canon 358, § 1, which, in listing those who are to be called to the diocesan synod, names the diocesan consultors or the cathedral chapter in second place, after the vicar general.

160 This is the place given him in the list of those who must be called to a diocesan synod.—canon 358, § 1.

161 "Vicarius foraneus . . . praecedit omnibus parochis aliisque sacerdotibus sui districtus."—canon 450, § 2. See below for more detailed discussion, page 279.

162 "Sicut parochus ecclesiae cathedralis . . . praecedit omnibus aliis dioecesis parochis. . . ."—canon 478, § 1.

163 "Vicarii substituti et adjutores praecedunt, dum in munere manent, vicariis cooperatoribus. . . ."—canon 478, § 2.

u) assistant vicars (assistants);[164]

v) other priests attached to a parish church.[165]

There seems to be some doubt whether the titular bishops and archbishops constitute a rank separate from that of residential archbishops and bishops. The Code itself makes no particular distinction between residential and titular bishops and archbishops. Since this is true, it seems safe to adopt the opinion of those authors who do not make any distinction between the two.[166] It may serve some utility, however, to consider the contrary opinions.

---

164 ". . . vicariis cooperatoribus; hi aliis sacerdotibus ecclesiae paroeciali addictis."—canon 478, § 2.

165 See below for greater detail, p. 234, note 46. The foregoing outline is basically that which is given by Michiels, *De Personis,* pp. 689-90. For more detail, see the outlines on pages 258, 262, 266, 272, 274.

166 This is, in fact, the practice followed in the determining of precedence on the part of the American hierarchy as it is given in *The Official Catholic Directory*. There the criterion which determines the precedence of the bishops and archbishops, residential and/or titular, is the date of their promotion in consistory. When two or more are named on the same date, the order of their publication in the *Acta Apostolicae Sedis* is generally adopted. Presumably, then, the order in the *Acta* reflects for them the order in which they were named in the consistory itself.

A consistory is a meeting of the Curial Cardinals with the Roman Pontiff. Such a meeting may be either public (or extraordinary), secret (ordinary), or semi-public. The public consistory is conducted with great solemnity. In addition to the cardinals, other prelates or secular leaders and civil officials are admitted to the public consistory. This consistory is merely for the performing of more solemn acts, such as the conferring of the red hat for cardinals, and the solemn declaration of canonization. Only the cardinals attend the secret consistory. Bishops and abbots are admitted to the semi-public consistory. At the present time much of the work formerly done in consistory is distributed among the various Roman Congregations, with the result that the secret (or business) sessions are not held as often as formerly. Sometimes they are held as rarely as once a year. It is in these secret consistories that new cardinals are created, consistorial benefices (all benefices to which episcopal power is attached) conferred, pallia granted, legates *a latere* appointed, and allocutions of the Roman Pontiff delivered on subjects of great importance to the conduct of Church affairs.—Sipos, *Enchiridion Iuris Canonici,* p. 163; cf. note 196, p. 147, for more detail on the conferral of consistorial benefices.

Zitelli (+1887) gave an indication that some difference might exist between the two positions when he mentioned that in Rome there was a titular bishop who was completely equal to residential bishops in precedence. The time of promotion alone determined his precedence among other bishops, even residential, unless the other bishops were assistants to the papal throne[167]

This distinction is maintained, according to Michiels, by those authors who hold that *gradus* indicates a genus, whereas *ordo* indicates the species or subordinate class or group within the *gradus.* Two examples are given: the *gradus* of cardinals comprising the orders of bishop, priest, and deacon, and the *gradus* of bishops comprising the orders of bishops, residential and titular.[168] In the discussion regarding the various schools of thought on the meaning of *gradus* and *ordo* it was pointed out this school's opinion could not be accepted, since it not only made the provisions of canon 106 repetitious, but also implied the legislator's using the same word in two different meanings in the same canon.

In 1850 the Sacred Congregation of the Council was asked to solve a doubt about titular bishops and their relation to suffragan bishops in a council. In the given case, a titular bishop resided in the metropolitan see subsequently to his resignation from a see in another province. He had been appointed to his see earlier than any of the suffragans of the present province. The Congregation answered, admitting some evidence in favor of his precedence over the suffragans, on the basis that the *Caeremoniale Episcoporum* (lib. 1, cap. 31) did not distinguish between titular and residential bishops in implementing its norms for precedence in councils. The Congregation held that the *Caeremoniale* applied the same principle ". . . *episcopis omnibus, sive cum iurisdictione sive mere titularibus, cum in presenti lege nulla fiat distinctio.*" But the Congregation preferred to follow a different and more cogent line of reasoning which warranted

---

167 Z. Zitelli, *Apparatus Iuris Ecclesiastici in Usum Episcoporum et Sacerdotum praesertim Apostolico Munere Fungentium* (Romae, 1886), Appendix, p. 107, note 1; cf. *infra*, p. 244, for a brief description of assistants to the papal throne.

168 *De Personis,* p. 688, citing Perathoner, Leitner, Maroto and Toso.

the suffragan bishops to precede all titulars because of the authority of the former to legislate with a deliberative vote, whereas the latter had no such vote.[169]

In his special study of the provincial council, Murphy cited Vermeersch-Creusen's opinion that titular bishops, attending a council on the free invitation of the fathers of the Council, follow the same rules of precedence as suffragan bishops, not only among themselves but also in relation to the suffragan bishops. According to this opinion, titular bishops would not yield in precedence to those suffragan bishops whom they outranked according to the time of their promotion to the episcopacy. The proponents of this opinion admit that a titular bishop may be subject to some particular suffragan bishop by reason of domicile or quasi-domicile; but they assert that the participation of titular bishops in the council is based, not on their domicile or quasi-domicile, but on their possession of the episcopacy. The only norm of precedence stated for bishops at councils is that which looks to seniority in the episcopal dignity.[170]

However, neither the *Caremoniale Episcoporum,* nor the authentic interpretation of Nov. 10, 1925, ad II (basing precedence for suffragans solely on the date of their preconization) mentions titular bishops specifically. The Pontifical Commission's answer seems rather to exclude titular bishops, since it explicitly mentions only suffragans. In addition, residential bishops and not titular bishops are the ordinary members of councils; titular bishops often possess only a consultative vote. As a conclusion, Murphy argues that even the *Caeremoniale* prescinds from the question of the precedence of titular bishops, on the basis of the response from the Congregation of the Council in 1850, stating that titular bishops do not precede suffragan bishops at a provincial council.[171]

Poblete likewise states that ". . . titular archbishops and titular bishops, who have no authority properly or specifically at the council, follow . . ." residential bishops and archbishops.[172]

169 S. S. Conc., *Aquensium Archiepiscopo,* 24 aug. 1850—*ASS,* III (1867) 310.

170 *Legislative Power of the Provincial Council,* p. 112.

171 *Loc. cit.*

172 *The Plenary Council,* p. 43.

This seems to be contrary to the official precedence in a plenary council as given in the *Ordo in Concilio Plenario Servandus.* This states that archbishops and bishops, even titular, take their precedence according to the date of their promotion to the archiepiscopal or episcopal rank.[173] Although Nabuco agrees with this norm of precedence in the plenary council, he gives a lower place to titular bishops in the provincial council just after the suffragan bishops, unless the titular bishop enjoys a deliberative vote. In this case, the titular bishop goes with the suffragan bishops and determines his precedence solely according to the time of his preconization in consistory.[174]

The basic norm for those who give the titular bishops a special rank below that of residential bishops seems to be the notion of their authority in the council. If these titular bishops enjoy a deliberative vote, they also enjoy precedence with the residential bishops, and determine their own precedence in the same way. Otherwise, they have a special rank just below that of the residential bishops, but among themselves use the date of their promotion to the episcopacy to determine their precedence.

There are more authorities to support the view that titular bishops never have a special lower rank, however. A decree of the Congregation of Rites in 1656 granted precedence to a titular archbishop over other bishops and archbishops who were his juniors by consecration, and even over bishops who were his senior by consecration but were promoted to the rank of residential archbishop at a later date.[175] The following year, the same Congregation declared that the titular archbishop and titular bishop were to receive the same honors and reverence as the residential bishop[176]

The letter of Pius IX establishing the precedence for the Vatican Council in 1869 made no distinction between the titular and residential archbishops and bishops.[177]

---

173 Page 11; cf. Nabuco, *Pontificalis Expositio,* III, n. 19.

174 *Op. cit.,* III, n. 20.

175 S. R. C., *Ephesina,* 9 apr. 1656—*D.* n. 1006.

176 S. R. C., *Leodien.,* 1 dec. 1657—*D.* n. 1046; S. R. C., *Pragen.,* 1 dec. 1657—*D.* n. 1045.

177 Litt. ap., *Multiplices,* 27 nov. 1869—*Coll. Lac. VII,* Acta et Decreta Sacrosancti Oecumenici Concilii Vaticani, n. IV, col. 20.

Vermeersch-Creusen state specifically that the precedence of the suffragan bishops at a council is determined solely from the date of their preconization to the rank of bishop, and conclude with: "Idem valet de episcopis titularibus, tum inter se tum relate ad suffraganeos."[178] In another place they explain how a *gradus* in some general sort of way is determined according to a certain preeminence of title or name, without any special attention being paid to the effectiveness of the office, whether it be real or honorary. Thus, they say, although the titles are merely honorary, the Latin primate and patriarch have a rank of their own. So also, even though their titles too are only honorary, titular archbishops enjoy the rank of archbishop just as the residential archbishops do. In the same way, a residential archbishop without suffragans enjoys precedence of the same rank as that of a metropolitan archbishop when he is outside his province.[179]

Coronata refers to the former practice of the titular bishop yielding precedence to the residential bishops, but says "Id non amplius servari, sed archiepiscopos extra suam provinciam inter se et episcopos extra suas dioeceses inter se sive residentiales sunt sive titulares praecedere iuxta prioritatem promotionis ad sedem archiepiscopalem et respective episcopalem."[180]

The various grades or ranks discussed above are attached in some way to an official position of some authority in the Church. In accordance with Michiels' definition, there are other sources for rank which are merely honorary titles of preeminence. Examples of this type of rank which are found in the United States are the titles of protonotary apostolic, domestic prelate, and papal chamberlain. These will be discussed in the commentary on canon 106, 7°, which refers to the special norms of precedence for members of the papal household.

In the absence of any authority of one person over another, rank or grade will be the prime factor which determines the precedence of the one over the other. Whoever has the higher rank, according to the list given above, will have greater pre-

---

178 *Epitome,* I, n. 398.
179 *Op. cit.,* I, n. 230.
180 *Institutiones,* I, n. 401

eminence, and therefore also will have precedence over the other with lower rank and less preeminence.

In regard to the rank accorded to bishops, archbishops, cardinals, and all others appointed in consistory, it must be noted that the very fact of this announcement in consistory is sufficient to give the person concerned the precedence proper to that rank. However, if episcopal consecration is ordinarily a contributing factor to the preeminence of the rank as for bishops, those members of the grade who are consecrated will have precedence over those who are not. This will be true between the consecrated and unconsecrated cardinals within the order of cardinal-priest,[181] as well as between archbishops, bishops, abbots and prelates *nullius*, vicars and prefects apostolic, who are or are not consecrated. In a similar way, bishops promoted to the rank of archbishop, with or without suffragans, will take their place after all other archbishops who have taken canonical possession of their archdiocese, until they themselves have taken canonical possession of their own territory.[182] No such limitation was mentioned by authors in relation to the precedence of bishops or others who must take canonical possession of their territories. However, it does not seem out of place to make a similar distinction if there is to be no episcopal consecration.

B. Precedence and Higher Order

According to canon 106, 3°, the basic norms for determining precedence among those without authority over one another are grade, Orders, and age. Precedence is given to the person with the highest rank. When the rank of two or more people is the same, precedence is acknowledged for the person who is in the higher Order.

It was determined earlier that the more common interpretation of Order in this canon is the strict interpretation, which considers it ordinarily as the effect of a sacred rite. Order can include tonsure, as well as the minor and major Orders, and the consecration of a bishop.[183]

---

181 See below, p. 254.

182 Michiels, *De Personis,* p. 690; Berutti, *Institutiones,* II, n. 25; Beste, *Introductio in Codicem, sub canone* 106, 3°.

183 Canon 950.

In view of this, clerical seminarians have a right to precedence based on their respective Orders. Vito mantains that clerical seminarians are a part of the moral person of the cathedral chapter, and should go in procession under the cross of this chapter.[184] If other moral persons attend the procession, each with its own cross, the seminarians will have precedence over all other clergy by reason of being a part of the cathedral chapter.[185] If all persons in the procession go under one and the same cross, Moretti commonly gives the clerical seminarians a place just after the secular clergy. This gives the seminarians precedence over the religious and all pious associations of the faithful. If the cathedral chapter has its own cross in the procession, immediately after this cross come the chanters, the seminarians and the canons. The following is a typical processional arrangement given by Moretti:

a) thurifer;
b) cross-bearer and two acolytes;
c) chanters;
d) clerical seminarians;
e) parish priests;
f) canons;
g) bishop[186]

Another arrangement includes religious, and shows the precedence given to seminarians over them:

a) cross-bearer;
b) chanters;
c) religious;
d) clerical seminarians;
e) secular clergy;
f) college of pastors;
g) collegiate chapters *(non-insignis);*

---

184 Pasquale Vito, *Note Canoniche sulla Precedenza,* (Verona, 1924), p. 48.

185 *Loc. cit.*

186 See also *Caeremoniale Episcoporum,* Lib. II, cap. XXXIII, n. 5 for similar precedence of seminarians in a *Corpus Christi* procession.

h) collegiate chapters *(insignis);*
i) first dignitary;
j) cathedral chapter.[187]

Order is a secondary norm for determining precedence among several persons, all of whom are of the same rank or grade. Among cardinals, all enjoy the same rank; whoever is in the higher order, therefore, has precedence, with some exceptions that will be discussed in the treatment of cardinalitial precedence.

In the rank of bishops, although those who are consecrated will take precedence over those who are elected but not yet consecrated, bishops-elect (those not yet consecrated) also take their precedence over other clerics who have not been so named to the episcopal rank, because the bishop-elect holds a higher rank. Among themselves, these un-consecrated bishops have the same rank; they take their precedence, therefore, from the date on which they were named in consistory. If they were nominated on the same day, the order in which they were nominated must be observed for the determining of their mutual precedence.[188] As soon as one of the group has been consecrated, however, he takes precedence over all those who are not yet consecrated. This is true, even though he might have been the most recently named, and had therefore been preceded by all the others up to the time of his consecration. Once a second or third person from the group has been consecrated, these newly consecrated bishops determine their mutual precedence according to the date of their promotion in consistory while still taking precedence over those promoted before them but not yet consecrated. Once they are all consecrated, they will all determine their mutual precedence solely from the date of their promotion in consistory.

Persons holding certain positions, such as abbots and prelates *nullius,* or vicars and prefects apostolic, have by the very fact of their positions a certain rank, as was noted above. However, when, as happens not infrequently, any one of these is consecrated a bishop after being named to a titular see in consistory, his

187 Cf. Moretti, *De Sacris Functionibus,* III, nos. 2166, 2183, 2335, 2351, 2359, 2362, 2411, 2444, and 2479 for typical processional arrangements.

188 Berutti, *Institutiones,* II, n. 25.

precedence is no longer determined by the original rank of vicar apostolic or prelate *nullius;* the date of his promotion to the rank of titular bishop in consistory becomes the sole criterion, and he takes his precedence among the bishops.

SECTION 3—PRIOR PROMOTION TO A RANK OR ORDER AND AGE

In the event that two or more persons are of both the same rank and the same Order (such as two consecrated bishops, two pastors, or two vicars), canon 106, 3°, directs that the third criterion for determining precedence among them shall be priority of promotion to the grade or rank. Promotion is ordinarily a historical fact which can be proved from written documents and records.

The date of promotion to the rank of cardinal is the date on which the names were published by the Roman Pontiff in consistory.[189] An exception to this rule is found in the case of cardinals whose names the pope does not choose to publish in the consistory. Since only the will of the Roman Pontiff is required to create a cardinal, there is no essential need for the publication in consistory.[190] Therefore, if the pope has reserved the name of a cardinalitial candidate *in pectore,* the candidate nonetheless, has been officially created by this very fact. He may not enjoy the privileges of a cardinal in the external forum, however, until the creation becomes public through announcement in consistory. At this time, the right of precedence, which depends on the date of creation as a cardinal, goes into effect retroactively, as it were. The new cardinal then takes his precedence from that date of creation *in pectore* over others named before him in consistory, but after the date of his own creation *in pectore.*[191] If the Roman Pontiff should die before announcing in consistory the act of his earlier creation *in pectore,* then all cardinalitial rights and privileges are lost.

Bishops and archbishops, residential or titular, vicars and prefects apostolic, abbots and prelates *nullius,* likewise determine their mutual precedence from the date of their announce-

189 Canon 233, § 1.

190 Wernz-Vidal, *Ius Canonicum,* II, n. 469.

191 Canon 233, § 2.

ment in consistory.[192] "Inter episcopos autem consecratos, qui in eodem consistorio praeconizati sint, praecedentia attenditur ex ordine quo in illo suae quisque ecclesiae praefectus fuerit."[193]

For the members of the hierarchy in the United States and Canada, the order of promotion can be conveniently determined from "A List of Cardinals, Archbishops and Bishops in the United States in the Order of their Seniority" and a similar list for Canada (although these lists are not authentic, they are reliable), found in the annual publication, *The Official Catholic Directory.* This includes all those consecrated as bishops, whether they hold the position of abbot or prelate *nullius,* vicar or perfect apostolic, apostolic administrator, titular or residential, bishop or archbishop.

The authentic dates of promotion (not given in the Catholic Directory list) can be found in the official commentary of the Holy See, the *Acta Apostolicae Sedis,* in the section dealing with the acts of the Sacred Congregation of the Consistory. It could not be determined absolutely that the order of appointments in the *Acta* which are made on the same day, is the same which was (will be) followed in the consistory itself. It is probably the only reliable source readily available for determining prior promotion to these ranks, however. Athough the annual publication of the Holy See, the *Annuario Pontificio,*[194] as well as some of the recent editions (not 1959) of the *National Catholic Almanac*[195]

---

192 S. R. C., *Segobricen.,* 21 mart. 1609—*D.*, n. 270; S. R. C., *Regni Sardiniae,* 2 mart. 1641—*D.*, n. 734; S. R. C., *Terulen.,* 20 nov. 1677—*D.*, n. 1606; S. R. C., *Iaren.,* 15 apr. 1904—*D.*, n 4133; S. C. Conc., *in una vic. Africae Meridionalis,* 14 mart. 1909—*Fontes,* n. 4353

193 Berutti, *Institutiones,* II, n. 25.

194 The *Annuario Pontificio* is the best supplement to the Code as a criterion for determining precedence whenever the Code itself is inadequate; but nowhere is its use prescribed. To use it to determine precedence is, therefore, optional. It is the norm in use for determining precedence in Rome itself, especially in the papal household. It is not necessarily valid elsewhere, in virtue of the provisions of canon 106, 7°.—S. Goyeneche, *Quaestiones Canonicae de Iure Religiosorum* (2 vols.; Neapoli: M. D'Auria, Pontificius Editor, 1954-55), I, 92 (hereafter cited as *De Iure Religiosorum*).

195 "Biographies of the Hierarchy of Continental United States and American Bishops who have resigned their Sees," *The National Catholic Almanac* (Paterson: St. Anthony's Guild Press, 1904).

both have the dates of appointment of the hierarchy of the United States, neither make it possible to determine the mutual precedence of two or more persons of the same rank promoted on the same day.

The date of any other promotions made by the Holy See in consistory[196] or outside consistory[197] will also determine the precedence of the individual according to the principle of priority of promotion. On a similar basis, the date on the rescript of an appointment from lesser superiors will indicate to the recipient the time of his promotion. Thus, the priority of all appointments made by the ordinary of the place, such as diocesan officials, pastors, and all vicars, will be determined by the date found thereon. Should the dates of two or more appointments to the same rank be identical, recourse might be had to the protocol

---

196 The benefices which are conferred in consistory (canon 1411, 1°) are those to which episcopal power is attached, although the individual upon whom they are conferred may not have episcopal consecration. Sometimes these consistorial benefices of canon 1411, 1°, are conferred outside of a consistory because of the rather rare convocation of consistories in the present day. When this is done, the conferral of the benefice must be published in the consistory.—Coronata, *Institutiones,* II, n. 975. Haydt lists four types of consistorial benefices in the United States: those of the metropolitans, the bishops, the apostolic administrators, and the abbots *nullius.*—*Reserved Benefices,* The Catholic University of America Canon Law Studies, n. 161 (Washington, D. C.: The Catholic University of America Press, 1942), p. 118. In view of the fact that consistories may be held as rarely as once a year (Sipos, *Enchiridion,* p. 163), and because the announcement of the conferral of this type of benefice appears regularly in the official commentary of the Apostolic See, the *Acta Apostolicae Sedis,* it appears that the publication of these conferrals in consistory follows the order in which the names have appeared in the *Acta.* There is no definite information to confirm this, however.

197 Besides all consistorial benefices and all dignities in cathedral and collegiate churches in accordance with the norm of canon 396, § 1, there are reserved to the Apostolic See, even though this itself should be vacant, the following: 1° all benefices vacated by cardinals, papal legates, major officials of the Sacred Congregations, tribunals and offices of the Roman Curia, and even honorary members of the household of the Roman Pontiff [domestic prelates and papal chamberlains]; 2° benefices left vacant by the death of the incumbent in Rome; 3° benefices conferred invalidly because of simony; 4° benefices dealt with by the Roman Pontiff or his delegate in any one of several ways.—canon 1435.

number, if there is one. It is conceivable, however, that appointments issuing from any superior subordinate to the Roman Pontiff would not have such a number. In that event, it might be possible to have recourse to the order in which these promotions were named in the official diocesan publication where the announcement was made, much as one would consult the *Acta Apostolicae Sedis* for appointments made by the Holy See.

This last norm may prove to be less reliable and less satisfactory, in view of the fact that in all likelihood less attention is paid to proper precedence in the diocesan publication than in the *Acta*. The mutual precedence of pastors in a given diocese could then be determined from the list of those present at the diocesan synod, if it was known that the list was so compiled according to the rules for precedence, or from a similar list in the diocesan directory.[198] In the absence of accurate information regarding the priority of promotion to a rank, it is necessary to have recourse to the fourth criterion for determining precedence among those who have no authority over each other: priority of promotion to the same Order.

In this matter of ordination (or episcopal consecration, according to canon 950), it would be possible to argue a right to precedence even from the hour of the day if two persons were promoted to the same Order on the same day, or from the sequence in which they were called to Orders.

---

198 Such a list may be highly recommended as a step towards relieving the confusion that might otherwise arise if such information were not readily available. It would also give less foundation to whatever excuses are proffered for the non-observance of proper precedence. It should simply list the diocesan officials in the order of precedence given them by the Code and the ordinary in view of canon 106, 6°, the protonotaries apostolic, domestic prelates, and papal chamberlains, according to their dates of promotion within each rank, as well as all pastors, in the order of their first promotion to the rank of pastor (just as bishops are listed according to their first promotion to the rank of bishops, even if it was only to a titular see, and they have been transferred since then).—Michiels, *De Personis,* p. 690.). The same could be done with the various kinds of vicars, although it would be practical only for the assistant vicars (assistants), since the other kinds of vicars have lesser permanence in their assignment. Such a list could include the ordination date as well, in case it became necessary to invoke that norm to determine proper precedence.

There is an exception to the rule of priority of ordination which the lawgiver provides: the existence of this exception will itself be exceptional. Two clerics hold the same rank, are in the same Order, and have been promoted to the given rank and Order on the same day in such a way that it cannot be determined who was promoted first. Ordinarily the one who was promoted to the Order first would have precedence. The exception is this: if one was ordained by the Roman pontiff, he has precedence over the other who was ordained by some lesser prelate, even though the former may have been ordained more recently.[199] This can also be true if the Pope has specifically delegated someone to ordain a cleric of his own choice. This does not seem to hold true of everyone ordained by a papal legate, however.[200]

If no distinction can be based on the rank or Order, nor on the time of promotion to either, then the final criterion offered by the Code is that of age: the one born first will have precedence over the one who was born later. In the rare case where even this fact in the lives of two or more people is identical, no norm is provided by the lawgiver. However, there is no reason why the ordinary, in view of the power given him in canon 106, 6°, could not determine the relative precedence of the persons concerned "*. . . ratione habita principiorum iuris communis, legitimarum dioecesis consuetudinum et munerum ipsis commissorum. . . .*"

The provisions of canon 106, 3°, for determining the relative precedence of people who have no authority over one another can be summarized in the following five norms:

1) higher rank or *gradus;*

2) higher order when two or more have the same rank;

3) prior promotion to the rank, when rank and Order are the same;

4) prior promotion to the Order, when rank, Order, and promotion to rank are the same, with this exception: he who was ordained by the pope has precedence;

5) senior by age.

199 Canon 106, 3°.

200 Coronata, *Institutiones,* I, n. 157; Chas. Augustine [Bachofen], *A Commentary on the New Code of Canon Law.* (8 vols., St. Louis, London, 1919-22), II, 39. (hereafter cited as *Commentary*).

Article 4. The Determination of Precedence Among Persons of Different Rites

Canon 106, 4°. *In praecedentia diversitas ritus non attenditur.*

The notion of equality among the various rites in the Catholic Church, as far as precedence is concerned, was expressed in nearly the same terms the Code uses, by Benedict XIV in his constitution *Etsi pastoralis.*[201] The same provision for the mutual precedence of the rites is found in the present-day Oriental legislation.[202] The wording of canon 37 of the *motu proprio* is almost identical with that of canon 106 of the Code of Canon Law. The norms of canon 491 of the Latin Code are used as the basis for canon 6, §§ 1, 2, of the Oriental legislation for religious.[203] The fact that this Oriental canon is more comprehensive, including, as it does, those norms of canon 106 of the Latin Code which are applicable, may have been necessary in view of the fact that the Oriental legislation on persons had not yet been promulgated. However, in the opinion of the present writer, this arrangement has much to commend it, as does the change in wording in some places. The phraseology of the Latin Code in Canon 106, 5°, which has caused some differences of opinion among Latin commentators, has been clarified through being changed from *"Inter varias personas morales eiusdem speciei et gradus . . ."* to read: *"Inter religiones eiusdem condicionis iuridicae. . . ."* Whereas it is not clear from Canon 491 of the Latin Code that its norms for the precedence of religious and clerics are applicable only when these individuals proceed as part of moral persons or collegiate groups, the Oriental canon 6, § 3, on religious provides specifically for precedence *"inter singulos autem clericos et religosos. . . ."*

There are likewise particular norms for precedence similar to those in the Code of Canon Law; but these are, of necessity, more numerous because of a more complicated arrangement of

---

201 Const. 26 maii 1742, § IX, n. XVII—*Fontes,* n. 328; *Bull. Rom. Taur.,* I, 167-185.

202 Pius XII, motu propr. *Cleri sanctitati,* 2 iunii 1957, canon 37—*AAS,* XXXXIX (1957), 446-447.

203 Pius XII, motu propr. *Postquam Apostolicis Litteris,* 9 febr. 1952—*AAS,* XXXXIV (1952), 68.

the Oriental hierarchy to include jurisdictional patriarchs of various rites as well as different concepts of the office of metropolitan and archbishop. There are special norms, too, for the Oriental titular metropolitans and archbishops; the Latin Code provides no special norm for these members of the hierarchy.

The scope of this study does not permit a detailed consideration of the Oriental hierarchy, much less a comparative study of the Oriental grades with the Latin equivalents. It will be sufficient to state that, in virtue of the Latin canon 106, 4°, the clergy of the Oriental rites will not be separated in any way from their Latin counterparts. The same norms of authority, grade, Order, and age will apply to them as equals, which they are. Similarly, the same norms apply to the Oriental proxies, moral persons, and members of the papal household.

The practical application of this is evident in the seniority list of the hierarchy in the United States as found in *The Official Catholic Directory*. There it will be noted that the precedence of the Oriental hierarchs of Pittsburgh (exarch, equivalent to a Latin vicar apostolic who is consecrated), Philadelphia (metropolitan, with the same precedence that a Latin archbishop has), and Stamford, Connecticut (an eparch, the equivalent of a Latin bishop), is determined according to the date of their promotion in consistory, regardless of their rite. As a result, their names are found intermingled with those members of the Latin hierarchy who were promoted before and after them.

CHAPTER VI

THE PRECEDENCE OF MORAL PERSONS OF DIFFERENT SPECIES

In Article 7 of the previous chapter, in Section 1, the precedence of moral persons is discussed in a general way as they come under the norms of canon 106, 3°. In number 5 of canon 106, more specific norms of precedence are provided for all moral persons of the same species and rank; but canon 106 omits any such norms for moral persons of different species and ranks. It is evident that such different moral persons exist, otherwise no such distinction would be made at this point.

The difference in the species of moral persons depends on the juridic grade to which they belong. This, in turn, is determined by the prescriptions of the canons, such as canon 491, which specifies the various species of religious institutes and orders.[1] In actual fact, there are three different types of moral persons for which the Code has determined some of the more general norms of precedence: chapters of canons, religious institutes, and pious associations of the faithful.[2]

Each of these species of moral persons has its particular norms for precedence in addition to the use of the general norms of canon 106. In giving these particular norms, the lawgiver likewise determines the various hierarchical grades of these types of moral persons. For instance, the chapters of canons have their precedence specified in canon 408, which divides them into those who belong to the cathedral church and others who belong to some collegiate church. This canon likewise divides these chapters into those which are signal or eminent *(insignia)* and those which are not *insignia.* Similarly, canon 491 provides the norms for determining the relative precedence of moral persons of different rank and species, including the various species of religious institutes. Finally, canon 701 divides the

1 Berutti, *Institutiones,* II, n. 26.

2 Canons 408, 491, and 700, respectively.

genus of pious associations of the faithful into three species: third orders secular, confraternities, and pious unions.

However, the provisions of canon 408 and canons 700-701 are not formally treated in this study. It seems proper, therefore, to treat at least of canon 491 at this point. Thus a study of the precedence of moral persons of a different species or grade will precede the consideration of the precedence of moral persons of the same species and grade, as provided in canon 106, 5°.

Article 1. The Application of the Norms of Precedence to Members of Moral Persons

Before all treatment regarding the precedence of the various religious institutes and orders among themselves, it will be necessary to clarify a distinction which must be kept in mind whenever the rights of precedence for religious or for the members of any other moral persons are being determined. A member of a moral person or of some collegiate group takes the precedence of that moral person or group only in the following instances:

1) when, together with other members of the moral person, he is present at function specifically as a part of the moral person, or

2) when he officially represents the moral person at some function.[3] Moretti[4], Coronata[5], and Jone[6] require that the members of the moral person who attend a function should be present and enter as a moral person, in some sort of group (". . . *aliquo modo colligatae personae* . . .").

When would this requirement ordinarily be met? It seems to the present writer that normally the members of religious institutes or orders who are engaged in the care of souls in a diocese would attend most diocesan functions as individuals *(ut singuli)* rather than as members of their institute or order.[7] As individuals, their rights of precedence would be determined ac-

3 Regatillo, *Institutiones,* I, n. 650.

4 *De Sacris Functionibus* I, n. 151.

5 *Institutiones,* I. n. 160.

6 *Commentarium,* I, *sub canone* 491, §1.

7 Jone, *loc. cit., et sub canone* 106, 5°; Coronata, *loc. cit.*

cording to the norms of canon 106, 1°, 2°, 3°, and 4°.[8] But a group of religious, or an individual from a religious house (or from any other moral person) who attended any function, would be there as a representative of the house or of the moral person of the institute. As a collegiate group, or as a representative (following the rules of a proxy in canon 106, 1°), they would follow the norms of precedence proper for their species of moral person; e.g., canons regular, monks, mendicants, or congregations, as found in canon 491, §1.[9]

Another explanatory remark should be made by way of an introduction to the precedence of religious. Canon 490 provides that both men and women are understood in the term "religious." But canon law, when it speaks of precedence in relation to processions and other similar functions, is concerned directly with men. Therefore, the established rules are applicable only to women religious among themselves, for they should be in separate

---

8 Regatillo, *op. cit.*, I, n. 650; Berutti, *op. cit.*, III, n. 10; Sipos, *Enchiridion*, p. 83.

9 Although the Code in canon 491 speaks of canons regular, monks, and regulars, these are not to be understood in the sense of being taken as individuals. This follows from the last two clauses of paragraph 1 of this canon, in which these apparent references to individual religious are put in opposition to religious congregations, rather than to members of religious congregations.

The argument can also be based on canon 106, 5°. This number is concerned, in the first place, with the external precedence of moral persons of the same species and grade; it clearly contrasts the first principles of number 5 with the second group, which regulates the internal precedence among the members of some moral person. It is only logical that the legislator intended the same interpretation (for moral persons as such) to be applied to canon 491: viz., he was determining the external precedence of the moral persons of different species, just as he had determined the external precedence of moral persons of the same species and rank in canon 106, 5°. Canon 106 provides norms for both moral and physical persons, but number 5 is specifically limited in its first part to moral persons. Therefore, one can use all the other norms of canon 106 to determine the precedence of individuals in the Church, without any distinction as to their status as members of a moral person, be they of the secular or the religious clergy, or as clerical or lay religious, or merely as members of the laity. Their individual rank as a cleric or a lay person is the only basis for determining their precedence. Cf. Larraona, "Commentarium Codicis," *CpR*, IV (1923), 212, and note 421 (hereafter cited as Larraona, *CpR*).

parts of a procession or of any similar function.[10] There may be some acts for which a definite division should be made between the secular and the religious clergy, between men and women religious, and between women religious and the laity. There is no reason why proper precedence should not be observed in such circumstances, and proper honor shown to the religious state, that is, to women religious inclusively with men religious.[11]

Article 2. The Species and Grades of Moral Persons

There may be some confusion as to the exact intentions of the lawgiver in using the terms *species* and *gradus* in canon 106, 5°. Prior to any attempt to list the various kinds of moral persons according to species and rank, it will be helpful to see with what limitations a species may be considered to be divisible into grades.

Moral persons can be of different species; they may have a specific difference to distinguish them from others of the same genus, which is the supreme classification.[12] Within the species, some types of moral persons can be subdivided into grades, which have less significant differences among themselves than do the species, or, a fortiori, the genera.

Genera, the supreme classification, would include the chapters of canons, religious institutes, and pious associations of the faithful. For instance, within the genus of chapters of canons are the two species, cathedral chapters and collegiate chapters. Within the genus of pious associations of the faithful, confraternities, pious unions and third orders secular are different species. Within the genus of religious institutes are all the species listed in canon 491, such as canons regular, monks, congregations of pontifical approval, and the others. When one congregation is a clerical institute and the other a lay institute, this is considered to be a specific juridic difference, and each is considered a species rather than a subdivision or grade of the species i. e., the congregation.

---

10 *Rituale Romanum*, tit. IX, c. I, n. 4.

11 Larraona, *ibid.*, note 413.

12 Coronata, *Institutiones*, I, n. 159.

Within some of the species there are further subdivisions referred to as grades, or the lowest classification for the purpose of differentiation, at least in regard to precedence. Within the species of confraternity, for instance, there are the grades of archconfraternity and confraternity; pious unions are further divided into primary pious unions and other pious unions which are not primary; a collegiate chapter (which is a species under the genus chapter) can be either *insignis* or *non-insignis.* These are the more obvious examples of genus, species and grades of moral persons. Not every type of moral persons can be easily divided into its various species and grades, and be accurately labelled.[13]

Michiels recognizes the difficulty when he states: "Quaenam vero sint gradus illi et species, quaenam sit illorum graduum et specierum series hierarchica ordinata, non una regula determinari potest."[14] He claims that a wide interpretation of the term "moral persons" is to be accepted here. Such an interpretation would include all colleges and ecclesiastical institutions which might lack juridic personality in the strict sense.[15] Such groups of persons Michiels divides into three species in matters of precedence:

1) secular clerics as a body generally precede religious in a body (canon 491, §§1, 2):
   a) chapters of canons;
      (1) cathedral chapter
      (2) collegiate chapter
      (3) *insignia* and *non insignia* chapters (c. 408, §1)
   b) clerical societies of members living in common without vows;
   c) [clerical secular institutes should be inserted here].
2) religious precede laymen (canon 491, §§1, 2):
   a) clerical religious institutes precede lay religious institutes;
   b) canons regular precede monks;
   c) monks precede other regulars;

---

13 Cf. Coronata, *Institutiones,* I, n. 159; Regatillo, *Institutiones,* I, n. 218; Jone, *Commentarium,* I, *sub canone* 106, 5°.

14 *De Personis,* p. 693.

15 *Ibid.,* note 2.

d) regulars precede religious congregations;
e) congregations of pontifical approval precede those of diocesan approval.

3) precedence of associations of the faithful (canon 701, §1):
a) third orders secular;
b) archconfraternities;
c) confraternities;
d) primary pious unions;
e) other pious unions.

Larraona in his "Commentarium Codicis" on canon 491[16] clears up much of the problem in regard to moral persons which are religious institutes. Canon 491 lists species, but for this particular type of moral person there is no grade. Only such moral persons as chapters of canons, confraternities and pious unions can have grades to distinguish cathedral from collegiate chapters, archconfraternites from confraternities, and primary from other pious unions.

There is considerable agreement that the institutes of laymen and those of clerics are in different species;[17] the same holds true for a cathedral chapter and a collegiate chapter[18] and the various kinds of religious institutes and orders that receive mention in canon 491, §1.[19]

Article 3. Introductory Notions About Religious

By divine instituton the clergy are distinct from the laity in the Church. Both of these classes of persons in the Church may reflect the status of religious.[20] Canon 491 provides for the precedence of religious over laymen. Briefly, a religious is someone

16 *CpR,* IV (1923), 214, note 433.

17 Coronata, *Institutiones,* I, n. 159; Jone, *Commentarium,* I, *sub canone* 106, 5°; Sipos, *Enchiridion,* p. 83; Berutti, *Institutiones,* II, n. 26; Michiels, *De Personis,* p. 693.

18 Coronata, *loc. cit.;* Berrutti, *loc. cit.;* Michiels, *loc. cit.;* Jone, *loc. cit.* Sipos, however, calls this distinction a *gradus* within the species of clerical chapters—*Loc. cit.*

19 Coronata, *loc. cit.;* Berutti, *loc. cit.;* Michiels, *loc. cit.;* Larraona, "art. cit.," *Loc. cit.*

20 Canon 107.

who lives a permanent mode of community life by which the faithful undertake to observe, not only the precepts common to all, but also the evangelical counsels, by way of the vows of obedience, chastity, and poverty.[21] In strict parlance, then, novices and postulants are not to be classified as religious, though they share some of the rights and privileges of religious and, in favorable matters, are to be honored and considered as religious.[22] It is proper that a type of honor be shown to the religious state for three reasons: (1) because it derives substantially from the teaching and example of Christ; (2) because of its excellence, requiring that religious offer themselves a holocaust, through their prayers and penances, in the quest for Christian perfection; (3) because of its great value to the Church and its spiritual, intellectual, and material benefit to mankind.[23] There are some basic notions connected with a study of religious that should be explained.

An institute *(religio)* is a society approved by legitimate ecclesiastical authority, and its members, in accordance with its laws, take public vows either perpetually, or for a time, with the intention of renewing them after their expiration.[24]

Such a religious institute enjoys a moral personality conferred by ecclesiastical law. As such it has the positive approbation of the Church, and a Rule or constitution which defines its special purpose and proper form of government; it evinces a profession of public and perpetual vows, which are either simple or solemn; its members have the duty to strive for perfection.[25]

An institute in which the members of at least one class profess solemn vows is an order and its members are called Regulars.[26] Such an institute is called an order even if only some of the members profess solemn vows; in some cases its members profess only simple vows (some members of the Society of Jesus) which, by apostolic dispensation, are considered to have the same effects

21 Canon 487; canon 488, 7°.

22 Coronata, *Institutiones,* I, n. 505.

23 Abbo-Hannan, *The Sacred Canons,* I, 482.

24 Canon 488, 1°.

25 Coronata, *Institutiones,* I, n. 501.

26 Canon 488, 2°; *Annuario Pontificio* (1959), p. 871.

as solemn vows.[27] But a solemn vow is simply a vow which is both recognized as such by the Church and acknowledged to have definite juridical effects. In the absence of such recognition, all vows are simple no matter what other effects are recognized for them.[28]

The religious institute whose members profess only simple vows (temporary or perpetual) is called a congregation, and its members are called religious of simple vows.[29] These names for the members of religious institutes are applicable to both men and women who are members of the respective institutes. There are some designations which are applicable only to women who belong to religious institutes. Sisters are religious with simple vows; nuns are religious with solemn vows, and also those whose vows, according to the constitutions of their institutes, should be solemn, but which, by Apostolic provision, are simple in certain regions.[30]

Juridically, religious institutes are divided into different categories corresponding to the various forms which the religious life has assumed in the course of history.[31]

Canons regular are religious who have taken solemn vows and who are principally devoted to maintaining the splendor of the divine worship. They are so called because they have united and fused together the regular or religious life with the dignity and office of canons.[32]

Those Regulars are called monks or hermits who, although they have lived in common for centuries, follow the rules composed by the first patriarchs of the religious life for the direction of the hermits of Egypt and of Syria. Translated into Latin, coordinated and modified by such men as St. Benedict, these rules serve as the rules of the monasteries of Europe. Monks, unlike the mendicants, may own property in common.[33] The other

27 Coronata, *Institutiones,* I, n. 503.

28 Canon 1308, § 2.

29 Canon 488, 2°, 7°.

30 Canon 488, 7°.

31 *Annuario Pontificio* (1959), p. 871.

32 *Ibid.,* p. 877.

33 L. Fanfani, *De Iure Religiosorum* (3. ed.; Rovigo: Istituto Pandano di Arti Grafiche, 1949), n. 7.

Regulars include the mendicant orders, and the clerics regular whose principal aim is the apostolic ministry. The first religious congregations in the modern sense of the word date only from the sixteenth century.[34] A religious institute is said to be of pontifical approval *(iuris pontificii)* when it has obtained from the Holy See a decree either of approbation or of commendation *(decretum laudis)*.[35] If the institute was merely established by means of a decree of the local ordinary and has not yet obtained even a decree of pontifical commendation *(decretum laudis)*, it is said to be of diocesan approval *(iuris dioecesani)*.[36]

Religious institutes may be either clerical or lay. They are clerical if a notable part of their members are priests. But the mere number of religious either clerics or laymen, is not sufficient to determine the legal character of the institute. The institute would remain clerical even though it admitted lay brothers in greater number than it did clerics, provided that the former remained subordinate to the latter (clerics) in the constitution and the government of the institute. Examples of this are the clerics of St. Viator.[37] Chelodi (1880-1922) maintained that this clerical character could be determined likewise by the purposes of the institute;[38] Larraona holds that the same is true from an observation of the activities of the institute, whether they be

---

34 Creusen-Ellis, *Religious Men and Women in the Code,* n. 24, 3°.

35 When a new institute has developed sufficiently, and has shown by the test of time the value of its religious spirit and unity, it may ask of the Holy See a positive approbation. Practically, the steps of approbation in the Roman Curia are the following: (1) decree of commendation of the institute (*decretum laudis*); (2) decree of approbation of the new congregation; (3) approbation of the constitutions, first provisional, then final. Frequently the temporary approval of the constitutions is given together with the decree of praise. As soon as the decree of commendation (1) is obtained, the institute becomes one approved by the Holy See.—Creusen-Ellis, *op. cit.,* n. 27.

36 Canon 488, 3°. A diocesan congregation, although it extends in the course of time into several dioceses, nevertheless remains diocesan as long as it is without either pontifical approval or a decree of commendation from the Holy See (*decretum laudis*), and is entirely subject to the jurisdiction of the ordinaries according to law.—canon 492, § 2.

37 *Annuario Pontificio* (1959), p. 909; Creusen-Ellis, *op. cit.,* n. 10.

38 J. Chelodi, *Ius Canonicum de Personis* (5.ed. curavit Pius Ciprotti; Vicenza: Societa Anonima Tipografica, 1947), n. 245.

characteristic of the priesthood or not.[39] This clerical state of an institute is the first norm of canonical precedence.[40]

The following are clerical religious institutes: canons regular, monks (who are also called Regulars), and all other Regulars, mendicant and non-mendicant (clerics regular). Congregations of either pontifical or diocesan approval may be either clerical or lay institutes, according to the norms given above.[41]

There is still another form of community life which is not strictly that of a religious institute, because its members do not take public vows;[42] these are the so-called communities of members who live in common without the three customary public vows, as described in canons 673-681.[43] Such a group can also be either clerical or lay; it, like a religious institute, can be of either pontifical or diocesan approval, according to the norms of canon 488, 3°, 4°. Even if such societies are lay, they enjoy the privileges of clerics,[44] although they do not have the privileges of religious,[45] unless they have a special mandate.[46] One of the privileges of clerics, however, is reverence,[47] and precedence is one way of showing this reverence. Therefore, members of these

39 *CpR*, II (1921), 284 ff.

40 *Annuario Pontificio* (1959), p. 872.

41 Vermeersch-Creusen, *Epitome*, I, n. 597.

42 Canon 488, 1°.

43 In such a society of men, or of women, the members imitate the manner of life of religious by living in a community under the government of superiors according to approval constitutions, but they are not bound by the three customary public vows. Since these institutes do not make any profession of public vows, they are not properly religious institutes (canon 488), and their members are not properly designated as religious. The Congregation of the Mission (Vincentians) have the three ordinary vows plus a fourth, but they are private vows. The Oratorians of St. Philip Neri have no vows. The White Fathers [and the Sulpicians—Abbo-Hannan, *The Sacred Canons* I, 684, note 2] merely take an oath of obedience or perseverance. The Pallotines make a promise of stability together with the private vows of poverty, chastity and obedience.—Vermeersch-Creusen, *Epitome*, I, n. 829, 2°.

44 Canons 119-123.

45 Canons 613-625.

46 Canon 680. The Pallotine Fathers have a very liberal indult granting them many of the privileges of religious. — Vermeersch-Creusen, *op. cit.*, I, n. 838.

47 Canon 119.

societies living in common without vows are entitled to a right of precedence. Though they are not religious in the strict sense, they will be discussed in this article with the religious institutes after the pattern adopted by the *Annuario Pontificio,* which includes them among the "states of perfection."[48]

Article 4. Precedence Among the Religious Institutes

Canon 491, §1. *Religiosi praecedunt laicis; religiones clericales, laicalibus; canonici regulares, monachis; monachi, ceteris regularibus; regulares, Congregationibus religiosis; Congregationes iuris pontificii, Congregationibus iuris dioecesani; in eadem specie servetur praescriptum canonis 106, 5°.*

In canon 491, the lawgiver determines the relative rights of precedence for religious and laymen, for the various religious institutes, and for the religious and secular clergy. Nothing is said here about the order of precedence among religious of the same institute or order. The rules of canon 106, 5°, will apply to that question.

SECTION 1—RELIGIOUS PRECEDE THE LAITY

Ordinarily, religious, whether singly or as part of the moral person, precede laymen, who are also considered either singly or gathered in a group.[49] It may happen that, either by law or through custom, clerics and religious both will yield precedence to a layman who has been elevated to some ecclesiastical or civil dignity. This is especially true if the clergy and religious are of a lower rank,[50] as when the layman is the head of State, or a member of the parliament.[51]

It makes no difference if the laymen are members of a pious

---

48 1959 ed., pp. 930-38.

49 Canon 491, § 1. Cf. Jone, *Commentarium,* I, *sub canone* 491, § 1. This precedence of religious is generally conceded to be a juridic consequence of the honor and respect of which the Church considers them worthy because of their public and complete profession of evangelical perfection. It is likewise the result of the participation of the religious in the privileges of the clergy, according to canon 614 and canons 119-23.—Larraona, *CpR,* IV (1923), 173, note 410.

50 Michiels, *De Personis,* p. 693.

51 Sipos, *Enchiridion,* p. 92.

association such as a pious union, confraternity, or third order secular. The comparatively larger number or prior time of institution or approbation of the lay moral person will not matter in regard to this absolute principle of precedence: religious always precede laymen.

The societies of persons living in common without vows may be either clerical or lay; like congregations, they may also be of pontifical or diocesan approval.[52] Yet, any religious institute or order would have precedence over such a society which was merely a lay moral person. The fact that the society enjoyed the privileges of clerics would not give it any particular precedence in this case, because the religious institute enjoys the same privileges, which puts the two on equal bases, and allows the norm of canon 491, §1, to give precedence to the religious. On the other hand, this type of lay society would have precedence over other lay societies or laymen as individuals, because it shares in the privileges of clerics, among which is the right to the reverence of the faithful.[53] However, if this society without vows were a clerical society (and not a lay society as the above examples presuppose), its precedence would be determined by the rules of the next section dealing with the precedence of clerics over laymen.

If in either group, religious or lay, there is more than one religious or lay institute of the same species, the norms of canon 106, 5°, must be invoked.

SECTION 2—CLERICAL RELIGIOUS PRECEDE LAY RELIGIOUS

The next part of canon 491, §1, provides that all clerical religious institutes of any kind have absolute precedence[54] over all lay religious institutes of whatever kind, unless there are some special privileges favoring the lay religious institute, and these privileges have not been revoked.[55] It was this principle which

52 Canon 673, § 2.

53 Canon 680. Cf. T. Schaefer, *De Religiosis ad Normam Codicis Iuris Canonici* (2.ed.rev.; Muenster: Ex Officina Libraria Aschendorff, 1931), n. 57.

54 Larraona, *CpR*, IV (1923), 274, note 456.

55 According to canon 4, pre-Code privileges even in the matter of precedence, remain intact after the promulgation of the Code, if they are not expressly revoked by it.

originally gave the canons regular precedence over the monks, for the monks were laymen in the beginning, while the canons regular were priests.[56]

No attention need be paid to the type of vows or the time of institution of either moral person.[57] Accordingly, a clerical congregation, even though it is only of diocesan approval, precedes not only a lay congregation of pontifical approval, but even a lay order with solemn vows, whether either of these is exempt or not.[58]

The various kinds of religious institutes, *viz.*, canons regular, monks, other Regulars, and congregations of diocesan or pontifical approval, may all be clerical in nature. Some may be either clerical or lay. But according to the general norm, all clerical groups of each of these species will come before all the lay groups (even if some clerics are members of these lay groups) of each species. The lay group may never just follow immediately after its respective clerical group of the same species to form a unit of one species embracing both groups, clerical and lay. Such an arrangement would violate the absolute principle of this canon: for some lay institutes of a higher species (congregation of pontifical approval) would then be given precedence over some clerical institute of a lower species (congregation of diocesan approval).

Thus there is precedence even in the application of the norms of precedence: the norms of canon 491, §1, are to be applied in the order in which they are given:

a) of several kinds of moral persons, religious moral persons will always precede lay moral persons;

b) among the religious, those institutes which are clerical will precede all those which are lay, regardless of the species of lay institute.[59]

---

56 G. Cocchi, *Commentarium in Codicem Iuris Canonici ad usum Scholarum* (3. ed. rev., 8 vols.; Taurinorum Augustae: Marietti, 1925-1940), IV, n. 9 (hereafter cited as *Commentarium*); Wernz-Vidal, *Ius Canonicum,* III (Romae, 1933), n. 53.

57 Berutti, *Institutiones,* III, n. 10; Schaefer, *De Religiosis,* n. 57.

58 Larraona, *CpR,* I (1920), 77.

59 Thus all the lay institutes of any of the species mentioned in canon

But it may be asked whether a clerical institute has precedence over lay religious everywhere: that is, whether clerical religious would precede lay religious even in the churches of the latter. There seems to be some doubt, for paragraph 2 of canon 491 expressly acknowledges such precedence only for secular clerics over lay religious in their own church, while paragraph 1 says nothing about a similar precedence on the part of clerical religious over lay religious in such circumstances. By juridic analogy, the same right of precedence seems applicable to clerical religious that is applicable in paragraph 2 for secular clerics: even within their own churches lay religious must yield precedence to clerical religious.[60]

On the other hand, a clerical religious institute has a right to precedence in its own church over other religious[61] in the same way it has precedence over the secular clergy in such circumstances.[62] If there were some individual lay members in a clerical religious institute which had precedence over another clerical religious institute, these individual lay members, too, as part of the clerical moral person, would precede the individual clergy of the lay institute; the clerical moral person always precedes the lay moral person. But there must always be a question of precedence for the moral person as such, and not for the individual members; the individual persons *"ut singuli"* are to be judged on their personal qualifications when precedence is determined for them as individuals.[63]

If there is more than one clerical or lay institute of the same species, one must invoke the norms of canon 106, 5°, to deter-

---

491, § 1, will all follow after all the clerical institutes of these same species, so as to form two groups: one clerical group, arranged according to the precedence of the various species of this canon, and one lay group, arranged in the same order. See below, pp. 178-79, for a continuation of this schematic delineation which includes the other norms of canon 491.

60 Canon 20. Cf. Larraona, *CpR,* IV (1923), 214; Coronata, *Institutiones,* I, n. 599.

61 Even over monks and canons regular. — Jone, *Commentarium,* I, *sub canone* 491, § 1; Sipos, *Enchiridion,* p. 274.

62 Canon 491, § 2. Cf. Wernz-Vidal, *Ius Canonicum,* III, n. 53.

63 Larraona, *CpR,* IV (1923), 211, note 417.

mine their relative precedence among themselves within the same species.

SECTION 3—THE PRECEDENCE OF CANONS REGULAR OVER MONKS

This rule of canon 491, §1, which grants precedence to canons regular over all other religious, dates back at least as far as 1564, when the canons regular of St. Augustine were given specific precedence over the Benedictines.[64]

Originally this precedence was based on the fact that fundamentally *(per se)* canons regular were priests, whereas monks usually were not.[65]

Although the Code designates canons regular, monks and regulars, they are to be reckoned with not as individuals, but insofar as they compose a body and proceed in a body.

Larraona notes that the Code is here concerned only with true canons regular, not with those who are merely titular. Thus, the religious congregation of canons regular does not precede the orders, but takes its place among the other religious congregations.[66]

The canons regular listed in the *Annuario Pontificio* (1959) according to seniority include the following:

1) Sacer et Apostolicus Ordo Canonicorum Regularium S. Augustini [There are four congregations of these true canons regular: that of the Lateran, for the Austrians and the Swiss, and the Congregation of St. Nicholas and Bernard].

2) Candidus et Canonicus Ordo Praemonstratensis (O. Praem.—Norbertine)

3) Ordo S. Crucis (O.S.Cr.—Crosier Fathers)

4) Canonici Regulares Sanctissimae Crucis a stella rubea.[67]

---

64 Pius IV, const. *Sedes apostolicae,* 18 febr. 1564 — *Fontes,* n. 104. Cf. also Pius V, const. *Ex supernae,* 16 aug. 1567 — *Fontes,* n. 122: *Bull. Rom Taur.,* VII, 584; Pius V, const. *Cum ex ordinum,* 23 dec. 1570 — *Fontes,* n. 137; Benedictus XIII, const. *Militantis Ecclesiae,* 21 iunii 1727 — *Fontes,* n. 294. All of these granted precedence to the canons regular of St. Augustine over other canons or monks.

65 Wernz-Vidal, *Ius Canonicum,* III, n. 53; Cocchi, *Commentarium,* IV, n. 9.

66 *CpR,* IV (1923), 212, note 422. Cf. Schaefer, *De Religiosis,* n. 57. Cf. *Annuario Pontificio* (1959), p. 916.

67 *Annuario Pontificio,* pp. 878-79.

So far as the present writer knows, only the Norbertines and the Crosier Fathers have houses in the United States. On the basis of canon 491, §1, then, these canons regular would have precedence over all other religious in the United States in the absence of a contrary custom. Between them precedence would be determined according to canon 106, 5°.

SECTION 4—THE PRECEDENCE OF MONKS OVER OTHER REGULARS

The question here is of the ancient monks properly so-called.[68] Monks, therefore, in virtue of the rule already existing prior to the Code[69] and accepted from antiquity, precede friars, both mendicant and non-mendicant. Now, from the Code, they precede not only friars, but all regulars, even clerics regular, who before the Code had precedence over monks.[70]

Monastic orders at the present time can be reduced to five general groups: two from the West, the Benedictine type and the Carthusian type; and three from the East, the Pauline, Antonian, and Basilian types.[71]

In listing the various orders, the *Annuario* lists the Benedictine Conferedation as a unit in first place. Within this confederation, the precedence of the fifteen member congregations[72] is determined by the *"Lex Propria."* With a special deference shown to the Congregation of Monte Cassino out of respect for the founder, the other member congregations take their precedence according to the time of their founding. Among the Benedictine

---

68 Monks are a second kind of Regulars who are given precedence over the other Regulars ". . . *ob eorum venerandam antiquitatem. . . .*" — Cocchi, *Commentarium,* IV, n. 9. Those religious institutes which are not orders but congregations, and likewise lay institutes of religious ought not be considered as monastic religious institutes for matters of precedence. — Larraona, *CpR,* IV (1923), 212, note 423.

69 Schaefer, *De Religiosis,* n. 57. "Praecedentiam monachis semper et ubique tribuere debent fratres mendicantes." — S. R. C., *in Monopolitana,* 23 martii 1619 — *D.* n. 374; Clemens VIII, const. *Regis,* febr. 1598 — *Bull. Rom. Taur.,* X, 471.

70 Larraona, *CpR,* IV (1923), 212; DeHerdt, *Praxis Pontificalis,* II, 215.

71 *Annuario Pontificio* (1959), p. 880.

72 By a monastic congregation is meant the union of several independent (*sui iuris*) monasteries under one and the same superior, for example, the

Congregations in the United States are the following, in the order of their priority of foundation:

a) Congregatio Angliae;

b) Congregatio Americana Casinensis;

c) Congregatio Helveto-Americana.

The Benedictine Congregations which do not (as of 1959) belong to the Confederation are the following: the Camaldolese, the Vallombrosian and Sylvestrine Congregations, and the Congregation of Mt. Olivet.[73] Two congregations which follow the Benedictine rule are the Mechitarists in the Armenian Rite, one in Venice, and the other in Vienna.

After the Benedictine monks, the *Annuario* lists the Cistercians, who also follow the Benedictine rule. The original group of Cistercians was called an order, as are the reformed Cistercians (O.C.R.) or the Cistercians of the Stricter Observance (O.C.S.O.), known as the Trappists. Two other groups in Italy have formed into congregations, but they are monastic congregatons and therefore they are listed among the monks by the *Annuario.*[74]

The other group of monks in the western Church, according to the *Annuario,* is the Order of Carthusians. Even these are sometimes identified with the Benedictine family. As a matter of fact, St. Bruno (1032-1101) did not give his monks a rule. Later on, their customs were codified into a primitive rule, which combined certain elements of the Benedictine Rule with other regulations which are quite distinct from the latter.[75]

The Oriental rites have the three types of monks: the Pauline (Order of Brothers of St. Paul, the First Hermit), four different Antonian Orders (three among the Maronites, one among the

---

Benedictines of Monte-Cassino, of Beuron, of Solesmes. A monastic congregation differs from a religious congregation in the relative independence of the houses which compose it. The fact that there is one superior gives rise only to a very loose bond between the houses by reason of the very restricted powers which are ordinarily conferred on the superior of such a congregation.

A religious congregation is an institute whose members make profession of simple vows only, whether perpetual or temporary. — Creusen-Ellis, *Religious Men and Women in the Code,* nos. 7, 8.

73 *Annuario Pontificio* (1959), pp. 882-86.

74 1959 ed., p. 887-88.

75 Creusen-Ellis, *Religious Men and Women in the Code,* n. 24.

Chaldeans), and five different groups of Basilians (Grottaferrata, St. Josaphat, the Melkite Order of the Holy Saviour, and one of St. John, and another of Aleppo.[76]

The list of monastic orders as given in the *Annuario* is arranged as follows:

I. The Benedictine Confederation (O.S.B.)
  a) Congregatio Casinensis
  b) Congregatio Angliae
  c) Congregatio Hungarica
  d) Congregatio Helvetica
  e) Congregatio Bavarica
  f) Congregatio Brasiliensis
  g) Congregatio Gallica (Solesmensis)
  h) Congregatio Americana Casinensis
  i) Congregatio Beuronensis
  j) Congregatio Casinensis a primaeva observantia (Congr. Casin, p. o. O.S.B.)
  k) Congregatio Helveto-Americana
  l) Congregatio Austriaca ab Immaculata Conceptione
  m) Congregatio Ottiliensis O.S.B. pro missionibus exteris
  n) Congregatio Belgica ab Annuntiatione B.M.V.
  o) Congregatio slava S. Adalberti

II. Camaldolese
  a) Congregatio Monachorum Eremitarum Camaldulensium O.S.B.
  b) Congregatio Eremitarum Camaldulensium Montis Coronae

III. Congregatio Vallis Umbrosae Ordinis S. Benedicti

IV. Congregatio Silvestrina

V. Congregatio S. Mariae Montis Oliveti, O.S.B.

*VI. Armenian Rite Benedictines
  a) Ordo Mechitaristarum Venetiarum Monachorum sub regula S.B.
  b) Ordo Mechitaristarum Vindobonnensis

---

76 *Annuario Pontificio* (1959), pp. 888-91.

VII. Cistercians
- a) Sacer Ordo Cisterciensis (S.Ord.Cist.)
- b) Congregatio Cisterciensis S. Bernardi in Italia
- c) Congregatio Casamarensis S. Ordinis Cisterciensis
- d) Ordo Cisterciensium Reformatorum seu Strictioris Observantiae (O.C.R., O.C.S.O.—Trappists)

VIII. Ordo Cartusiensis (Carthusians)

*IX. Ordo Fratrum S. Pauli primi Eremitae (O.S.P.P.E.)

*X. Antonian Orders
- a) Ordo Antonianus Aleppensis Maronitarum
- b) Ordo Libanensis Maronitarum
- c) Ordo Antonianus S. Isaiae Maronitarum
- d) Ordo Antonianus S. Hormisdae Chaldaeorum

*XI. Basilians
- a) Ordo Basilianus Italiae, seu Cryptoferratensis
- b) Ordo Basilianus S. Josaphat
- c) Ordo Basilianus SSmi Salvatoris Melkitarum
- d) Ordo Basilianus S. Iohannis Baptistae, seu Baladitarum
- e) Ordo Basilianus Aleppensis Melkitarum[77]

SECTION 5—THE PRECEDENCE OF REGULARS OVER RELIGIOUS CONGREGATIONS

Ordinarily, the term "Regulars" includes three classes of religious institutes: canons regular, monks, and all other regulars. This third group includes both mendicants and non-mendicants or clerics regular. Since the precedence of canons regular and monks has already been treated, the mendicants and clerics regular are the specific object of study in this Section.

As far as the Code law is concerned here, there is no difference among the institutes of this third group of regulars; no law of precedence is in any general way acknowledged for any one group of Regulars over another group, except for the canons

---

77 *Annuario Pontificio* (1959), pp. 882-91. Those divisions which are headed by Roman numerals marked with asterisks (*) represent Oriental orders.

regular and monks, as mentioned earlier.[78] Therefore, all mendicants and non-mendicants, such as the military orders, hospitallers and clerics regular now constitute a single category for precedence, at least according to the Code law. These institutes would therefore determine their mutual precedence according to the norms of canon 106, 5°. The Code itself simply vindicates an absolute precedence to all these orders of regulars over religious congregations.[79]

Cocchi explains this right of precedence for Regulars on the basis that they profess solemn vows, while the members of congregations profess only simple vows.[80]

Within the species of Regulars who are neither canons nor monks, a distinction must be considered which is not found in the Code law. The mendicants, one group of Regulars, have received some privileges of precedence in the course of centuries. In virtue of canon 4, these privileges still retain their force, according to Larraona.[81] This distinction in favor of the mendicants is likewise acknowledged in the *Annuario Pontificio*.[82]

What then, are these privileges which serve as the bases for precedence of mendicants over other Regulars in this third group of Regulars? It seems that the question of a special precedence for mendicants received its impetus from a constitution of Pius V (1566-72), which gave the Order of Preachers (Dominicans) precedence over all other relgious except monks of the ancient orders

---

78 Although the Code law makes no distinction, the privileges of the mendicants still remain in force in virtue of canon 4. — Larraona, *CpR,* IV (1923), 212, note 426. This is noted in the list of general curias of religious institutes given in the *Annuario Pontificio* (1959), p. 876, which names, in the order of their precedence: orders (canons regular, monks, mendicant orders, clerics regular), clerical religious congregations, societies of the common life without vows, lay religious congregations, and secular institutes.

79 Before the Code, clerical religious congregations were considered like the secular clergy, and took their precedence from them. — Schaefer, *De Religiosis,* n. 57. This is still true of the clerical societies whose members do not have public vows.

80 *Commentarium,* IV, n. 9; cf. canon 488, 2°.

81 *CpR,* IV (1923), 214, note 426.

82 "General Curias," *Annuario Pontificio* (1959), p. 876.

and canons regular.[83] In 1584 Gregory XIII (1572-85) promulgated the constitution, *Exposcit,*[84] which established the principle of peaceful quasi-possession[85] of the right of precedence to settle any controversies in this matter among the mendicants in general.

It was not clear in the minds of some whether the norms of this constitution of Gregory XIII included the Dominicans or not, in view of their special privilege. Ferraris (+1763) and others were of the opinion that it did.[86] If this is true, the Dominicans determine their precedence with other mendicants according to the rule of quasi-possession as originated in Gregory's constitution. Ferraris reasoned that this constitution had as its purpose the settlement of the controversies regarding precedence among the mendicants, which category or species included the Dominicans. To give them a special precedence would not have contributed to the solution of difficulties about precedence. A decree of the Sacred Congregation of the Council in 1867 seemed at first to defend this position.[87] But one of its explanatory footnotes allows for an exception for the Dominicans on the basis that the constitution of Gregory XIII should indeed be considered the common law for mendicants ". . . *nisi aliquid aliunde obstet. . . .*" But in regard to the Dominicans, ". . . *obstaret constitutio Pii V quae incipit 'Divina' qua generaliter dedit iisdem praecedentiam ante alios mendicantes.*"

An explanatory note before the text of the constitution *Divina* in the *Bullarium Luxemburgense* sums up the historical development of the precedence of the Dominicans quite succinctly, and according to an interpretation followed quite commonly today:

> Haec declaratio, quae circa processiones mutata videtur ex constitutione Gregorii XIII *Exposcit* fuit postea a Clemente VIII ampliata in constitutione *Inter cetera* ubi Ordini Predicatorum ubique concedit quoad omnes

---

83 Const. *Divina,* 27 aug. 1568 — *Bull. Lux.,* II, 285.

84 15 iulii, 1584 — *Bull. Lux.,* II, 501.

85 Cf. *infra,* the commentary on canon 106, 5°, pp. 193 ff.

86 *Prompta Bibliotheca,* s.v. *praecedentia,* n. 46. Cf. also Bassi, *Bibliotheca,* s.v. *praecedentia,* n. 9; Augustine, *Commentary,* III, *sub canone* 491, § 1; Matthew Ramstein, *A Manual of Canon Law* (2.ed.rev.; *Hoboken, N. J.*: Terminal Printing and Publishing Co., 1948), p. 137.

87 S. C. C., 27 iun. 1867 — *ASS,* III (1867), 308.

religiosos tam mendicantes quam non mendicantes, post canonicos et clericos saeculares ac antiquos Ordines Monacales.[88]

A similar explanatory note before the constitution *Exposcit* in the *Bullarium*[89] recalls the special precedence of the Order of Preachers based on Pius V's constitution *Divina,* and the extension or restoration of this right of precedence by Clement VIII's constitution *Inter cetera.*[90]

Moreover, a formidable list of modern canonists maintain that the privilege of special precedence given the Dominicans is still in force.[91] The *Annuario Pontificio* for 1959 records this opinion as the one adopted by the Roman curia for matters of precedence by listing the Order of Preachers first among the mendicants[92] who follow the monks in the order of precedence in Rome.[93]

However, this will only explain the precedence of one mendicant order, the Dominicans. What is to be said for the other mendicants and the precedence attributed to them in the *Annuario Pontificio* and by at least one author?[94] It seems that the notion of the interparticipation of privileges must be invoked if one is to explain this division of "other Regulars" into mendicants, and non-mendicants or clerics regular, although no authority was found which specifically verified this conclusion.

Ordinarily, some juridic proportion must exist between the beneficiaries of privileges when they are acquired through

---

88 *Loc. cit.*

89 *Bull. Lux.*, II, 501.

90 Const. 25 sept. 1592 — *Bull. Lux.*, III, 17.

91 Jone, *Commentarium*, I, *sub canone* 491, § 1; Wernz-Vidal, *Ius Canonicum*, II, n. 54; Coronata, *Institutiones*, I, n. 508; Schaefer, *De Religiosis*, n. 61; Beste, *Introductio in Codicem, sub canone* 491, § 1; Cocchi, *Commentarium*, IV, n. 9; S. C. Ep. et Reg., *Romae*, 4 sept. 1733 — *Collectanea in Usum Secretariae Sacrae Congregationis Episcoporum et Regularium* (cura A. Bizzarri; Romae, 1863), p. 364.

92 Page 893.

93 *Ibid.*, p. 846.

94 Vito, *Note Canoniche sulla Precedenza*, p. 55.

interparticipation.[95] This principle seems to be verified among all the mendicant orders.[96] Several papal constitutions specify which orders are to be considered as mendicants over and above the Friars Minor of the Observance and the Capuchins; only these two were recognized as mendicants by the Council of Trent.[97] Others named subsequently were the Order of Preachers, the Hermits of St. Augustine, the Carmelites, the Servants of Mary (Servites),[98] and the Order of Minims of St. Francis of Paul.[99] Vasto concludes that these six mendicant orders share reciprocally ". . . *in forma aeque principali* . . ." in regard to both past and future concessions of privileges that concern places or persons.[100] Later, in listing the mendicant orders as they are acknowledged today, Vasto adds the following to the original six named above: the Trinitarians, [101] Mercedarians (Order of Mercy, not the Mercy Fathers),[102] and the Hospitallers of St. John of God.[103] Teutonic Order of St. Mary in Jerusalem.[104]

---

95 Raymond Matulenas, *Communication — A Source of Privileges*, The Catholic University of America Canon Law Studies, n. 183 (Washington, D. C.: The Catholic University of America Press, 1943), p. 151, citing Julius II, const. *Alias ad supplicationem*, 1 iunii 1509 — *Bullarium Ordinis FF. Praedicatorum* (ed. Thomas Ripoll et Antonius Bremond, 8 vols.; Romae, 1729-40), IV, 258.

96 Larraona, *CpR*, IV (1923), 212, note 426.

97 Session XXV, *de regularibus*, c. 3.

98 Pius V, const. *Romanus pontifex*, 3 oct. 1567 — *Bull. Lux.*, II, 256; for the Servites, cf. also Gregory XIII, const. *Dum ad uberes*, 20 apr. 1578 — *Bull. Rom. Taur.*, VIII, 205.

99 Pius V, const. *Apostolicae Sedis benignitas*, 9 nov. 1567 — *Bull. Lux.*, II, 260.

100 *De Communicatione Privilegiorum praesertim inter Religiones* (Aquilae in Vestinis: Italia, 1936), p. 18.

101 Paulus V, const. *Ecclesiae Catholicae*, 15 dec. 1609 — *Bull. Rom. Taur.*, XI, 608.

102 Alexander VIII, const. *Inscrutabili*, 21 iulii 1690 — *Bull. Rom. Taur.* XX, 62.

103 Pius V, const. *Licet ex debita*, 1 ian. 1572 — *Bull. Rom. Taur.*, VII, 959. Cf. Vasto, *De Communicatione Privilegiorum*, pp. 29-31.

104 1959 ed., p. 899.

The mendicant orders, according to the order of precedence followed in the *Annuario Pontificio,* is as follows:

a) Ordo Fratrum Praedicatorum (O.P.)
b) Ordo Fratrum Minorum (O.F.M.)
c) Ordo Fratrum Minorum Conventualium (O.F.M. Conv.)
d) Ordo Fratrum Minorum Capuccinorum (O.F.M. Cap.)
e) Tertius Ordo Regularis S. Francisci (T.O.R.)
f) Ordo Fratrum Eremitarum S. Augustini (O.S.A.)
g) Ordo Recollectorum S. Augustini (O.R.S.A.)
h) Ordo Fratrum Eremitarum Discalceatorum S. Augustini
i) Ordo Fratrum B.M.V. de Monte Carmelo (O. Carm.)
j) Ordo Fratrum discalceatorum B.M.V. de Monte Carmelo (O.C.D.)
k) Ordo SSm̃ae Trinitatis redemptionis captivorum (O.SS.T.)
l) Ordo Servorum Mariae (O.S.M.—Servite Fathers)
m) Ordo Minimorum
n) Ordo Hospitalarius S. Joannis de Deo (O.S.J. de D.)
o) Fratres Ordinis Teutonici Sanctae Mariae in Jerusalem[105]

Precedence among these various mendicant orders is determined primarily according to the principles of canon 106, 5°. An exception is made for the Dominican Fathers; according to most commentators, their privilege of preceding all other mendicants still obtains. The Franciscans determine their relative precedence by a particular law given them by Pope St. Pius X.[106]

The second group included among the "other Regulars" of canon 491, §1, have been called clerics regular. As the foundation of their priestly apostolate they employ the regular life, which they adapt to the different needs of the times, without however making it less secure.[107] The clerical state, which for monks was considered something secondary, and for mendicants was intended to be equal to the rule, for canons and clerics regular was

105 *Annuario Pontificio* (1959), pp. 893-99.

106 Motu propr. *Seraphici Patriarchae,* 15 aug. 1910 — *AAS,* II (1910), 713. Cf. *infra,* p. 196, on the treatment of canon 106, 5°, for the details of this particular norm.

107 *Annuario Pontificio* (1959), p. 899.

something primary. For them the priesthood was not joined to the rule; the rule was joined to the priesthood.[108]

These clerics regular, like the mendicants, have precedence over all religious congregations.[109] In the order listed in the *Annuario Pontificio,* this group includes the following:

a) Ordo Clericorum Regularium vulgo Theatinorum (C.R.)
b) Congregatio Clericorum Regularium S. Pauli, Barnabitarum
c) Societas Jesus (S.J.)
d) Ordo Clericorum Regularium a Somascha (C.R.S.)
e) Ordo Clericorum Regularium Ministrantium Infirmis (M.I.—Camillians)
f) Ordo Clericorum Regularium Minorum (C.R.M.)
g) Ordo Clericorum Regularium a Matre Dei (O.M.D.)
h) Ordo Clericorum Regularium Pauperum Matris Dei Scholarum piarum (S.P. o Sch. P.)[110]

In the event that more than one of the foregoing institutes are in attendance at some function where precedence is being observed, their relative precedence will be determined according to the norms of canon 106, 5°.

SECTION 6—THE PRECEDENCE OF RELIGIOUS CONGREGATIONS

Toward the end of the XVI and through the XVII century there appeared several institutes of clerics and laymen who lived in a community without any desire to become real religious orders. Besides their personal perfection, there were the apostolate and various works of charity to occupy them. In these associations the members either did not take vows, or else they took vows which were not solemn (either perpetual or temporary).[111] These latter were the religious congregations; the former were the societies without the profession of vows.[112] In the former and broad sense of the term, the first congregation was founded by St. Philip Neri (1515-1595) in 1566, which came to be called the

---

108 Vermeersch-Creusen, *Epitome,* I, n. 586.
109 Canon 491, § 1.
110 *Annuario Pontificio* (1959), pp. 899-902.
111 Canon 1308, § 2.
112 *Annuario Pontificio* (1959), p. 903.

Oratorians.[113] In this Section, the specific object of study is congregations in the more strict sense of a religious institute of at least simple vows.

These congregations of religious can be either clerical or lay. Between the two, the right of precedence will always be given to the clerical group, according to the norm given in canon 491, §1. There is another distinction, explained in more detail above, which divides these congregations into those of pontifical approval, and those with only diocesan approval. The fact that the Code distinguishes between their relative precedence suggests a similarity to the special preference given to a cleric ordained by the Roman Pontiff over one ordained by a lesser prelate.[114]

Among the congregations of pontifical approval, as among Regulars who are not canons regular or monks, the Code law indicates no diversity of species in matters of precedence. Nevertheless, the juridic nature of the matter seems to indicate the validity of some distinction concerning their relative precedence for this reason: some congregations can only be considered as being in the first stages of pontifical approval (there are three stages).[115] It is only indirectly by their decree of commendation *(decretum laudis)* that they are subject to pontifical law. They can be called pontifical in the full sense of the term only when they have obtained final approval of their constitutions.[116]

Congregations of pontifical approval do not require any right of precedence over the non-exempt congregations in consequence simply of their own exemption;[117] all congregations of pontifical approval precede those of diocesan approval, regardless of the

---

113 Vermeersch-Creusen, *Epitome,* I, n. 586.

114 Cocchi, *Commentarium,* IV, n. 9.

115 These three stages are: (1) receiving the decree of commendation *(decretum laudis)* (2) the decree of approbation of the new congregation; (3) the decree of provisional, and then final approval of the constitutions. — Creusen-Ellis, *Religious Men and Women in the Code,* n. 27.

116 Larraona, *CpR,* IV (1923), 213, note 429. In the *Annuario Pontificio* (1959), however, the congregations are listed according to the date on which they first received the simple approbation *(decretum laudis).* — *Annuario Pontificio* (1959), p. 903.

117 Larraona, *CpR,* I (1920), 78, ad III; IV (1923), 213; Berutti, *Institutiones,* III, n. 10.

type of approval. In the same way, congregations of diocesan approval will always precede societies of lay persons living in common without public vows,[118] even if such societies are of pontifical approval.[119] This is in accord with the first criterion of canon 491, §1: a religious institute always precedes a lay institute.

The foregoing norm of precedence for institutes or moral persons must always be applied together with the other principle that clerical religious always precede lay religious. The norms of the precedence of religious may be applied in this order in a given case:

1) within each canonical species (canons regular, monks, other Regulars including mendicants and clerics regular, congregations of pontifical approval, congregations of diocesan approval, societies whose members live in common without vows) religious institutes always precede lay institutes.

2) among the religious institutes:

a) clerical religious precede lay religious;

b) of two clerical religious institutes, the one which has higher rank as a species, according to (1) above, will precede another institute of a lower species;

c) if the two institutes are both Franciscan, consult the special norms given under the treatment of canon 106, 5°;

d) if the two institutes are congregations, that congregation which has pontifical approval will precede the other which has only diocesan approval. Some would give precedence to the congregation with full pontifical approval over the congregation which has only received the decree of commendation *(decretum laudis)*. Among two congregations with exactly the same type of approval, or in the same stage of approval, the relative precedence may be determined according to the date on which they received their form of approval;[120]

---

118 Larraona, *CpR*. IV (1923), 213 note 431.

119 Canon 673, § 2.

120 Moretti, *De Sacris Functionibus*, I, n. 152, XXV. Note that the *Annuario Pontificio* (1959) lists only the congregations of pontifical approval, and in the order in which they received their first decree of commendation

e) after these distinctions have been made, if there are still two institutes whose right to precedence remains identical, one must invoke the norms of canon 106, 5°, in order to determine their relative precedence more accurately.

In the order of their seniority according to the date of their first pontifical approbation (simple approbation or the *decretum laudis*), the following are the clerical religious congregations listed in the 1959 *Annuario Pontificio:*

1) Congr. Presbyterorum doctrinae christianae

2) Congr. Piorum Operariorum Catechistarum Ruralium

3) Congr. Clericorum Regularium Marianorum sub titulo Immaculatae Conceptionis Bm̃ae Virginis Mariae (M.I.C.—Marian Fathers)

4) Congr. Clericorum excalceatorum SSm̃ae Crucis et Passionis D.N. Jesu Christi (C.P.—Passionists)

5) Congr. SSm̃i Redemptoris (C.SS.R.)

6) Congr. Sacrorum Cordium Jesu et Mariae necnon adorationis perpetuae Ss. Sacramenti altaris (SS.CC.—Picpus or Fathers of the Sacred Hearts)

7) Societas Mariae (S.M.—Marists)

8) Congr. S. Spiritus sub tutela Imm. C. Bm̃ae. V. M. (C. S. Sp.—Holy Ghost Fathers)

9) Societas Mariae Montfortana (S.M.M.—Missionaries of the Company of Mary, or Montfort Fathers)

10) Congr. Oblatorum Missionariorum B.M.V. Imm. (O.M.I.)

11) Congr. Oblatorum B.M.V. (O.M.V.)

12) Cong. Clericorum saecularium Scholarum Charitatis

13) Congr. Presbyterorum a Sancto Basilio (C.S.B.—Basilians)

14) Congr. Missionariorum a SS. Cordibus Jesus et Mariae (M.SS.CC.)

15) Congr. Clericorum Parochialium seu Catechistarum S. Viatoris (C.S.V.—Viatorians)

16) Societas Mariae (S.M.—Marianists)

17) Institutum a Charitatis (I.C.—Rosminians)

(decretum laudis); but the date of their final approval is also given. — Pages 903, 907, 908 for the principle, and two examples. Cf. the treatment of Canon 106, 5°, *infra*, pp. 192 ff.

18) Congr. Filiorum Mariae Immac. (C.M.F.—not the Claretians: cf. #28)

19) Missionarii S. Francisci Salesii de Annecio (M.S.F.S.)

20) Societas a Sancto Petro in Vinculis

21) Congr. Presbyterorum a St. Stigmatibus D.N.J.C. (C.P.S.—Stigmatine Fathers)

22) Congr. a S. Cruce (C.S.C.—Holy Cross Fathers)

23) Pia Societas Presbyterorum ab Assumptione aut Augustiniani ab Assumptione (A.A.—Assumption Fathers)

24) Congr. Filiorum B.M.V. Immac. (F.M.I.)

25) Societas Mariae pro educatione surdorum et mutorum

26) Congr. Presbyterorum a Ssmo Sacramento (S.S.S.—Blessed Sacrament Fathers)

27) Congr. a Resurrectione D.N.J.C. (C.R.—Resurrectionist Fathers)

28) Congr. Missionariorum filiorum Immac. Cordis B.M.V. (C.M.F.—Cordis Mariae Filius—Claretians)

29) Congr. Sacratissimi Cordis Jesu Infantis (S.C.J.I.)

30) Institutum Josephitarum Gerardimontensium (C.J.)

31) Societas S. Francisci Salesii (S.D.B.—Salesians of St. John Bosco)

32) Pia Presbyterorum Societas ab Immac. V.M. Conceptione

33) Missionarii SSmi Cordis Jesu (M.S.C.)

34) Congr. Fratrum a S. Vincentio a Paulo[121]

35) Congr. Fratrum a Caritate

36) Societas Presbyterorum Ssmi Cordis de Bétharram

37) Institutum Oblatorum S. Francisci Salesii (O.S.F.S.)

38) Congr. Canonicorum Regularium Immac. Conceptionis (C.R.I.C.—these are not true canons, but only titular)

39) Societas Patrum S. Edmundi Oblatorum S. Cordis Jesu et Immaculati Cordis Mariae (S.S.E.—Edmundite Fathers)

40) Missionarii B.M.V. a La Salette (M.S.)

41) Filii Sacrae Familiae Jesu, Mariae et Joseph (S.F.)

42) Congr. Sacerdotum a Sacro Corde Jesu (S.C.J.)

43) Pia Societas Taurinensis S. Joseph (C.S.J.)

44) Congr. Filiorum S. Cordis Jesus (F.S.C.J.—Sons of the Sacred Heart for African Missions)

---

121 These are not the "Vincentians" of the U. S. Cf. *infra*, p. 185, n. 3.

45) Societas Missionariorum a S. Joseph (S.S.J.—Josephites)
46) Congr. Presbyterorum a S. Maria de Tinchebray
47) Congr. Imm. Cordis Mariae (C.I.C.M.—Scheut Fathers)
48) Societas Verbi Divini (S.V.D.)
49) Fratres Tertii Ordinis S. Francisci Capulatorum a B.M.V. Perdolente
50) Congr. Filiorum S. Mariae Immaculatae (F.S.M.I.)
51) Societas Divini Salvatoris (S.D.S.—Salvatorians)
52) Pia Societas S. Francisci Xaverii pro exteris missionibus (S.X.—Xaverian Missionary Fathers)
51) Tertius Ordo Carmelitarum Discalceatorum Malabarensium (T.O.C.D.)
52) Pia Societas Missionariorum a S. Carolo pro Italis emigratis (P.S.S.C.—Scalabrinians)
53) Congr. Oblatorum S. Joseph, Astae Pompejae (O.S.J.—Oblates of St. Joseph)
54) Institutum Missionum a Consolata (I.M.C.—Consolata Society)
55) Congr. Missionariorum a S. Familia (M.S.F.)
56) Congr. Servorum a Charitate
57) Congr. parvae Missionis ad surdos-mutos
58) Congr. Missionariorum de Mariannhill (C.M.M.)
59) Congr. Missionariorum Filiorum SS. Cordis Iesu (M.F.S.C.)
60) Congr. pro operariis Christianis a S. Josepho (C. Op.)
61) Filii Charitatis
62) Institutum Missionariorum Opificum (M.O.)
63) Missionarii a Spiritu Sancto (M.Sp.S.)
64) Congr. Missionariorum SS. Cordium Iesu et Mariae (M. Ss.Cc.)
65) Pia Societas a Sancto Paulo Apostolo (S.S.P.)
66) Congregatio Sanctae Familiae a Nazareth
67) Institutum Filiorum a Caritate (F.d.C.C.)
68) Societas Christi pro Emigrantibus Polonis
69) Congr. a Fraternitate Sacerdotali (C.F.S.)
70) Congr. Religiosorum Tertii Ordinis Regularis Sancti Francisci Assisiensis "of the Atonement" (S.A.—Franciscan Friars of the Atonement)
71) Congr. Rogationistarum a Corde Jesu (R.C.J.)

72) Congr. Missionariorum Servorum SSmae Trinitatis (M.S. Ss.T.)[122]

Among congregations of diocesan approval, the general norms must be applied in determination of their relative precedence. A religious congregation will precede a lay congregation; a clerical religious congregation will precede a congregation of lay religious. If, according to these norms, two or more congregations of diocesan approval have the same right to precedence, the norms of canon 106, 5°, must be invoked.

The following are the congregations of lay religious, that is, congregations whose members, in large part, are laymen, in the order in which they were approved by Rome:

1) Institutum Fratrum Scholarum Christianarum (F.S.C.—Christian Brothers)
2) Fratres Scholarum Christianarum de Hibernia (Irish Christian Brothers)
3) Institutum Fratrum a Sancta Familia de Bellicio (F.S.F.)
4) Congr. Fratrum Immac. Conceptionis B.M.V.
5) Institutum Fratrum instructionis Christianae de Ploermel (F.I.C.P.—Brothers of Christian Instruction)
6) Institutum Fratrum B.M.V. a Misericordia (F.D.M.)
7) Congr. Fratrum B.M.V. Matris Misericordiae (F.M.M.)
8) Institutum Parvulorum Fratrum Mariae (P.F.M. or F.M.)
9) Filii Immac. Conceptionis
10) Congr. Fratrum Cellitarum seu Alexianorum (C.F.A.—Alexian Brothers)
11) Congr. Fratrum a Sancto Patricio (Patrician Brothers)
12) Fratres a Charitate (C.F.C.—Brothers of Charity)
13) Fratres de Misericordia (Brothers of Mercy—F.M.M.)
14) Fratres Piae Congr. a Praesentatione
15) Fratres a Sacratissimo Corde Iesu (S.C.—Brothers of the Sacred Heart)
16) Fratres N. D. Lurdensis
17) Fratres de Misericordia Sanctae Mariae Auxiliatricis
18) Institutum Tertiariorum Franciscalium a Sancta Cruce loci Waldbreitbach (T.F.S.C.)
19) Institutum Fratrum instructionis christianae a S. Gabriele

[122] *Annuario Pontificio* (1959), pp. 904-929.

20) Congr. Fratrum Pauperum S. Francisci Seraphici (C.F.P.—Brothers of the Poor of St. Francis)
21) Congr. Fratrum a Sancto Aloysio Gonzaga
22) Filii Matris Dei Dolorosae
23) Congr. Fratrum a S. Francisco Xaverio (C.F.X.—Brothers of St. Francis Xavier)
24) Congr. Fratrum Tertiariorum Franciscalium a Mount Bellew
25) Congr. Missionaria S. Francisci Assisiensis (C.M.S.F.)
26) Fratres christiani Immac. Conc. B.V.M. Matris Dei[123]

Any congregation not listed either here or in the list of clerical congregations above is not of pontifical approval. Although it will be evidently of diocesan approval, it must still be determined if it is clerical or lay before the proper precedence can be declared.

SECTION 7—THE PRECEDENCE OF SOCIETIES WITHOUT VOWS

Although the various norms for the precedence of societies without vows are discussed in earlier sections by comparison with religious institutes, it will be helpful to collect these norms in one separate section for the sake of clarity.

Inasmuch as the members of these societies do not take the three public vows of religious, neither the members nor the society itself are to be considered as religious in matters of precedence. The *Annuario Pontificio* (1959) groups religious institutes, societies without vows, and secular institutes together under the common title, "Pontifically Approved States of Perfection for Men,"[124] and for this reason only these societies are listed together with the religious. They are likewise treated in the Code in *Pars II: De Religiosis,* in the second book. A separate title is devoted to the treatment of such societies, and the first canon states specifically that such a society ". . . non est proprie religio, nec eius sodales nomine religiosorum proprie designantur."[125]

---

123 *Annuario Pontificio* (1959), pp. 939-946.
124 Pages 871 ff.
125 Canon 673, § 1.

Like the congregations, these societies without vows may be either clerical or lay, and of either pontifical or diocesan approval, according to the terms of canon 488, 3°, 4°.[126]

Whether such a society is clerical or lay, it enjoys the privileges of clerics,[127] but not those of religious,[128] unless the society has a special indult.[129]

On the basis of these canons, it becomes clear that such societies, if they are clerical, will have the precedence of secular priests.[130] If they are lay societies without vows, they will have precedence over other lay moral persons because of their share in the privileges of clerics, one of which is precedence over the laity. In view of another general norm, such lay societies of the common life will be preceded by any religious institute: for religious always precede laymen.[131]

To determine the relative precedence of these societies when one is of pontifical approval and the other of diocesan approval, or when one is clerical and the other lay, the hierarchy of general principles must be recalled, and applied in the order of their importance:

1) a religious institute always precedes a lay society, even if the former is only of diocesan approval, and the latter of pontifical approval.

2) a clerical institute or society always precedes a lay institute or society, even if the same conditions are present as in (1).

3) an institute of pontifical approval precedes one of diocesan approval, only if the institutes or societies are equal in regard to the first two norms: e.g., both are clerical religious institutes, or

---

126 Canon 673, § 2.

127 Canons 119-23.

128 Canons 613-25.

129 Canon 680.

130 S. R. C., *Mechoacanen.*, 21 ian. 1769 — *D.*, n. 2485; Benedictus Ojetti, *Synopsis Rerum Moralium et Iuris Pontificii* (4 vols., 3. ed.; Romae, 1909-14), s.v. *praecedentia*, n. 3236 (hereafter cited as *Synopsis*); Beste, *Introductio in Codicem, sub canone* 491, § 2; Jone, *Commentarium*, I, *sub canone* 491, § 2; Larraona, *CpR*, IV (1923), 273-274; Cocchi, *Commentarium*, IV, n. 9; canon 491, § 2.

131 Canon 491, § 1. Cf. *infra*, pp. 186-88; Larraona, *CpR*, IV (1923), 210 and note 411.

both are lay religious institutes, or both are clerical societies of the common life, or, finally, both are lay societies without vows. If the two moral persons (societies without vows) are equal on the basis of all other criteria then the one which received its pontifical or diocesan approval first will have precedence over the other.

The following are such clerical societies without vows which have received pontifical approval, in the order in which they received their approval. All other such societies are of diocesan approval only.

1) Institutum Oratorii S. Philippi Nerii (C.O.—Oratorians)
2) Congr. Oratorii Jesus et Mariae Immac.
3) Congr. Missionis (C.M.—Vincentians or Lazarists)
4) Societas Presbyterorum a S. Sulpitio (S.S.—Sulpicians)
5) Societas Parisiensis missionum ad exteras gentes (M.E.P.—Paris Foreign Mission Society)
6) Societas Presbyterorum a Misericordia (S.P.M.—Fathers of Mercy)
7) Societas Apostolatus Catholici (S.A.C.—Pallotines)
8) Congr. Pretiosissimi Sanguinis (C.Pp.S.)
9) Congr. Jesu et Mariae (C.J.M.—Eudist Fathers)
10) Institutum Pontificium a Ss. Apostolis Petro et Paulo et a Ss. Ambrosio et Carolo pro missionibus exteras gentes (P.I.M.E.—Missionaries of Sts. Peter and Paul)
11) Missionarii Africae (P.A.—White Fathers)
12) Societas Missionum ad Afros (S.M.A.)
13) Socictas Missionariorum S. Joseph de Mill Hill
14) Societas de Maryknoll pro missionibus exteris (M.M.)
15) Institutum Hispanicum S. Francisci Xaverii pro Missionibus Exteris
16) Societas S. Columbani pro missionibus apud Sinenses
17) Societas Sacerdotum Missionariorum a S. Paulo Apostolo (C.S.P.—Paulists)
18) Societas pro missionibus exteris Provinciae Quebecensis
19) Societas Lusitana pro Catholicis Missionibus (S.M.P.)
20) Societas Sodalium Sancti Joseph a Sacro Corde (S.S.J.—Josephites)

21) Societas Missionum Exterarum de Bethlehem in Helvetia (S.M.B.—Bethlehem Missionaries)
22) Societas Scarborensis pro Missionibus ad Exteras Gentes (S.F.M.)
23) Institutum a Santa Maria de Guadalupe pro exteris missionibus (M.d.G.)
24) Societas Sancti Patricii pro Missionibus ad Exteros[132]

SECTION 8—THE PRECEDENCE OF SECULAR INSTITUTES

Secular institutes are societies, whether clerical or lay, whose members profess the evangelical counsels in the world, in order to attain Christian perfection and to exercise a full apostolate.[133] Historically, these institutes go back as far as the XVIII century, although juridically they were recognized by the Church only as recently as February 2, 1947, through the Apostolic Constitution *Provida Mater Ecclesia.*[134] The members of these institutes strive toward personal perfection through the practice of the evangelical counsels, and dedicate their lives to the apostolate in its most varied and modern forms. For this reason they are said to make profession of the State of perfection, but not of the canonical state of perfection, which is proper to religious. But they are not bound to the common life[135] and they do not take public vows. The term "secular" emphasizes that the persons professing this type of life do not change their social status which they had in the world. Hence, after their consecration to God, they remain either clerics or laymen, with all the juridical and practical consequences deriving therefrom. Hence, secular institutes can be either clerical or lay, and can enjoy either pontifical or diocesan status.[136]

---

[132] *Annuario Pontificio* (1959), pp. 931-938.

[133] "Lex Peculiaris Institutorum Saecularium," Art. 1 — *AAS,* XXXIX (1947), 120.

[134] *AAS,* XXXIX (1947), 114.

[135] This is one note that distinguishes them from societies without vows.

[136] *Annuario Pontificio* (1959), pp. 949-50. Cf. also Donnell Walsh, *The New Law on Secular Institutes,* The Catholic University of America Canon Law Studies, n. 347 (Washington, D. C.: The Catholic University of America Press, 1953), pp. 61-64. Cf. also, canon 488, 3°, 4°.

Secular institutes, precisely for the reason that they are secular, precede religious institutes according to norms which are similar to the norms for societies without vows. If the secular institute is clerical in nature, it will precede religious institutes either because it is secular or because it is clerical. If the secular institute is a lay institute, according to Larraona and Gutierrez, it still precedes a religious institute.[137] This is different than the principle given above for societies without vows, and the common interpretation of canon 491, §1. For the secular institute as such does not enjoy the privileges of clerics as the society without vows does.[138] This was the basis for giving precedence to the lay society without vows over an institute or moral person composed of laymen. Here no such basis exists. Larraona and Gutierrez do not give any reason for assigning such a right of precedence to the lay secular institute; they merely state in the footnote that this principle goes contrary to that ordinarily applied to societies without vows.[139] Although it is not stated explicitly, Lemoine implies the same precedence by stating: "Les membres laiques des Instituts, individuelement n'ont aucune préséance vis-á-vis de Religieux."[140] To state that lay members of a secular institute do not have precedence over religious *"ut singuli"* is to imply that as a body the secular institute would have precedence over the religious institute, even if the secular institute was made up of laymen.

Although Larraona and Gutierrez do not offer an explanation for the precedence of a lay secular institute over a lay religious institute, the present writer sees a reason based on the following factors. Both the religious institute and the secular institute represent states of perfection.[142] Canon 491, §2, provides for the

---

137 "Iurisprudentiae pro Institutis saecularibus hucusque conditae summa lineamenta," *De Institutis Saecularibus* (1 vol., incomplete, cura et studio *CpR,* Romae, 1951), I, 207.

138 Canon 680. Larraona and Gutierrez, "art. cit.", *ibid.,* p. 227.

139 *Ibid.,* p. 207, note 22.

140 Robert Lemoine, *Le Droit des religieux du Concile de Trente aux Instituts seculiers* (Bruges: Desclée de Brouwer, 1956), p. 519.

142 "Secular institutes, even though their members live in the world, still by reason of the full dedication to God and to souls which they profess with the approval of the Church, and by reason of the internal interdiocesan and

precedence of secular clerics over religious (or non-secular) clerics. Only by analogy, and through the adoption of a new, still un-canonical term, may the lay member of the secular institute be referred to as being in a "secular state of perfection" (someone striving for perfection in the world in a way juridically approved by the Church), as distinct from a "non-secular (religious) state of perfection" (someone striving for perfection while withdrawn from the world, in a way juridically approved by the Church). On the basis, then, of canon 491, §2, that secular precedes non-secular (religious), it may be said that a secular layman in a secular institute precedes the non-secular layman of a religious institute.

The following are the secular institutes which had received pontifical approval as of 1959 according to the order in which they received it:

1) Societas Sancti Pauli;
2) Societas Sacerdotalis Sanctae Crucis et Opus Dei;
3) Sacerdotes operis dioecesani Sacrae Cordis Jesu;
4) Societas Cordis Jesu.[143]

Article 5. The Relative Precedence of Secular Clerics and Religious

Canon 491, §2. *At clerus saecularis praecedit tum laicis tum religiosis extra eorum ecclesias atque etiam in eorum ecclesiis, si agatur de religione laicali; Capitulum vero cathedrale vel collegiale eisdem praecedit ubique locorum.*

If religious precede laymen,[144] even more should clerics precede laymen, whether the latter are considered singly or in a group. Larraona expresses the opinion that this norm might have been inserted more fittingly in title II of Book II of the

universal hierarchical organization which they can have in varying degrees, are according to the Apostolic Constitution, *Provida Mater Ecclesia* (Pius XII, apost. const., 2 febr. 1947 — *AAS*, XXXIX [1947], 114) rightly and properly numbered among the states of perfection which are judicially constituted and recognized by the Church." — Pius XII, motu propr., 12 martii 1948 — *AAS*, XL (1948), 283, n. V.

143 *Annuario Pontificio* (1959), pp. 949-50.

144 Canon 491, § 1.

Code, where the other privileges of clerics are given.[145] This second series of norms in canon 491 is simply an application of canons 107-109, and canon 408.

The secular clergy have this precedence both absolutely and universally over religious in general.[146] But the precedence of the secular clergy is not so absolute in relation to the clerical religious. As a body, the secular clergy will precede the religious clergy. When the members of either group are considered singly, seculars may precede religious or be preceded by them, according to the rules of canon 106.[147]

The norms of canon 106, 3°, apply equally to secular and religious in the Church if both are considered singly or as individuals.[148] This excludes the case wherein the religious is acting as a representative of his community at some function. There he would follow the norms of canon 106, 1°, which would be determined according to the precedence of the particular religious institute or order as mentioned in canon 491, §1,[149] and canon 106, 5°.

However clear the theoretical principle may be in this matter, the practical application is not so easy in some instances. There is no provision in the law for a basis or a guide that one could use to determine the relative importance of grades or ranks in religion with those found among the secular clergy. There is no problem when the religious holds a position or fills an office that can be held by a secular priest, such as pastor, assistant, or some similar position. Here the religious merely takes his precedence according to the date of his promotion to the given

145 *CpR,* IV (1923), 273, note 449. These privileges are listed in canons 118-23. Cf. canons 107-109.

146 Lay religious are not separated from clerical religious if they proceed in a body with the clerics of their own clerical religious institute. The same is true of clerical religious who belong to a lay institute. — Larraona, *CpR,* IV (1923), 273, note 450.

147 That is, in abstraction from the difference in rite (4°), but in consideration of their relative authority (2°), their representation (1°), grade, order, time of promotion to the grade, time of ordination, and age (3°).

148 Jone, *Commentarium,* I, *sub canone* 106, 3°, *et sub canone* 491, § 1; Michiels, *De Personis,* p. 691; Berutti, *Institutiones,* III, n. 10; Sipos, *Enchiridion,* p. 83; Larraona, *CpR,* IV (1923), 212.

149 Jone, *loc. cit.*

rank in the same way the secular cleric would. Naturally, this results in a mingling of religious and seculars in a function, but that is the provision of the law as it is commonly interpreted.

The difficulty arises when one tries to determine the relative rank of the various religious superiors with the various grades found among the diocesan clergy. The following is a solution agreed on by both Michiels[150] and Jone:[151]

a) vicar general;

b) major religious superiors of canon 488, 8°;

c) vicars forane (rural deans);

d) superiors of local religious houses;

e) pastors

An exception that is quite obvious will occur when one of the major superiors is a consecrated bishop and the vicar general is not.

Even as a body, the secular clergy do not precede religious clerics everywhere. For instance, only the cathedral or a collegiate chapter precedes religious clerics of a particular institute when they are in their own religious churches. By implication, other chapters or bodies of clerics will cede their places to the religious clerics within the churches of clerical religious, even though the seculars will precede lay religious in their churches.[152]

The pre-Code law for all religious is retained by the Code only for lay religious: the secular clergy precede the lay religious everywhere even within their own churches.[153]

The rule of this canon for the cathedral chapter is simply an application of the general principle of canon 408, according to which the cathedral chapter precedes all other moral bodies everywhere within the diocese. It must be noted that the canon does not distinguish between the various kinds of collegiate chapters when it allows for their precedence over religious within

---

150 *De Personis,* p. 691.

151 *Commentarium,* I, *sub canone* 491, § 1.

152 Canon 491, § 2.

153 It may be recalled here that Larraona is of the opinion that clerical religious institutes, like the secular clerics, may precede lay religious institutes, even in the church of the lay institute, on the basis that clerical institutes precede lay institutes (canon 491, § 1). — *CpR,* IV (1923), 274, and note 456.

their own church. It seems, then, that such precedence must be acknowledged for all collegiate chapters of whatever kind, anywhere.

It may be asked whether this right of precedence extends to the proper church of the lay religious institute, or whether the precedence of the chapter is restricted to the limits of its proper diocese. It is probably not the common practice for a chapter to attend an extra-diocesan function *collegialiter;* it may assist through its representative however. He would enjoy the same honors as the chapter itself, according to the norms of canon 106, 1°. What would these be?

The words of the canon ". . . *ubique locorum* . . ." from the context may be taken in this sense: both within and outside the church of the religious institute. This is a conclusion based on a distinction implied by the canon itself. The secular clergy ordinarily precede religious only outside of their church, unless the religious are of a lay institute. On the other hand, cathedral and collegiate chapters are given precedence over religious everywhere, that is, outside their church as well as within. This could possibly lead one to conclude that this special precedence of the chapter is limited to the territory of the diocese.

Nonetheless, the words of the canon are general. In addition, the old law admitted general precedence for the chapter. Therefore, it seems that these chapters do obtain precedence within the churches of religious, even if these are outside the proper diocese of the chapter. Certainly, contrary arguments can be found.[154]

Aside from the exceptional cases mentioned, the secular clergy will always precede the members of a religious institute when these are present as a group, or *collegialiter.*

---

154 Larraona, *CpR,* IV (1923), 275, and note 462.

CHAPTER VII

THE PRECEDENCE OF MORAL PERSONS OF THE SAME SPECIES AND GRADE

Canon 106, 5°. *Inter varias personas morales eiusdem speciei et gradus, illa praecedit quae est in pacifica quasi-possessione praecedentiae et, si de hoc non constet, quae prius in loco, ubi quaestio oritur, instituta est. . . .*

It can happen that the intrinsic criteria of species and grade will fail to distinguish two moral persons sufficiently to determine their relative precedence. What is to be done if this occurs? Canon 491, §1, prescribes the application of the extrinsic criteria of canon 106, 5°, when religious orders or institutes are in question. The latter canon, by its own wording, includes all other moral persons of the same species and grade. It provides that among the various moral persons of the same species and grade, whether they be religious or lay, that moral person precedes which has peaceful quasi-possession of precedence.[1] If there is no certainty about this quasi-possession, or if it is not a peaceful possession, or, finally, if there has not been sufficient time to acquire quasi-possession, that moral person which was first established in the place where the question arises enjoys precedence over the other.[2]

These first two principles of quasi-possession and prior institution in the place of controversy are taken from Gregory XIII's constitution *Exposcit*,[3] which was originally meant to determine the precedence among the mendicants in processions only; today these same norms have been extended to apply to all religious institutes for all matters of precedence.[4] There are

[1] It is called quasi-possession because of the nature of the right, which is non-corporeal. The holding of a corporeal object is called possession. — Vermeersch-Creusen, *Epitome*, III, 90; cf. canon 1695, § 1.

[2] Canon 106, 5°.

[3] Const. 15 iulii 1584 — *Bull. Lux.*, II, 501.

[4] Larraona, *CpR*, IV (1923), 217, note 446.

special provisions, however, for the Dominicans[5] and the Franciscans.[6]

ARTICLE 1. THE DETERMINATION OF THE SAME GRADE AND SPECIES

A discussion of the various species and grades of moral persons is found in Chapter VI, Article 2.[7] At that place are given the various criteria by which it can be determined how one moral person differs from the other, and which species of moral persons may be subdivided into various grades. Here it may be asked, whether, besides the species of religious institutes, grades can also be found in each separate species for the purpose of determining precedence according to canon 106, 5°. Canon 491, §1, seems to exclude such grades for religious orders and institutes when it specifically states that ". . . *in eadem specie* . . ." recourse must be had to the norms of canon 106, 5°, to determine the rights of precedence more precisely. The wording of canon 106, 5°, is broader, referring to both species and grade, because it intends to provide norms for other moral persons (as well as for religious) which can be subdivided into grades: chapters, confraternities, pious unions and the like.[8]

Allowing for special provisions for some of the mendicants, the norms of canon 491, §1, will help determine which religious moral persons are in the same species. If two or more of them are in an identical species, then the norms of canon 106, 5°, must be resorted to, but only then. It is to be a norm of last resort for determining precedence of all moral persons, not just the precedence of religious moral persons.

ARTICLE 2. THE PEACEFUL QUASI-POSSESSION OF PRECEDENCE

The possession of a right of precedence which is called quasi-possession[9] is present when that precedence has been claimed

---

5 They are to be preceded only by secular clerics, canons regular, and monks. — Pius V, const. *Divina,* 27 aug. 1568 — *Bull. Lux.*, II, 285; Clemens VIII, const. *Inter caetera,* 25 sept. 1592 — *Bull. Lux.*, III, 17.

6 Pius X, motu propr. *Seraphici Patriarchae,* 15 aug. 1910 — *AAS,* II (1910), 713 ff: cf. pp. 196 ff., *infra.*

7 Pp. 155 ff.

8 Larraona, *CpR,* IV (1923), 214, note 433.

9 Cf. canons 1695, § 1; 1697, § 3; 1698, § 1.

with the full intention of acquiring the right of precedence thereby.[10]

The right in question must be held peacefully, insofar as it has not been publicly challenged by protest, or judicial or administrative action, or reservation of the right.[11] This does not necessarily imply that the claim to the right is based on a legitimate title, or need be.[12] Rightly or wrongly, a moral person has merely assumed a right to precedence over another moral person for a period of time and has repeatedly exercised this right of precedence without any challenge or protest from the others whose rights of precedence may be violated.

Many authors maintain that the moral person need only show conclusively that it has enjoyed for four or five years, peaceful quasi-possession of the right of precedence over the party concerned.[13] Larraona seems to give an explanation that satisfies the majority of the authors and helps to explain the few who demand thirty, forty, or one hundred years to acquire quasi-possession of the right of precedence. He states that quasi-possession of one year as described in Canon 1695, §1, merely gives to the moral person a *"ius oeconomicum"* (a practical basis without a necessarily sound foundation) to precedence, which will be converted

---

10 Michiels, *De Personis,* p. 694.

11 Moretti, *De Sacris Functionibus,* I, n. 151.

12 Ojetti, *Commentarium,* II, 208; cf. canon 1696, § 1.

13 Regatillo, *Institutiones,* I, n. 218; Coronata, *Institutiones,* I, n. 160; Michiels, *De Personis,* p. 694; Moretti, *De Sacris Functionibus,* I, n. 151; Sipos, *Enchiridion,* p. 84.

Augustine *(Commentary,* II, 40*),* on the contrary, maintained that proof was needed that a moral person has had undisturbed and unchallenged precedence at least for the time required for prescription (thirty years, according to canon 1511, § 2). Capello *Summa Iuris Canonici* [3 vols., Vol. I, 5. ed.; Romae, Aedes Universitatis Gregorianae, 1951], n. 203) mentions first a period of one hundred years, or enough to make the practice immemorial (which induces a presumption about the concession of a privilege—c. 69, § 2), then compromises with thirty or forty years. None of the authors mentioned give any reason or source for his figure.

Although the law implies in canon 1695, § 1, that quasi-possession of a right can be acquired in one year, four or five years seems to be a safer norm, in view of the nature of the right of precedence which in many places may not be exercised more than once or twice a year.

into a "*ius absolutum*" when the requirements for prescription (thirty years) or custom (forty years) are fulfilled.[14] When this quasi-possession has been proved, this proof begets a presumption of a right to precedence.[15] The present writer prefers the requirement of four or five years for quasi-possession because of the nature of the right which, at least, in this country, is not often exercised in any one year.

It is further required that this possession be continuous, according to Cappello.[16] This opinion is modified somewhat by Berutti. He maintains that quasi-possession is lost only through an interruption caused by a canonical suppression, if this quasi-possession is not restored within one hundred years.[17]

This norm of quasi-possession is a primary one for determining precedence between two moral persons of the same species and grade. Practically, it would seem that the norm could be invoked in the United States only rarely, because of the great difficulty of proving such quasi-possession to the satisfaction of both parties. Canon 106, 5°, provides the solution to the doubt: ". . . *si de hoc non constet, quae prius in loco. . . .*"

Article 3. The Determination of Precedence From the Priority of Foundation in the Place

If there is no quasi-possession, either because the right was exercised at one time by one group, and at another time by a second group, or because there is a question of the first encounter of the two religious or other moral persons, or because there is not sufficient proof of the quasi-possession, or, finally, because the claimed quasi-possession has not been peaceful, then, with the criterion of quasi-possession duly relinquished, attention

---

14 *CpR*, IV (1923), 215; cf. also Michiels, *De Personis*, p. 694; canons 1508-1512. Cappello's one hundred years would imply that there is a clause in the laws of precedence prohibiting any future custom contrary to them. No such clause appears. Cf. canon 27, § 1.

15 Moretti, *De Sacris Functionibus*, I, n. 151. Factum possessionis praesumptionem iuris fundat. — Beste, *Introductio in Codicem, in praenotandis*, c.1693.

16 *Summa Iuris Canonici*, I, n. 203.

17 *Institutiones*, II, n. 26; cf. canon 102, § 1.

is directed to the time at which the house of each institute or other moral person was established in the place where the controversy now arises. On the basis of this time element, precedence belongs to that moral person which has been in the place for the longer period of time.

In accord with what was said about continuous time for quasi-possession, it must be pointed out here that the time of the first establishment in a given place furnishes the point from which to calculate, unless the institute was canonically extinct for more than one hundred years.[18] The accurate determination of this time will be based on the date of canonical erection of the individual religious house in the place of controversy, not the founding of the entire religious order or institute, or moral person.[19] However, if a second and third house of members of the same order or institute are erected in the same place, the members of the latter foundations will take their precedence from the date of the foundation of the first house.[20] The same will be true of a group of religious taking over a house given them by members of the same institute or order, though perhaps of a different congregation or family (e.g., the various Benedictine groups): they will take the precedence which the former residents rightfully enjoyed.[21] In no case it is necessary that this religious house be a *domus formata*.[22]

Particular norms have been given with a view to determining the relative precedence of the various families of Franciscans. Pius X, in the *motu proprio, Seraphici Patriarchae,*[23] prescribed the following four principles of precedence:

a) That Order of Friars Minor [whether simple Friars Minor, or the Conventuals or the Capuchins] which was in the city or place the longest precedes all other Friars Minor, unless it is certain that one of the Franciscan families which came at a

---

18 Michiels, *De Personis,* p. 695; cf. canon 102, § 1.

19 S. Goyenche, *De Iure Religiosorum,* I, 92; Berutti, *Institutiones,* II, n. 26.

20 Larraona, *CpR,* IV (1923), 216, citing Ferraris, s.v. *praecedentia,* nn. 48, 49.

21 *Ibid.,* citing Ferraris, s.v. *praecedentia,* n. 50.

22 Schaefer, *De Religiosis,* n. 57; cf. canon 488, 5°.

23 15 aug. 1910 — *AAS,* II (1910), 713 ff.

later date actually has quasi-possession of the right of precedence.[24]

b) If one of the Franciscan families had possession of precedence over all the others from January 1, 1900, to August 15, 1910, that one is to have precedence perpetually.

c) The right of precedence in a given place is lost by a family of Franciscans which has been extinct for fifty or more years in that place.

d) The precedence of the individual houses is to be calculated only for the city and its suburbs; if visiting houses are present at a function, that house which is in its own town takes precedence over all members of visiting houses. If none of the Franciscan families present has a house in the given place, their relative precedence is as follows: in first place, the Friars Minor; in second place, the Conventuals, and in third place, the Capuchins.

It may be asked whether in other cases, apart from the Franciscan family, the time of foundation is to be computed from the date when the two or more religious houses belonged to orders or institutes of exactly the same species, or absolutely from the calendar date of their foundation in the given place. For instance, if in a given place there are two congregations of clerical religious, one of pontifical and the other of diocesan approval, the pontifically approved congregation would have precedence because of its higher form of approval, even though in this given instance the congregation of diocesan approval was established earlier in the given place. When the congregation of diocesan approval receives its *decretum laudis* (which will place it in the same species as the other congregation), will it then, on the basis of its foundation in the place, take precedence over the congregation which had been pontifically approved earlier, even though it had once yielded precedence to it? Larraona thinks it should not. In other words, their precedence is determined by the answers to these questions: are they both congregations? clerical? of pontifical approval? which has existed in

24 At first this seems to be an inversion of the Code principle that was to be promulgated seven years later; actually, it says the same thing in a different way.

this city *as a pontifically approved congregation* for the longest time?

Article 4. The Place of Controversy

It seems that the lawgiver had in mind a narrow meaning of the word "*locus*" in canon 106, 5°. From the source of the principle, Gregory's constitution *Exposcit,* it can be seen that the legislator had in mind two or more religious houses in a given city.[25] At any rate, the use of the word "*locus*" seems to be somewhat relative to the area represented by or interested in the function, so that, if the function were a local city matter, a Corpus Christi procession, or something similar, the date of establishment in the given city would be the criterion of priority. On the other hand, if it were a diocesan synod or some other function of interest to the entire diocese, then the date of foundation in the diocese would help all religious houses in the diocese to determine their proper precedence. The same would be true if the function had a special meaning for the whole province. Any function of wider interest, such as a plenary council or some sort of national or international congress, or some such similar affair, would necessitate having recourse to the date of establishment of the whole order or institute in the Church.[26]

It may very well happen that some moral persons who attend an ecclesiastical function will not have a house in the place wherein the controversy arises. In this case, they may have neither quasi-possession nor prior foundation in that place. If the function is of a scope that goes beyond the city itself, as a diocesan synod, quasi-possession or prior foundation in the diocese may be used as criteria. If some function is held in a diocese in which a moral person has neither quasi-possession of

---

25 15 iulii 1584 — *Bull. Lux.,* II, 501; Larraona, *CpR,* IV (1923), 215; s.v. *praecedentia,* n. 44.

26 Larraona, *CpR,* IV (1923), 218, note 447; Regatillo (*Institutiones,* I, n. 218), on the contrary, would have the ordinary of the place in which the function takes place, determine the precedence when the function has more than a diocesan interest, rather than have recourse to the date of establishment of the whole institute in the Church; cf. Michiels, *De Personis,* p. 695; Berutti, *Institutiones,* II, n. 26.

precedence nor prior foundation, and the function has interest for the whole province, such as a provincial council, then quasi-possession or prior foundation in the province may be used as a criterion, and so on, until the date of foundation or institution in the Church becomes the final criterion in the absence of all other criteria. Such a progression of principles or norms is not provided for in the law: but by analogy it seems to be permissible.[27] Such an analogy seems applicable in three cases:

a) when the religious institutes whose precedence is controverted have no house in the place of controversy;

b) when the function or public act is independent of the place in which it happens to be celebrated, such as a plenary council or Eucharistic congress;

c) when a whole province rather than a local house is represented inasmuch as the provincial superior rather than the local superior attends the function.[28]

When the norm of quasi-possession is used it is quite evident that in one town or diocese one order will precede the other, while in a second town or diocese, the order of their precedence may be reversed, depending on the date of their foundation in each town or province. It must always be kept in mind, however, that norms of quasi-possession of the right of precedence and the prior foundation in the place of controversy are in reality the ultimate or final criteria; when any of the higher criteria are applicable, they are the first to be used. These norms of canon 106, 5°, are to be used only "*inter personas eiusdem speciei et gradus. . . .*"

---

27 Larraona, *CpR,* IV (1923), 217, note 445.

28 *Ibid.*, p. 218.

CHAPTER VIII

PRECEDENCE AMONG THE MEMBERS WITHIN A GIVEN MORAL PERSON

Canon 106, 5° . . . *inter sodales vero alicuius collegii, ius praecedentiae determinetur ex propriis legitimis constitutionibus; secus ex legitima consuetudine; qua deficiente, ex praescripto iuris communis.*

In this second part of the fifth numerical division of canon 106, the law determines the internal precedence of any moral person in the most general terms by naming, in the order in which they may be invoked, the three basic criteria for determining such precedence:

a) proper legitimate constitutions;

b) legitimate custom and

c) the prescripts of the current universal law.

The colleges or bodies of persons which the lawgiver has in mind need not be moral persons in the strictest sense of the term:[1] they may be a religious house,[2] a confraternity, a pious union, or the provincial house[3] of a religious institute.[4]

The scope of the first two criteria forbids a detailed study of them even for the more important moral persons in the Church. It will be for the superior of the moral person to see to the observance of the proper precedence of the members of the moral person when they attend any function as a body His acquaintance with the constitutions or other norms and customs of the moral person will qualify him better than anyone else.

The three criteria of canon 106, 5°, may be used only in the order in which they are named in the canon: as an earlier mentioned norm becomes ineffective, the next mentioned norm may be invoked. Therefore, local customary usage should not

---

1 Canons 99 and 100.

2 Canon 488, 5°.

3 Canon 488, 6°.

4 Michiels, *De Personis,* p. 692.

be a criterion for precedence if it is contrary to the direct prescriptions of the legitimate constitutions, unless it has fulfilled the requirements for the establishment of a legitimate custom.[5] It may happen that the constitutions will not determine precedence, or that they may not have taken a particular situation into consideration. In the absence of such a constitutional norm, the local customary usage of the moral person may and should be invoked as an alternate criterion. When this norm is not available, the prescripts of the current universal law as enacted in canon 106 and canon 491 must be used, either as they stand, or analogically if they provide no norm any other way.

If the norms of the universal law must be invoked, they have been treated above: the notions of authority in canon 106, 2°, will determine the precedence of the superiors over their subjects; canon 106, 3°, will provide the norm that superiors among themselves go according to their relative rank, as do the members among themselves. Certain basic notions will be seen to give rank to members of the religious institutes: ordination, religious profession, reception of the religious habit, or the time of their arrival at the particular house.

Within non-religious moral persons, the norms of canon 106 may be applied, either literally or analogically: they may be proxies, superiors, various ranks of members with different times of promotion or different ages. Such moral persons may have special norms for precedence in their constitutions.

Article 1. The Determination of Precedence from Legitimate Constitutions

The term "constitution" here includes all similar bodies of regulations which guide the operations, duties, and privileges of the members of a moral person, whether they are called rules, ordinances, statutes, by-laws, or constitutions.[6] If these

---

5 Canons 25-30.

6 Rules and constitutions are terms that are often used indiscriminately, especially in more recent times. Strictly taken, however, the term "rule" is applicable only to the more or less ancient collections of regulations for the religious life composed by the great exponents of its values, i.e. Saints Basil, Augustine, Benedict, and Francis of Assisi. "Constitution" in the strict sense

constitutions have been legitimately approved[7] they become particular norms for the moral persons, and must be abided by even if they are contrary to the Code law.[8] Their legitimate approval and the specific provisions of canon 106, 5°, seem to make this clear.[9]

Therefore, if the order of precedence is determined solely from the time of admission as a member of the moral persons, or from the office or position held, this order is to be followed.[10] The following are some examples of norms of precedence in individual constitutions which are contrary to the norms of the Code law:

a) the Servites do not acknowledge any special precedence because of the priesthood;

---

designates the particular statutes added by the various orders or monastic congregations to these famous rules. When the Holy See no longer required the adoption of an ancient rule by new religious institutes, the body of regulations give the new institutes was sometimes called "rule," and sometimes "constitution."—S. C. de Relig., 6 martii 1921—*AAS,* XIII (1921), 316, cited by Abbo-Hannan, *The Sacred Canons,* I, 492-93.

7 By the ordinary of the place, or by the Apostolic See, depending on the nature of the institution; cf. canons 410, § 2; 488, 1°; 689, § 1.

8 Canon 489 provides for the abrogation of rules and particular constitutions of all institutes which were in force but contrary to the Code at the time of its promulgation. However, canons 4 and 5 permits the continuation of those provisions of the constitutions which were derived from privileges or centenary customs even though they were contrary to the Code. Immediately after the Code was promulgated, all religious institutes of pontifial approval and societies without vows were required to submit their rules and constitutions after they had been modified according to the norms of the Code (S.C.Rel., decr. 26 iunii 1918 — *AAS,* X (1918), 290). Either such revised constitutions which were re-approved contain nothing contrary to the norms of the Code, or such contrary norms can be considered as approved particular law.

Coronata, however, maintains that anything in these constitutions which is contrary to the Code law is illegitimate, and therefore not to be used (*Institutiones,* I, n. 161, note 6). Michiels (*De Personis,* p. 692), on the other hand, rejects this opinion on the basis that the words of canon 106, 5°, which indicate recourse to the Code law as a separate or alternative criterion, would be unreasonable if this were true.

9 Larraona, *CpR,* IV (1923), 275. Cf. also Schaefer, *De Religiosis,* n. 59.

10 Berutti, *Institutiones,* II, n. 26; Schaefer, *loc. cit.*

b) the Camaldolese, Dominicans, and Redemptorists use the priesthood as their only criterion;

c) the following use all three major Orders as criteria for determining precedence: the Cassinese Benedictines of the Primitive Observance, the Trinitarians, the Pallotines, and the Missionaries of the Sacred Heart;

d) the French Benedictines, the Mercedarians, and the Oblates use all the Orders, major and minor, as bases for determining their precedence.[11]

Article 2. The Determination of Precedence from Legitimate Customs

When the particular rules or constitutions fail to give any norms for precedence, or when they are in need of interpretation, one may invoke lawful custom to determine proper precedence among the members of a moral person.[12] According to canon 26, only those communities which are capable of receiving an ecclesiastical law can induce a legitimate custom which has the force of law. Larraona maintains that the notion of custom in canon 106, 5°, is broader, and the requirements more lenient, than the provisions of canon 26 would allow. He holds that such a custom may be induced by a religious house, a whole province, or the institute itself.[13]

A right based on custom, like those based on quasi-possession, is sometimes difficult to prove and therefore sometimes unsatisfactory as a norm for precedence. In the event that this is true, or if there simply is no custom, the third and last criterion that is available for determining precedence within a moral body is the law and its provisions.

Article 3. The Code Law as a Criterion of Last Resort to Determine Precedence within a Moral Body

Where neither the special norms of the moral person, whether it be a rule or a constitution, nor its customs provide sufficient

---

11 Larraona, *CpR,* IV (1923), 276, note 464.

12 Canon 106, 5°.

13 *CpR,* IV (1923), 276, note 465.

norms for determining precedence within a moral body, recourse must be had to the norms of the Code itself.[14]

Just which norms of the Code law are meant by the lawgiver in canon 106, 5°, is not clear in the minds of the commentators: their opinions vary from Beste's limiting the Code law to mean only canon 106, 3°,[15] to Coronata[16] and Jone[17] who include the first four numbers of canon 106. Coronata is careful moreover, to distinguish between clerics and laymen. These four norms apply to laymen only by analogy in some cases. He permits the use of the norms of authority, and of seniority in promotion and age to determine the layman's precedence.[18]

The types of situations which will require recourse to the Code law norms cannot be foreseen with all their variations. Since the Code itself does not distinguish, it seems that any norm of precedence provided by the Code may and should be used, whether it be mentioned in canon 106, or outside it, whether it be used in its strictest interpretation or by analogy.

Often the Code norms of canon 106, 3°, will be applied according to the individual needs and circumstances in each religious institute or other moral body. According to their rank, then, novices will precede postulants, while the professed members will precede the novices. Clerical novices, because of their Orders, always precede lay novices on the bass of canon 107 and canon 491. Among novices, precedence is determined by the time of their admission or by their age. Those in solemn or perpetual vows precede those in temporary or simple vows. When two or more professed members are in the same class and type of profession, the time of profession is used. Usually the date of the first or temporary profession serves as the criterion. If this is the same, then admission to the novitiate, and, finally, ordination to the priesthood, are called upon as criteria for determining their relative precedence.[19]

---

14 Canon 106, 5°.

15 *Introductio in Codicem, sub canone* 106, 5°.

16 *Institutiones,* I, n. 161.

17 *Commentarium,* I, *sub canone* 106, 5°.

18 *Institutiones,* I, n. 161.

19 Schaefer, *De Religiosis,* n. 59.

Article 4. A Detailed Notion of the Internal Precedence of Religious

It sometimes happens that constitutions or rules do not provide for any norms of precedence among the members of a moral person, lay or religious. In regard to religious, Larraona made a detailed study of several constitutions in connection with his "Commentarium Codicis" on canon 491.[20] The result was a norm which might be followed when norms for precedence were incorporated in a constitution, or improved. This norm reflects the more or less general pattern of precedence as it was found in whole or in part in the various institutes. It is included here as a concrete example of the norms which have been given in theory. The footnotes merely cite examples, and are not in any way to be taken as a complete list of the religious institutes in which a particular norm is or is not found.

SECTION 1–THE PRECEDENCE OF SUPERIORS

A. The General Officers

The supreme superior, by whatever name he might be called, always precedes his religious subjects wherever they may be. This will be true even when the general chapter will elect his successor, until the new superior takes over. In some cases, however, the chapter is not presided over by the superior general; a president-designate takes his place.

Once the new superior general has been elected, the former superior cedes his right of precedence to his succssor. The various constitutions determine the former superior's precedence once he is out of office. Some become *ex officio* vice-presidents.[21]

---

20 *Commentarium pro Religiosis,* IV (1923), 172-73; 210-18; 273-80; 331-35; 360-67.

21 The Claretians and Mercedarians in particular, and quite generally most religious institutes give them this honor. — Larraona, *CpR,* IV (1923), 333, note 505.

In the Benedictine Confederation, the ex-abbots primate take their place immediately after the abbot-bishops and before the abbots-president of the various congregations. — "Lex Propria Confoederationis Congregationum Monasticarum Ordinis Sancti Benedicti," Article 18, annotation n. 31. — *Commentarium pro Religiosis et Missionariis* (Romae, 1935 —), XXXIII (1954), 4 (hereafter cited "Lex Propria" and *CpRM).*

Some former superiors general take a place just after the new general superior;[22] some are given no consideration at all once they are out of office.[23]

The precedence of the supreme superiors of religious institutes is complicated somewhat by the Confederation of Benedictines which was formed in 1893. The "Lex Propria" of this confederation established the following norms of precedence.

The abbot primate has a right of precedence in the confederation anywhere he might be.[24]

Although the precedence of the abbots president of the various congregations could more properly be treated under canon 106, 3°, and the rule of precedence among persons who have no authority over each other, it will be given briefly here to complete the picture of precedence among the highest officials of the confederation.

At a meeting of the confederation, the abbot primate is followed by the Abbot of Monte Cassino, the abbots-bishop, ex-abbots primate, and abbots president of the various congregations, abbots *nullius,* and finally by all other abbots of independent monasteries according to the time they were elected to the abbatial dignity.[25] Out of reverence for their founder, St.

---

22 The Carmelites, Dominicans and Friars Minor give them precedence just after the superior general. Others such as the Discalced Carmelites, acknowledge precedence for them only in general chapters. Some give some other limited form of precedence, according to the varying provisions of thir individual constitutions: the Servites, Trinitarians, Pallotines, and the Divine Word Missionaries. — Larraona, *CpR,* IV (1923), 333, note 505.

23 The Discalced Carmelites outside the general chapter, and many modern congregations whose constitutions make no provisions for former superiors general, such as the Claretians, give them no special precedence. — *Loe. cit.*

24 The abbot primate is a true major superior according to canon 488, 8°, and within the limits set by particular law he has authority over all congregations and monasteries in the confederation; therefore the application of canon 106, 2°, is posible here. — "Lex Propria", annotation n. 30 to Art. 17 — *CpRM,* XXXIII (1954), 9.

25 Among themselves, the abbots-president determine their mutual precedence from the time of their congregation's erection or approval. Any congregations joining the confederation later will determine the precedence of their abbots-president from the date of their admission into the confederation. *Ibid.,* Articles 18-19, p. 4.

Benedict, the Confederation acknowledged a special precedence for the Abbot of Monte Cassino, who also presides over the election of the abbot primate.[26]

The **vicar general,**[27] whenever he is exercising his office according to the constitutions because of the death, absence or inability of the superior general of the place, takes the first place of the superior general as a proxy. The same is true of the visitator general and others who may be taking the place of the superior general on occasion.[28] In addition the vicar general, either as first assistant or because of his habitual participation in the supreme power of the superior general, usually precedes all other superiors and subjects. Former vicar generals usually are given consideration similar to that of former superiors general.

Definitors general, also called assistants or consultors, do not always have the same precedence in all religious institutes. In many congregations of more recent origin, they often precede all other superiors and officials, other than the vicar general and the visitator, no matter where they might be, whether forming a collegiate group with the general or singly. In other institutes, they are granted precedence only in general acts, such as general chapters, and that just after the general, if it is a function taking place in the general motherhouse, or when they are in the company of the superior general; otherwise they are preceded by those who have actual authority in the place, such as the provincial, the superior of a house, or his vicar in the superior's own absence. In older institutes, particularly,

---

26 Annotation n. 31 to Article 40 — *ibid.*, p. 9.

27 This officer is also known as first assistant in almost all modern congregations. In older orders he is customarily called a procurator general. — Larraona, *CpR,* IV (1923), 333, note 56, and p. 334, note 509.

28 The visitator has this special precedence only during the time of visitation, and in the place of visitation. If he has this office habitually, then his precedence is also habitual. This right will be acknowledged more carefully, on the actual occasion of a visitation because of the authority he exercises at that time. In the monastic orders it is customary on other occasions to give him the same precedence which Regulars and congrations give their definitors or assistants. In non-monastic orders the office of visitator will sometimes not take this degree of importance—Larraona, *ibidem,* note 508.

there are also some officials, such as the procurator general (who is often called the vicar general), who precede the definitors. Former definitors usually are granted some form of special precedence in the older religious institutes, not in others.

Among themselves these definitors determine their mutual precedence in one of three ways. Among the Friars Minor, Mercedarians, and Redemptorists, the date of profession is the factor determining the precedence of the definitors. Among the Trinitarians, Discalced Carmelites, and Oblates, the time of their election is used as a basis. The third basis which is used in some religious institutes is the dignity of the individual, as among the Reformed Cistercians.[29]

Three of the general officials who are commonly found in religious institutes of both men and women today are the procurator general,[30] the secretary general,[31] and the econome general.[32]

A procurator *apud S. Sedem* is found in some monastic orders and generally in all mendicant orders.[33] This procurator general precedes not only all general officials but also the definitors or assistants if he is serving as vicar general in the case of the death or absence of the superior general. Otherwise, he is merely first among the assistants or definitors.[34] However, in some men-

---

29 Larraona, *CpR,* IV (1923), 335, note 518.

30 Only male religious have a procurator general *apud Sanctam Sedem* (canon 517, § 1). — *Ibid.*, p. 360, note 520.

31 Cf.*infra*, p. 209-10, for details.

32 There are other offices in some religious institutes, but they are peculiar to one or two, and not important for this comparative-study. — *Ibid.*, note 521.

33 Order of Friars Minor, O.F.M. Conventual, O.F.M. Cap., Augustinians, Carmelites, Servites, and Minims. — *Ibid.*, note 528.

34 This is true among the Cassinese Benedictines of the Primitive Observance, the Order of Friars Minor, O.F.M. Conventual, O.F.M. Cap., Augustinians and Carmelites.

On the other hand, there are some religious institutes in which the procurator may not be named vicar general, such as the Minims and Dominicans. Sometimes this procurator does not belong to the *Consilium Generale* or *Definitorium Generale.* This is true among the Cassinese Benedictines, Augustinians, and Servites. Another variation is found among the Friars Minor and the Capuchins, as well as among the Carmelites: although their procurator is not one of the definitors, by law he does belong to the

dicant orders, especially those which were reformed[35] and in orders of clerics regular, the procurator general commonly has at least a place just after the definitors.[36]

In religious congregations the procurator general is never the vicar general, nor does he ordinarily precede the consultors or have a place among them;[37] he does commonly precede the other general officers, such as the secretary and econome general.[38] There are some congregations in which he follows either one or both of these general officers.[39]

The office of **secretary general**, especially in the congregations, should and can be joined with that of the assistant or definitor. In this case there would be no new problem of precedence for him. The rules for assistants or definitors would have to be followed.[40] If the secretariate is not so joined to either of the other two positions, it is merely a private office as in the case of the secretary of the superior general.[41] There would be no special precedence for such a secretary on the basis of authority over others.

If, however, the secretary general holds a public position, which is separate from other general offices, he has his special precedence before the econome and after the procurator general ordinarily.[42] There are some different practices in regard to this

---

Consilium Generale. One final variation is found among the Brothers Hospitallers of St. John of God: their procurator is first among the consultors. — *Ibid.*, note 524.

35 Discalced Carmelites, Trinitarians, and Mercederaians. — *Ibid.*, p. 361, note 525.

36 Barnabites and Theatines. — *Ibid*, note 526.

37 Oblates, Pallotines, Divine Word Missionaries, Missionaries of the Sacred Heart. — *Ibid.*, note 528.

38 Divine Word Missionaries, Pallotines, Missionaries of the Sacred Heart. — *Ibid.*, note 529.

39 He follows both in the Marists. Among the Oblates, the econome general usually precedes the procurator general. — *Ibid.*, note 530.

40 This is the practice among the Theatines. — *Ibid.*, note 531.

41 The Discalced Carmelites have such a secretary general. It should be noted here that the secretary of the *Definitorium* is not the same as the secretary general. — *Ibid.*, note 532.

42 This is the case with the Missionaries of the Sacred Heart of Jesus and the Pallotine Fathers. — *Ibid.*, p. 362, note 534.

type of secretary general, however.[43] It is rather common for the secretary general to precede the provincial superior outside his proper province.[44] In any case, unless he himself is a definitor, the secretary general will always come after the definitors or assistants.

The office of **econome general** does not exist in the religious orders today in the sense commonly understood. Insofar as it does exist, it is ordinarily held and exercised by the procurator general. Even where it does exist in some orders, this office lacks sufficient juridic importance to be a reason for precedence.[45]

When the econome general in religious congregations has a separate office, he customarily takes precedence after the procurator and secretary general.[46] The relation of the econome general with the provincial superior resembles that of the secretary general. Outside the province, the provincial superior usually cedes his place to the econome.[47]

Of the three officers just discussed, only the ex-procurator general is customarily given more or less precedence by those religious institutes which also give former definitors some form of precedence. There is no special precedence given to the former secretary or econome general.[48]

B. Provincial Officers

The highest officer in the province is the **provincial superior.** His precedence differs according to whether he is within or outside his proper province, in line with the general norm about

---

43 Among the Marists, the secretary precedes the procurator general. The econome general among the Marists, Missionaries of the Divine Word and the Claretians precedes the secretary general. — *Ibid.*, note 535.

44 This is true among the Marists and the Missionaries of the Divine Word. The Claretian and Pallotine secretaries general always precede the provincial superiors, even in their own provinces. — *ibid.*, note 536.

45 *Ibid.*, note 539.

46 This is not true among the Marists, Claretians, and the Missionaries of the Divine Word, where the econome general precedes the secretary general. — *Ibid.*, note 535.

47 The Marists and the Missionaries of the Divine Word observe this procedure. The Claretian or Pallotine econome general precedes the provincial superior even within his own province. — *Ibid.*, note 536.

48 *Ibid.*, p. 335, note 519.

precedence based on authority which is limited to a specified territory.

Within his province the provincial superior yields precedence to various superiors above the provincial level. These would include the superior general or his vicar and the visitator. He may likewise have to cede the right of precedence to a definitor general.[49]

Outside his own province the provincial superior comes after a definitor general and usually even after all the members of the general government.[50]

The determination of precedence among the provincial superiors as a group is more properly the matter of canon 106, 3°; but like the precedence of abbots-president of the congregations, it seems better to discuss it briefly here to complete the picture of precedence among the superiors of religious.

Here, again, it makes a difference whether the matter is considered outside of or within the province of one of the superiors whose precedence is being determined. If they attend some function outside the province of all of them, such as a general chapter, their precedence is determined by three different principles, depending on the religious institute to which they belong. Among the Dominicans, Mercedarians and Claretians, the precedence of these provincial superiors is determined from the time their provinces were established.[51] Among the Ursuline nuns, the date of election to the office of provincial superior is the determining factor. A third group of provincial superiors determine their relative precedence among themselves on the basis of their own ages: the Barnabites. Ex-provincial superiors are given precedence for a limited period of time and within

---

49 Among the Discalced Carmelites, the definitors general are the only general officers to whom the provincial superior yields after the superior general. The provincial superior of the Augustinians and other Carmelites must yield to all members of the general government of the order. — *Ibid.*, p. 363, note. 545.

50 Among the Trinitarians they even follow the provincial definitors. The provincial superior does precede the superior of local houses, however, in the case of the Dominicans, Servites, and Claretians. — *Ibid.*, note 547.

51 *Ibid.*, note 548.

their own province by the Dominicans, Order of Friars Minor, Servites and Pallotines.[52]

Within their own territories, certain other major regional superiors have precedence similar to that of the provincial superiors among the Dominicans, the Order of Friars Minor, the Oblates, the Pallotine Fathers, and the Missionaries of the Divine Word. Such officers are variously called vice-provincials, quasi-provincials, or superiors of the missions.[53] When such regional superiors, inferior to the provincials, are outside their own territory, they follow the provincials among the Dominicans, Augustinians, Discalced Carmelites and the Oblates.[54]

In an independent territory which has not as yet been formed into a province, the superior is often called either a provincial vicar or vice-provincial. The same norms are used for the determining of the precedence of the vicar-provincial that were used for the vicar general: whenever he is exercising his office according to the constitutions because of the death, absence or incapacity of the provincial superior, he takes the first place in the province, normally taken by the superior himself. As first assistant or because of his habitual participation in the power of the provincial superior, he customarily precedes all lesser superiors and subjects. The same comparison of the provincial with the supreme or general officer can be made in regard to the provincial visitator.

The comparison of the two levels, general and provincial, is not so close with reference to the definitors or assistants. Among some religious the precedence of the provincial definitor is limited to the province.[55] Sometimes these provincial definitors are even placed after the local superiors.[56] In some religious institutes the provincial definitors are preceded by all general

52 *Ibid.*, note 550.

53 *Ibid.*, note 551.

54 *Ibid.*, note 552.

55 Order of Friars Minor, Discalced Carmelites, and Marists. — *Ibid.*, p. 364, note 555.

56 This is the case among the Servites and Oblates, whose definitors general are given precedence over local superiors in their own houses. — *Ibid.*, note 556.

officers. In others they are preceded even by some of the provincial officials

Among themselves the provincial definitors determine their precedence according to the same rules which are used for the definitors general: from the date of their election, the date of their profession in religion, or some particular basis determined in the individual constitutions.[57]

Lesser provincial officials include the provincial secretary and econome, the novice master, the spiritual director, the masters of theology, the prefects of studies, and the lectors.

The **provincial secretary's** position is usually filled by one of the provincial consultors; he does not have any special precedence. If the secretariate is a separate office, its occupant frequently goes ahead of the provincial econome, just as the secretary general goes before the econome general.[58]

The **provincial econome** offers no special problem in matters of precedence. It is not customary to join this office to that of provincial consultor. In some religious institutes he is given last place among the provincial officials; in some he is placed even farther down in the general list.[59]

The precedence of the **novice master**, if any obtains, is often limited to the novitiate house itself, as among the Dominicans. The Carmelites and Marists acknowledge precedence for him for the province, and sometimes beyond.[60] Among the Discalced Carmelites, the Trinitarians, the Redemptorists, the Missionaries of the Sacred Heart, and the Claretians, the novice master is given no precedence. By contrast, the other Carmelites, the Friars Minor and the Oblates give him a place just after the vice-rector or local assistants. A few groups such as the Camaldolese, the Pallotines, and the Divine Word Missionaries, place him right

---

57 *Ibid.*, p. 335, note 518; cf. *supra*, p. 208 ff.

58 Secretaries general precede the economes general among the Marists, the Missionaries of the Divine Word, and the Claretians. — *Ibid.*, p. 362, note 535; cf. also p. 364, note 560.

59 No special precedence is acknowledged here by the Pallotines, the Divine Word Missionaries, or the Missionaries of the Sacred Heart. — *Ibid.*, p. 365, notes 561-64.

60 *Ibid.*, note 565.

after the local superior.[61] Outside their own houses the novice masters of the Marists precede local superiors; some institutes have their novice masters precede even the provincial consultors.[62]

Many religious institutes, e.g., the Dominicans and the Oblates, give the **spiritual director** a precedence equivalent to that of the novice master.[63]

Masters of theology, prefects of studies and **lectors** all have some sort of precedence among the Dominicans, the Augustinians, and the Friars Minor.[64]

C. Local Officers in Religious Institutes

It is quite common for the **local superior** to have precedence in his own house over all who do not actually exercise greater authority there.[65] In some religious institutes he yields to the general or provincial superiors, vicars and visitators. Others require the local superior to yield precedence to definitors and other officials of both the general and provincial government of the order.[66]

When the local superior is outside his own house, the Missionaries of the Divine Word and the Pallotine Fathers give him precedence immediately after the local superior of the house he is visiting.[67] Others place him immediately after the vice-superior, the master of novices or the local consultors of the house he is visiting.

Among themselves the local superiors outside their own houses sometimes determine their precedence in relation to each other according to the foundation date of their house or the degree of its dignity.[68] Other local superiors determine their mutual pre-

---

61 *Ibid.*, note 568.

62 *Ibid.*, notes 569 and 570.

63 *Ibid.*, note 571.

64 *Ibid.*, p. 366, note 572.

65 *Ibid.*, p. 335, note 516, and p. 366.

66 *Ibid.*, p. 366.

67 *Ibid.*, note 576, p. 366.

68 The Camaldolese, the Trinitarians, the Discalced Carmelites and the Marists follow this norm. — *Ibid.*, note 578.

cedence either from the date of their election, or from the time of their profession.[69]

The **vice-superior** referred to above takes the place of an absent superior, although he does not always take the same precedence.[70] When the superior is present, the vice-superior is preceded by the superior general and provincial superior, as well as by the consultors and other officials, both general and provincial.[71] Outside his own house this official rarely has any particular precedence by reason of his position.

The **local definitors** often get no precedence.[72] Generally, however, these local definitors precede all other priests, local economes, and the novice master within their own house.[73]

Ordinarily, the **local econome** will have no precedence. However, some religious institutes, because of the care and authority he has over the brother helpers, acknowledge that he does have a part in the local regime, and therefore is entitled to some precedence, as is true among the Claretians.[74]

With due allowance made for the numerous exceptions given in the footnotes, the following represents, in a general way, the relative authority, and therefore the relative precedence, of religious superiors, supreme, provincial, and local. While a more detailed understanding may be gained from a reading of the foregoing treatment, it cannot be urged too strongly that an authentic chart be prepared by each group from its proper constitution or book of rules in actual practice.

GENERAL OFFICIALS:

The Supreme Superior

(In the Benedictine Confederation)

Abbot Primate

---

69 *Ibid.*, note 580. The Barnabites and Claretians follow the norm of the time of profession. — *Ibid.*, note 580.

70 *Ibid.*, note 581.

71 Cf. *ibid.*, p. 335, note 516.

72 Cf. the Camaldolese, all the Carmelites, the Marists, the Servites, the Redemptorists and the Pallotine Fathers. — *Ibid.*, p. 367, note 584.

73 The Oblates and the Missionaries of the Sacred Heart provide examples of such precedence. — *Ibid.*, note 585.

74 *Ibid.*, note 586.

Abbots President
Abbot of Monte Cassino
Abbots-Bishop
Ex-Abbots Primate
Abbots President of the Congregations
Abbots *Nullius*
Vicar General (First Assistant or Procurator General)
Visitator General
Definitors General
Procurator General *apud Sanctam Sedem*
Secretary General
Econome General

PROVINCIAL OFFICIALS:
Provincial Superior
Provincial Vicar
Provincial Definitors
Provincial Secretary (if it is a separate office)
Provincial Econome
Novice Master
Spiritual Director
Masters of Theology, Prefects of Studies, Lectors

LOCAL OFFICIALS:
Local Superior
Vice-Superior
Local Definitors

What has been said above in great detail can at most furnish an outline idea of the various grades of authority in the Church, both jurisdictional or public, and private or domestic (dominative). From these examples and principles one can intelligently apply the norms of canon 106, 2°, to vindicate a proper precedence over their subjects to those who possess some kind of authority over them.

SECTION 2–THE PRECEDENCE OF MEMBERS OF A RELIGIOUS INSTITUTE

A. The Precedence of Postulants or Aspirants

In some institutes the postulants or aspirants are kept apart from the other members as guests. After they have been admitted to exercises of the community, they take the last place after the novices.

Among themselves postulants determine their precedence according to their clerical or lay state, or the state for which they are destined. Within either of these categories, the time of entrance into the institute will determine the precedence of each postulant. In some institutes the criterion will be age rather than the time of entrance.[75]

B. *The Precedence of Novices*

Novices generally precede postulants, in virtue of the rule[76] and are generally placed after the professed members of the same category (clerical or lay), so that clerical novices follow clerical professed members, and lay novices follow the professed lay religious.[77]

Precedence among novices is derived primarily from the category (lay or clerical) to which they belong. Thus clerical novices in higher orders precede novices in lower Orders or lay novices; if the lay novices began their novitiate before the clerical novices of higher Orders, the clerical novices still take precedence because they are clerics.[78]

Among those of the same category (clerical or lay), precedence is based on the time when the habit was received or when the novitiate began; among clerical novices precedence is usually given to those in a major Order.

If the novitiate was begun or the habit was received at the

---

75 Larraona, *CpR,* IV (1923), 277, notes 468-69. The principles of this section, unless they are indicated as drawn from elsewhere, are all taken from this continued article by Larraona.

76 Sometimes clerical postulants precede not only novices but also the professed who are only laymen, as among the Missionaries of the Divine Word. Others treat these clerical postulants as though they were not yet members of the community in the full sense: they are placed after the novices. This is the practice among the Carmelites, the Missionaries of the Sacred Heart, and the Pallotines. — *Ibid.,* note 470.

77 Some exceptions occur in respect to priests or clerics in major orders who, although they are novices, precede the professed who are not priests or are of a lower Order. This is observed by the Camaldolese, the Dominicans, and the Trinitarians. — *Ibid.,* note 471.

78 *Ibid.,* note 472; cf. canon 491, § 1.

same time, precedence is determined as deriving either from the time of admission[79] or from the age of the novice.[80]

In some religious institutes, clerical novices precede all professed lay members.[81] In many other religious institutes, all novices are preceded by all the professed, even if these professed members are only lay members.[82]

Even in the religious institutes wherein the professed lay members precede the clerical novices, exceptions are sometimes made for priests and clerics in major Orders, so that they may precede professed lay members.[83]

C. *The Precedence of Professed Members in General*

Professed religious generally precede novices and postulants, with due allowance made for exceptions when the latter are clerics. All clerical professed religious precede all lay professed members, regardless of the time of profession of either. When all the professed religious in a given group are either clerical or lay, precedence is given to those who have made the higher profession, namely solemn, or perpetual, or who have been in temporary vows for a longer period of time,[84] over others bound only by the lower profession, that of simple vows or bound in the past by temporary vows for a shorter duration of time.[85]

When all the professed are either clerical or lay, and all have made the same kind of profession (solemn, simple, perpetual or

79 Ferrarris, *Prompta Bibliotheca,* s.v. *praecedentia,* n. 31.

80 An example is found among the Missionaries of the Sacred Heart and the Pallotines. — Larraona, *ibid.,* p. 278, note 476.

81 The Dominicans, the Carmelites, the Theatines, the Missionaries of the Sacred Heart, the Missionaries of the Divine Word, the Pallotines, and others observe this norm. — *Ibid.,* note 477.

82 Examples of this practice are found among the Friars Minor, Conventual, the Trinitarians, the Servites, and the Claretians. — *Ibid.,* note 478.

83 This is the norm of the Trinitarians. It happens more frequently that priests and perhaps also clerics in major Orders are given precedence over professed clerics who are not priests, or not in major Orders, as among the Dominicans. — *Ibid.,* note 479.

84 The Carmelites have this practice. — *Ibid.,* p. 279, note 483; cf. the norms of canon 106, 3°: grade (professed), Order, prior promotion to grade.

85 This kind of precedence is temporary of its very nature, and changes as one advances through the stages of profession. — *Ibid.,* note 484.

temporary, with the vows binding for the same duration of time), precedence is based on the earlier time of profession.[86]

The first profession is usually considered as the sole basis for the computing of priority, even after the last or definite profession has been made.[87]

To facilitate the computation of the priority of profession, the various religious institutes have their different rules. As an example, the constitution of the Discalced Brothers of the B.V.M. of Mount Carmel acknowledges priority of profession for a religious who made his profession before the other in the same house, even if both made their profession in the same hour. In other institutes, even if the professions were made in different houses, those who professed on the same morning, or in the same evening of the same day, have no priority over each other on the basis of their profession. Here priority is given to the older one.[88] In some other religious institutes, no distinction is made: whoever makes his profession first is considered to be the older;[89] on the other hand, there are some institutes in which all who make their profession on the same day are considered equal, regardless of the hour of their profession.[90]

Among these equals, precedence is decided differently according to the rules of the various religious institutes as deriving from the earlier reception of the habit, from prior acceptance,[91]

---

86 Ferraris, *op. cit.*, s.v. *praecedentia*, nos. 30, 34, 36, 37. This rule is absolute and does not yield even to a contrary custom, which is declared an abuse; it is not permitted to renounce this right of precedence which arises from the time of profession. — Larraona, *CpR*, IV (1923), 279, note 486.

87 This is true among the Dominicans, the Franciscans, and the Missionaries of the Divine Word, among others. — *Ibid.*, note 487. Note the similarity to the first promotion to the episcopal rank or pastoral office as a basis for precedence even after transfers to other sees or parishes.

88 *Ibid.*, pages 279-80.

89 This is the general norm found in constitutions: "Qui prius professionem emittit, antiquior censetur." — *Ibid.*, note 490.

90 The Claretians adopted this norm in their general chapter in 1922. — *Ibid.*, note 491.

91 Therefore, if several made their profession at the same moment, precedence is given to the religious who first received his habit, or who first began his novitiate; if all likewise received their habit at the same moment, precedence is acknowledged for him who was first accepted, even though all were

from more advanced age[92] or from a longer enjoyed ordination.[93]

Precedence among the professed religious, then, is for the most part, a general application of the norms of the Code law: higher rank, Order, and prior promotion. Special norms are provided with a view to determining the priority of promotion more uniformly within some institution.

D. *Precedence for Special Categories of Professed Religious*

The ratification of an invalid profession presents an unusual problem for precedence. Does the religious determine his precedence from the date of the invalid or of the valid profession? If the impediment was external and public, if it was likewise occasioned in bad faith, then priority for precedence is based on the day the profession was ratified.[94]

As a favor, when a novice cannot make his profession at the proper time for reasons beyond his control, priority for precedence is not infrequently computed as deriving from the date on which the novitiate was completed, and on which the profession could have been made.

For a lay religious who by apostolic concession transfers to the clerical state of the same institute, priority for precedence among the clerics is to be computed from the day of his profession in the clerical religious state, and not in the lay religious state.[95]

According to canon 640, §1, 2°, a religious who has received an indult of secularization has also been freed of his vows. If by

---

accepted in the same chapter or council. This norm resembles the norm which determines the precedence of bishops: their prior promotion in consistory. — *Ibid.*, note 492.

92 The Constitution of the Missionaries of the Sacred Heart provides for this criterion. — *Ibid.*, note 493.

93 The Pallotine Fathers use this norm. — *Ibid.*, note 494.

94 Schaefer, *De Religiosis*, n. 59. If the impediment is not external, then according to canon 586, § 2, a renovation of profession is not necessary. If the impediment is not public, there is no reason why the effects should be external and public. Canonical equity seems to forbid a privation of precedence in consequence of an invalid profession made in good faith. — Larraona, *ibid.*, p. 331, note 495.

95 Schaefer, *De Religiosis*, n. 59.

apostolic indult he is received again into the religious institute, he is required by canon 640, §2, to make a new novitiate and profession; he takes his place among the professed from the day of his new profession.[96]

If apostates, fugitives, and those who have been dismissed still retain their perpetual vows, they are not *ipso facto* deprived of their precedence by the full rigor of the law;[97] nevertheless, it is not only possible, but usual to deprive them of this right.[98]

In the case of transfer from one religious institute to another, or from one monastery to another, the religious computes his priority for precedence from the moment of profession in the new institute. If he returns to his original institute or monastery before profession in the second, he does not lose the precedence in the first religious institute,[99] at least not in consequence of any norms contained in the law of the Code.[100] When a religious transfers from one house or province to another within the same institute, there would seem to be no justification for a loss of precedence because of the transfer. However, particular law may provide for a deprivation of the rights of precedence when this transfer has the nature of a penalty. Otherwise, the precedence of a religious would continue to be based on the time of his profession in the first house or province, or on whatever norm was followed in the given institute, with due regard for particular legislation.

The deprivation of precedence is to be regarded as the gravest penalty of the internal religious penal law, especially if

---

96 Canon 542, 1°. Schaefer, *loc. cit.*

97 For those religious who enjoy the privilege according to which vows no longer bind after dismissal (canons 669, § 1; 672) readmission would require a renewal of their profession. Their priority for precedence would be based on the date of this renewal of profession. — Larraona, *ibid.*, page 332, note 499.

98 Schaefer, *loc. cit.* Cf. canons 2385, 2386. Such a deprivation of precedence is found among the Friars Minor, the Dominicans and the Discalced Carmelites. — Larraona, *ibid.*, note 500.

99 Schaefer, *loc. cit.*

100 If he returns to the original institute after making his profession in the new institute, this would constitute a second transfer, and therefore his precedence upon his return to the old institute would be determined from the date of renewed profession there. — *Loc. cit.*

it is perpetual. It should not be imposed except for the more grave delicts.

The determination of prior profession when the first profession was invalid will depend upon the nature of the cause of the invalidity. Sometimes canonical equity demands that a norm other than the actual time of profession be used for the determining of precedence if profession was postponed through no fault of the novice. Once the bond of religious profession has been severed, the precedence which was based on the time of that profession is also lost. This can happen through an indult of secularization or in consequence of a transfer to and profession in a second religious institute. Sometimes precedence is taken away as a penalty, even though the bond of profession remains.

CHAPTER IX

THE POWER OF THE LOCAL ORDINARY TO ESTABLISH PRECEDENCE AND TO SETTLE CONTROVERSIES

Canon 106, 6°. *Loci Ordinarii est in sua diocesi statuere praecedentias inter suos subitos, ratione habita principiorum iuris communis, legitimarum dioecesis consuetudinum et munerum ipsis commissorum; et omnes de praecedentia controversias, etiam inter exemptos, quatenus ii collegialiter cum aliis procedant, componere in casibus urgentioribus, remota omni appellatione in suspensivo, sed sine praeiudicio iuris uniuscusque.*

The principles of canon 106, 1° - 5°, may be said to be somewhat elastic. Efforts at determining precisely what was intended by each norm seem to justify this conclusion. But Michiels maintains that this indeterminate quality was intentionally put into the laws of precedence; the lawgiver realized that in some particular cases the general law would be difficult to apply: it must not be too detailed in regard to things which might vary greatly in different parts of the world. For this reason, the legislator has provided the ordinary of each diocese with a twofold power to solve, at least temporarily in some cases, all questions of precedence of any kind, not only among his own subjects, but also among others, even among the exempt religious.[1] This twofold power not only assigns to the ordinary of the place the task of determining beforehand by positive action, the rights of precedence for his subjects; it also enables him to settle promptly any difficulties regarding precedence which may arise among exempt religious as well as his subjects, under given conditions.[2]

---

1 *De Personis*, p. 695.

2 Coronata (*Institutiones*, I, n. 162) and Michiels (*De Personis*, p. 696) explain that the legislator intended with the aid of this canon to forestall scandal among the faithful who could suffer disedification at seeing the clergy and religious disagreeing over places of honor in public. Cf. canon 1295.

Article 1. The Ordinaries of Places in their Dioceses

Canon 198, §1, lists certain persons, all of whom are local ordinaries, with due exception made for religious superiors.[3] Included in this group, besides the Roman Pontiff, are:

a) residential bishops;

b) abbots and prelates *nullius;*

c) the vicars general of the foregoing, within the proper territory of their ordinaries;

d) administrators apostolic;

e) vicars and prefects apostolic, and

f) those who succeed any of the foregoing either by prescription of law, or according to approved constitutions.[4]

In a diocese in the United States, either the ordinary or his vicar general may use the powers of canon 106, 6°. During the vacancy of the see, the board of consultors, acting *collegialiter,* may use this same power until it has elected an administrator.[5]

The diocesan administrator may use this power, for instance, to determine the rights of precedence at the funeral of the deceased Ordinary, or for some other function for which, when it takes place in the interregnum, precedence had not been determined earlier.

In vicariates or prefectures apostolic, the vicar or prefect has the same powers in this matter of determining precedence as do the residential bishops;[6] when these ordinaries vacate their sees, their pro-vicar or prefect is entitled to use this power, but not while the vicar or prefect is still in office.[7] If no one was selected as pro-prefect or pro-vicar, or if either of these failed to observe canon 309, §3, the rule of the vacant vicariate or pre-

---

3 Canon 198, § 2.

4 This group also includes the diocesan consultors, who elect a diocesan administrator as their representative. — cf. canons 427 and 432, § 1. Also included are the pro-prefects and pro-vicars apostolic mentioned in canon 309, § 2, and the successor of an apostolic administrator according to the norms of canons 317 and 429 ff. An example of succession by approved constitutions would be the provisory government that takes command during the vacancy of an abbacy or prelacy *nullius,* as described in canons 321 and 324.

5 Canon 431, § 1.

6 Canons 215, § 2; 198, § 1; 294, § 1.

7 Canon 309, § 2.

fecture is undertaken by the priest who has served the territory the longest.[8] He is "de iure" a delegate of the Holy See and he has the powers of a titular or pro-titular of the territory.[9]

In the abbacy or prelacy *nullius,* either the abbot or the prelate, and their vicars general are entitled to determine precedence and settle controversies concerning it.

In all the foregoing the exercise of the powers listed in canon 106, 6°, is necessarily limited to the territory of the ordinary. This paragraph states specifically that the ordinary may use this power only ". . . *in sua dioecesi.* . . ." According to canon 215, §2, the term "diocese" includes the territories of abbots or prelates *nullius.* At this point there seems to be conflict in terminology. For canon 293, §1, reads: "Territoria quae erecta non sunt in dioeceses reguntur per vicarios aut praefectos apostolicos." However, the following provides the norm:

> Vicarii et prafecti apostolici iisdem iuribus et facultatibus in suo territorio gaudent, quae in propriis dioecesibus competunt Episcopis residentialibus, nisi quid Apostolica Sedes reservaverit.[10]

For the sake of clarity, then, canon 106, 6°, should perhaps read: *"Loci Ordinarii est in suo territorio* . . ." instead of ". . . *in sua dioecesi.* . . ."

The limitation of this canon is imposed not on the exercise of the powers granted, but on the territory in which the exercise may take effect, unless the power is exercised as judicial power.[11] If the ordinary determines or settles precedence in an administrative procedure, he is using non-judicial power. Such jurisdiction or power may be used by the ordinary even when he is outside his proper territory, or over his subjects when they are absent from the territory.[12] In the light of this principle it

---

8 If two have served equally long in the territory, the senior by ordination should assume the rule of the vicariate or prefecture according to canon 309, § 4. If this were not enough to single out one of the two, then recourse would be had to the factor of age, the only other norm of canon 106, 3°, which remains, unless one of the two had been ordained by the pope. — Vermeersch-Creusen, *Epitome,* I, n. 429.

9 Canons 294; 309, § 4; 310, § 2.

10 Canon 294, § 1.

11 Canon 201, § 2.

12 Canon 201, § 3.

seems that the ordinary may solve a controversy over precedence or determine this right for his subjects in any of the following circumstances:

a) when both ordinary and subject are in the ordinary's proper territory;

b) when the ordinary is outside his proper territory, for the subject in the proper territory;

c) when both ordinary and subject are outside their territory.

d) when the subject is outside and the ordinary is in his own territory.

Article 2. The Determination of the Subjects of Ordinaries of the Place

A person may become the subject of a superior in various ways, according to the Code. By baptism, everyone is the subject of universal Church law, and therefore a subject of the Roman Pontiff.[13] In a stricter sense, the baptized person becomes the subject of the local ordinary by reason of his own domicile or quasi-domicile in the territory of the ordinary.[14] In some instances even those without domicile or quasi-domicile in the territory of the ordinary may be his subjects in certain matters concerning the public order or the solemnities of acts.[15] Those who have no domicile or quasi-domicile anywhere are the subjects of the ordinary of the place in which they happen to be.[16]

In theory, there seems to be no doubt that the provisions of canon 106, 6°, apply to all these groups mentioned (those with domicile or quasi-domicile, those who have either of these outside the territory, and those who have neither domicile nor quasi-domicile anywhere). If the persons involved are not subjects of the local ordinary in someway, they are engaged in a public act which must be carried out in an orderly and peaceful manner.

---

13 Canons 12, and 87.

14 Canon 13.

15 Canon 14, § 1, 2°. Regatillo (*Institutiones,* I, n. 72), in treating of *peregrini* and the notion of public order as mentioned in canon 14 cites among the specific examples of laws which affect public order those ". . . *quae bonum ordinem externum spectant, ut processionem ordinantes* (canon 1295). . . ."

16 Canon 14, § 2.

Precedence becomes a matter of public order, for which the final judge is the local ordinary. In this way, by reason of their participation in the function at which precedence is to be observed, they become in some way a subject of the local ordinary, for the sake of peace and order.[17]

In actual fact, the ordinary will usually determine precedence only for his clergy, or for lay moral persons in his diocese. The clergy are his subjects through incardination, domicile or quasi-domicile. What, then, if the clergy from another diocese or territory come into the ordinary's territory? Although they are not bound by these particular laws on precedence[18] it is to be assumed that they will, at least for this occasion, follow the norms of precedence established locally; if they do not, and a controversy arises over the matter, the local ordinary is empowered to settle it for the single occasion anyway, on the basis of the power given him in the second part of canon 106, 6°.

The fact that the people whose precedence is determined are his subjects will not be of primary importance; for the ordinary will very likely determine the precedence to be acknowledged for certain positions or offices in the diocese. Whoever has one of these positions will enjoy the right of precedence attached to it.

The same will be true of lay people. The only precedence that can be determined for them will be in connection with the pious associations of the faithful which exist in the territory of the ordinary. Here again, the relationship is not so much with the ordinary who determines the precedence, but with the membership in one of these groups for which precedence has been determined. It appears most recommendable that a mention of their proper precedence be included in the decree of erection of all moral persons in the diocese.[19] As for those lay associations of the faithful which come from another territory for an occasion which is of more than diocesan interest, their precedence can be determined by the local ordinary only if the requirements of the second part of canon 106, 6°, are met: there must be some controversy which requires settlement.

---

17 Canon 14, § 2.

18 Canon 14.

19 Berutti, *Institutiones*, II, n. 27.

Article 3. The Basis for Determination of Precedence by the Ordinary of the Place

The legislator has carefully taken precautions against the establishment of any arbitrary norms of precedence. Abuse in this matter is forestalled by means of the requirement that any norms added to those already outlined in the Code must conform to three standards:

a) the norms of precedence as established by the Code itself;

b) legitimate diocesan custom;

c) the nature of the offices to which a certain type of precedence is being attached.[20]

Michiels points out that the use of the ordinary's power to determine precedence is restricted to those offices for which the Code has not already established definite rights of precedence.[21] Otherwise, the ordinary would, as a legislator subordinate to the Roman Pontiff, be legislating contrary to the provisions of the Code law. But, as Berutti points out, there would be no objection to the local ordinary's legislating on matters of precedence beyond or outside the norms of the universal law, or even contrary to the particular law or local custom.[22] He suggests, for example, that the ordinary might well determine a specific right of precedence for the diocesan judge *(officialis)* or the chancellor, for whom the Code has not provided any norm.

The Code itself specifically provides for the rights of precedence with reference to the ordinary of the place in canon 347, for the coadjutor or auxiliary bishops in canon 106, 2° or 3°, for the vicar general in canon 370, §1, and for the vicars forane within their own deaneries, according to canon 450, §2. It likewise provides norms for determining the precedence of the pastor of the cathedral, other pastors substitute or auxiliary vicars, and assistant pastors.[23] The priests of the diocese who are members of the papal household (protonotaries apostolic *ad instar,* domestic prelates, and papal chamberlains) are given norms

---

20 Canon 106, 6°.

21 *De Personis,* p. 695.

22 *Institutiones,* II, n. 27.

23 Canon 478. The precedence of pastors is only a logical conclusion drawn from the norms of this canon.

for their precedence in special provisions allowed for by canon 106, 7°, which are discussed in the next chapter.

No place seems quite as logical for the ordinary to determine these rights of predecence as in the synod. Several dioceses in the United States have done this since the promulgation of the Code in 1917.[24] The list which resulted from the application of these norms showed considerable uniformity as to those in the highest and lowest positions. There was a great variety, however, among the others, both as to position and as to who was given precedence. Some recognized a special precedence for the *officialis;*[25] others gave special recognition to the diocesan consultors.[26] Most statutes recognized the difficulty of singling out the individual curial officials below the rank of vicar general, *officialis* and chancellor. They merely put them all into one body or rank just after the vicar general or sometimes lower in rank; they determined the mutual precedence of these officials according to the date they were promoted to the body of curial officers. A similar solution was adopted when it could not definitely be determined who had the greater right of precedence among the deans, the pastor of the cathedral, and the irremovable rectors; between chaplains and assistants; and among the various diocesan officers who were not strictly members of the curia,[27] such as the bishop's secretary, the diocesan superintendent of schools, the members of the council of vigilance, the diocesan athletic director, and others.

The following plan of precedence determined for a diocese in the United States is suggested by the present writer. Such a plan is in line with the norms of the Code law. It may require

---

24 The statutes of these dioceses (in a synod held in the year indicated in parentheses) were found to have some legislation on matters of precedence (this list is by no means exhaustive): Crookston (1921), Des Moines (1923), Wheeling (1923), Harrisburg (1928), Trenton (1931), Richmond (1933). Lincoln (1934), Toledo (1941), and Erie (1942).

25 Statutes of the Dioceses of Harrisburg, Richmond and Toledo.

26 All the dioceses named above except Richmond and Trenton.

27 The curia consists of the vicar general, the *officialis,* the chancellor, the promoter of justice, the defender of the bond, the synodal judges and examiners, the parish consultors, the auditors, the notaries, the messengers, and the beadles of the court. — canon 363, § 2.

some changes in view of extant local custom or already existing diocesan statutes. Since it is specifically intended for the situation in the United States, the plan makes no provision for the precedence of chapters of canons and the special considerations that go with them. Some of the suggested norms reflect in their matter solely the mind of the present writer, namely in instances where in the Code law does not make any provision, and in the event that there are instances they are clearly indicated as such. Equally good reasons may be found for some other solutions with reference to these special problems of precedence. The plan is as follows:

1) the ordinary of the place;[28]

2) the coadjutor and auxiliary bishops in this order:

a) the episcopal vicar general;[29]

b) the other bishops in the diocese in the order of their promotion to the rank of titular archbishop or titular bishop, even if they are in retirement;[30]

3) the vicar general (if he is not a bishop);[31]

4) the *officialis*, in view of the fact that he shares the ordinary's

---

28 Canon 347; cf. *supra*, p. 134.

29 Canon 370, § 1.

30 "Ordinem, characterem et titulum semper inhaerere personae Episcopi consecrati quae numquam dimittit, nec dimittere potest: et ideo, licet administrationem Episcopatus quis dimittat, titulum et ordinem semper retinere; et consequenter debere praecedere omnibus aliis Episcopis post ipsum electis et consecratis." — S. R. C., *Minerbin.*, 4 mart. 1606 — *D.* n. 204.

"Haec quidem convenire videbantur episcopis omnibus sive cum iurisdictione sive mere titularibus, cum in praesenti lege nulla fiat distinctio; eo vel magis quod episcopus, qui resignavit simpliciter episcopatum, ordinis praerogativas, honorem et iura reverentialia retinet."—S. C. Conc., *Aquensium Archiepiscopo,* 24 aug. 1850—*ASS,* III (1867), 310, ad Dubium II.

31 Canon 370, § 1. The vicar general loses his office and consequently the basis of his precedence when he resigns, when he has his appointment revoked, or when the see is vacant. He is likewise deprived of his jurisdiction (and therefore his precedence) when the espiscopal jurisdiction is suspended in accordance with the law as stated in canon 371. In any of these circumstances, then, the vicar general loses his special precedence. If there is more than one vicar general, precedence is determined by higher order, prior promotion to this rank, or prior ordination.

judicial power in the same way the vicar general shares his voluntary jurisdiction;[32]

5) the protonotaries apostolic *ad instar,* according to the date of their nomination, regardless of the position they hold in the diocese, unless it be either number 3 or 4 above;[33]

6) the domestic prelates, with the same conditions, likewise according to the date of their promotion to the honor;[34]

7) the papal chamberlains, with the same condition and according to the same norms as in numbers 5 and 6;

8) the diocesan consultors as a body may be assigned the same precedence as the cathedral chapter;[35]

9) the curial officials listed in canon 363, §2, (unless they are included in numbers 5, 6, or 7 above) exclusive of the vicar general and *officialis.* The present writer suggests that they take their precedence as they are named in the Code, or according to the date of their promotion to the curia as a body. If the order of the Code is adopted by the local ordinary as a primary norm,[36]

---

32 The *officialis* does not lose his jurisdiction [the basis of his precedence] when the see is vacant. — canon 1573, § 6.

33 Cf. *infra,* p. 248 where members of the papal household are discussed.

34 A separate list of the protonotaries apostolic *ad instar,* of the domestic prelates, and of the papal chamberlains appears in the *Annuario Pontificio* each year, with the addition of the date of their promotion to the honor. This may be consulted when it becomes necessary to determine the proper precedence within each of these three groups of members of the papal household.

35 The cathedral chapter precedes all physical and moral persons in the whole diocese even in their own church (canon 491, § 2; canon 408, § 1), except the vicar capitular (canon 439) and the vicar general (canon 370 § 1), or those who are bishops. — Coronata, *Institutiones,* I, n. 450. By analogy, the present writer maintains that precedence may be given to the diocesan consultors on the basis that the chapter or diocesan consultors are listed just after the vicar general among those who, as mentioned in canon 358, § 1, must attend the synod. Cf. note 159, pp. 135, for more detailed arguments.

36 The last three types of curial officials mentioned in canon 363 (the notaries, messengers, and beadles) may be laymen instead of clerics. For this reason the local ordinary may prefer not to group them with the rest of the curial officers. Another possible solution with reference to the precedence of these three types of officials would be to list specifically which curial officials are to have precedence with this group, or to give a special place to these laymen elsewhere, or simply to exclude them.

then the date of promotion to one of the groups within the curia may be used as a secondary norm to determine the individual's precedence within the group., e.g., among the diocesan consultors.[37]

10) the rector of the major seminary;[38]

11) the vicar forane (rural dean) in his own deanery;[39]

12) the pastor of the cathedral;[40]

13) the vicars forane (rural deans) outside their proper deaneries and pastors of the see city, on an equal basis, forming one body; within this body precedence could be determined only according to the date of their promotion to the office of pastor (since the deans are not acting in their capacity as deans).

14) the pastors *emeriti,* all other pastors, military chaplains, and chaplains of Veterans' Administration Hospitals, according to the date of their promotion to that rank. No provision is made for retired priests in the Code, nor do any of the commentators even mention them. Yet they are found in many dioceses, and often enough they attend functions wherein proper precedence should be observed. Giving them precedence in this place would be a parallel to the precedence of retired bishops who retain their right of precedence based on their seniority in the episcopal rank.[41]

---

37 A practical application of the norms for internal precedence is mentioned by Woywod-Smith when they state the order of precedence within these bodies (cathedral chapter or the diocesan consultors) determines who is to administer the last rites to the local ordinary. — *A Practical Commentary on the Code of Canon Law* (rev. ed., 1957), pp. 190-91.

38 Canon 358, § 1, 3°.

39 Canon 450, § 2; cf. canon 358, § 1, 4°.

40 Canon 478, § 1. This right of precedence belongs to him as pastor over all other pastors as such. But nothing prevents their taking precedence over him in meetings where he is appearing not as pastor, but in some other capacity. Thus, the rector of the seminary will take precedence over him in a meeting of the seminary faculty. — S.C.Conc., *resolutio, Foroliven.,* 10 febr. et 9 iunii 1923, *votum consultoris ad questionem* I — *AAS,* XVI (1923), 400.

41 Nothing is said in the Code about a loss of precedence as such, except as a penalty (canon 2291, 11°), although the particular precedence of the vicar general, for instance, will change if he is no longer the vicar general. After this change, perhaps only the date of his ordination can serve as a basis for his precedence. If the date of pastoral appointment is not observed

15) the vicars econome (parish administrators) according to the time of their promotion to this rank, then by the date of their ordination, and finally by their age;[42]

16) the vicars substitute and the vicars auxiliary mentioned in canon 465, §§4, 5, and canon 475, forming one body; within this body, they take their precedence according to the date of their promotion to either of these two ranks, then according to the date of their ordination, and their ages;[43]

---

as a criterion for the precedence of the retired pastors, there remains only the date of ordination for them too. This could determine their precedence within some rank, but which one? In view of their years of service to their diocese and their seniority by ordination and pastoral appointment, it seems only canonically equitable that they be given a place the equal of which is here proposed.

Military chaplains are to be considered equal to and under the name of pastors with all parochial rights and obligations, with due regard for the special provisions of the Holy See. — canon 451, § 1, 3°. The Holy See has specifically provided for their pastoral status in two documents: S. C. Consist., Instruction on Military Vicars, April 23, 1951 — *AAS* XLIII (1951), 562, n. 10; S. C. Consist., Decree of Erection of the Military Vicariate for the United States, Sept. 8, 1957 — *AAS*, XLIX (1957), 970, n. 7.

42 This type of vicar is considered to have the same rights as a pastor in those things which pertain to the care of souls, according to canon 473, § 1. Canon 478, § 1, states that their precedence is determined according to the norms of canon 106, presumably according to paragraph 3° of that canon. However, Moretti (*De Sacris Functionibus*, I, n. 152), implies that they are to be considered as proxies. Sipos (*Enchiridion*, p. 267) states this specifically, and gives them the same precedence as if they were true pastors. On the other hand, Jone (*Commentarium*, I, *sub canone* 478, § 1) gives them a place after the pastors themselves. The present writer maintains that this seems to be more consistent with the limitation imposed on the administrator's equality with the pastor: ". . . *in iis quae animarum curam spectant*. . . ." Furthermore, for whom could they act as proxies when the pastor is deceased?

43 Canon 478, § 2. This is a departure from the pre-Code norm, which gave them precedence by reason of this position only when they were actually exercising the duties of a *vice-parochus*. — S.R.C., *Meliten.*, 23 febr. 1839 — *D.*, n. 2786; S.R.C., *Romana*, 12 iulii 1892 — *D.*, n. 3780. The vicar substitute is truly a proxy; a special form of canon 106, 1°, is established here for a proxy outside a council or similar gathering, which resembles more the norm for precedence in the council: in the same rank as the principal, but after all others of the same rank who are present personally. The vicar auxiliary, if he supplies for the pastor in all things, enjoys all the rights and obligations of the pastor, according to canon 475, § 2. He is therefore

17) the rectors of non-parochial churches;[44]

18) the vicars assistant mentioned in canon 476 (assistant pastors) precede all other priests who are simply attached to a parish; among themselves, precedence is determined from the date of their first appointment as assistant pastors or vicars assistant, then by the date of their ordination, and finally by their age, unless one of them was ordained by the Roman Pontiff;[45]

19) other priests who are attached to a parish;[46]

20) the chaplains of institutions who do not come under any of the categories named above, according to the date of their

---

entitled to a rank with greater precedence than the other vicars or assistants listed after him in canon 478, § 2.

44 The present writer maintains that the rank of the rector of a non-parochial Church as contemplated in canon 479 is higher than that of a vicar assistant, insofar as he is not subject to the pastor as the assistant is, and therefore has greater authority. Such a rector also enjoys a certain pre-eminence by the fact that to his church is attached a confraternity, a seminary, a hospital, a prison, or the like. — Sipos, *Enchiridion,* p. 267. It is also possible that such a rector will have parochial rights in regard to his church through Apostolic indult or lawful custom. — Veermeersch-Creusen, *Epitome,* I, n. 576. The local ordinary will best be able to determine if the rector of such a church should have a greater or lesser right of precedence.

45 Canon 478, § 2. "Vicarius paroecialis praecedit qui prius vicariatum obtinuit." — S.R.C., 28 apr. 1607 — cited by Adone, *Synopsis Canonico-Liturgica,* n. 1974.

"Ubi capitula cathedralia deficiant, concludendum esse videtur, ut vicarii paroeciales ecclesiae cathedralis sibi vindicare nequeant praecedentiam super ceteris vicariis." — Beste, *Introductio in Codicem, sub canone* 478, § 1. Cf. also Augustine, *Commentary,* II, 578.

It seems that no distinction should or could be made between those who are first, second, or lower assistants (except according to the date of their first appointment or promotion, and in the case provided for in canon 472, 2°), any more than a distinction is proper between pastors of small or large parishes, or for titular and residential bishops.

46 Canon 478, § 2. Just as there is no particular name for such priests in the Code, so there probably is no juridical act by which other priests may be attached to a parish. Such priests may or may not have residence in the parish rectory. It would be expected that they help with parish work to some degree, perhaps only on the week ends when they are not occupied with whatever it is that keeps the ordinary from assigning them to full time work in the parish. These priests may occupy themselves the better part of their

appointment to the position of chaplain, then by the date of their ordination, and finally from their age.[47]

21) other priests who are in no way attached to a parish;[48]

22) other clerics below the Order of priesthood, according to their Order and prior promotion to the same Order.

The foregoing list merely represents the present writer's conclusions as to the precedence which a bishop might usefully establish in his diocese. As can be seen, some have express canonical foundation; others are based only on analogy or some form of canonical equity. Equally good reasons might be found in support of a different arrangement of precedence in the diocese for those who have no special norms of precedence in the Code.

Article 4. Controversies over Precedence in Urgent Cases

The power to settle all controversies among subjects, nonsubjects, and religious (even if exempt,) was specified for ordinaries of places as early as the Council of Trent (1545-63).[49]

---

week with some other assigned or approved work, such as a non-residential chaplaincy or a position as principal, instructor or student in an institution of learning nearby. In view of these circumstances, and in the absence of any particular norms in the Code, it seems proper to determine the precedence of such priests, not from the time of their assignment or "attachment" to the parish, but from the date of their ordination, and then from their age.

47 The chaplains mentioned in canon 479, § 2, not infrequently have no other assignment upon which to base their precedence. Since they are not named among those called vicars in canon 478, and are not, in the supposed case, in any way attached to a parish, there seems to be no alternative but to give them their rank below those priests who are attached in some way to a parish, but are not named specifically in this canon. Included here would be the resident chaplains of hospitals (which are not Veterans' Administration Hospitals), schools of learning and correction, homes for the aged, orphanages, prisons and the like.

48 It may happen that a priest has retired either from work in the given diocese or in some other, and now lives in the parish without any particular connection with it. Some of the priests mentioned in the previous note may also have residence in a parish without being attached to it in any way. If no other precedence is given them under one of the categories listed above, they could take their places here after all the others, in the opinion of the present writer.

49 Sessio XXV, *de regularibus*, c. 13.

Any reasons advanced for this special power of the ordinary, repeated now in the Code in canon 106, 6°, would surely include the avoidance of scandal to the faithful at the sight of clergy and religious, who should be more concerned with the virtues of fraternal charity, justice, and humility, arguing among themselves over places of honor. These controversies are largely the result of ignorance on the part of one or both parties to the controversy. The lack of norms which are sufficiently detailed may result in similar difficulties. When the ordinary is able to use the power vindicated for him in canon 106, 6°, to establish practical and correct norms of precedence among his subjects, it is less likely that he will have to avail himself of this power to settle controversies among them.

If the litigant parties are subjects of the ordinary, there will be no problem about his right to proceed, administratively or judicially, to settle the difficulty. However, canon 106, 6°, recognizes the legal implications that arise if the controversy involves exempt religious or others not subject to the local ordinary. The extreme usefulness of the norm is the temporary suspension of the privileges of exemption for the common good, and the temporary subjection of persons who are not ordinarily subject to the local ordinary, for the sake of public order.[50]

SECTION 1—EXEMPT RELIGIOUS

Canon 615 grants the privilege of exemption from the jurisdiction of the local ordinary to all regulars, including the novices, whether they be men or women,[51] unless a special and expression exception is made. Regulars are those religious who are members of an order or of a religious institute in which, by the rule, there is a profession of solemn vows by at least some of the members, even though by direction of the Holy See such profession may not exist in fact.[52]

---

50 Canon 14, 2°, 3°; cf. Regatillo, *Institutiones,* I, n. 72.

51 Those nuns (*moniales*) who are not subject to regular superiors do not enjoy the privilege of exemption. Postulants are not included in this canon; in view of the explicit inclusion of novices, it seems safe to conclude that postulants are to be considered excluded. This conclusion was confirmed by the Code Commission in a reply of July 20, 1924. — *AAS,* XXI (1929), 573.

52 Canon 488, 2°, and canon 1308, § 2.

Ordinarily, religious of simple vows do not enjoy this privilege of exemption. In two exceptional cases, however, the Roman Pontiff has granted it to some of them: the Passionists and the Redemptorists enjoy exemption along with the regulars, although they are only congergations.[53] From these principles it is clear that the following religious are exempt, and therefore of special concern in the application of the norms of canon 106. 6°:

a) canons regular;[54]

b) monks;[55]

c) regulars (mendicants[56] and clerics regular);[57]

d) the two special congregations of the Passionists and the Redemtorists who, though professed with simple vows, nevertheless have the privilege of exemption.

When any groups of the above mentioned exempt religious are in a procession as a community, in some number, or *collegialiter*,[58] with other religious, even other exempt religious, with the secular clergy, or with the laity, whether they are his subjects or not, the local ordinary is competent to settle any controversies about their precedence, either with his subjects, or among themselves, so long as the controversy arises in his own territory.[59]

SECTION 2–URGENT CASES

The legislator is reluctant to lift the privilege of exemption too readily, however; the local ordinary is given this power over the exempt religious only in cases which are pressingly urgent. Such an urgency would be present if the celebration of a congress or a procession were about to be held which these exempt religious were going to attend.[60] This would become more justifi-

---

53 Creusen-Ellis, *Religious Men and Woman in the Code*, n. 313.

54 Cf. *supra*, p. 166 for details.

55 Cf. *supra*, pp. 167-70 for a list.

56 Cf. *supra*, pp. 171-76.

57 Cf. *supra*, pp. 175-76.

58 At least three are needed to form a collegiate moral person. — canon 100, § 2.

59 Canon 106, 6°. Cf. Berutti, *Institutiones*, II, n. 27. *Uti singuli*, the exempt, like other religious, follow the norms of canon 106, 1° to 4°, to determine their precedence with the others present individually.

60 Berutti, *loc. cit.;* Michiels, *De Personis*, p. 692.

able as the period of time for settling the case juridically before the competent superiors became shorter,[61] or as the exempt religious were increasingly at odds among themselves with the others over their precedence.[62]

SECTION 3—A JUDICIAL OR ADMINISTRATIVE PROCEDURE

Canon 106, 6°, uses the term *"appellatio."* Appeal and sentence are usually correlative terms and connote the fulfillment of complete judicial formalities.[63] However, this does not imply that an administrative procedure may not be admitted. If the law is to serve its purpose completely in settling controversies, even those which come up when it is too late for a judicial procedure must be capable of settlement.[64] The canon provides for this implicitly, permitting the ordinary to solve the problem either administratively or judicially. The common remedies against his solution will be recourse if he solved the controversy administratively, appeal *in devolutivo* or *suspensivo* if he settled it judicially, depending on what the law permits in the given case. In canon 106, 6°, the Code law forbids the use of appeal *in suspensivo,* implicitly permitting appeal only *in devolutivo.*

Possibly the administrative process will be used more often. By the very nature of his jurisdiction, the vicar general (as an

61 Fanfani, *De Iure Religiosorum,* n. 367. Among religious of the same clerical exempt institute in a province, the provincial superior or the abbot of an independent monastery would be the competent superior, the judge in the first instance. If the controversy extends beyond the province, the supreme moderator is competent. In the case of two different religious institutes, the ordinary of the place would be the judge of first instance according to the norms of canons 1560 ff. Regulars, moreover, who enter a controversy with other religious or with the secular clergy or the laity, are no longer exempt from the jurisdiction of the ordinary of the place. — Vermeersch-Creusen, *Epitome,* III, n. 39. Cf. canon 1579.

62 Blat, *Commentarium,* II, 38.

63 William Doheny, *Canonical Procedure in Matrimonial Cases,* 2 vols.; Vol. I, *Formal Procedure* (2.ed.; Milwaukee: Bruce Publishing Co., 1948), p. 212. Cf. canon 1601.

64 Fanfani, *op. cit.,* n. 367. Droste-Messmer (*Canonical Procedure in Disciplinary and Criminal Cases of Clerics* [New York: Benziger Bros., 1887], p. 148, note 2) indicate that it is the mind of the Church that the judicial process should be invoked only when the administrative procedure fails to achieve the desired end.

ordinary of the place) could solve such controversies only in this way.[65] In view of the urgency, the exempt religious as well as the subjects of the ordinary of the place must obey such administrative decrees emanating from any ordinary of the place;[66] later, if anyone feels that this decree has infringed upon his right of precedence, he can seek a remedy by having recourse *in devolutivo*.[67]

To whom this recourse is had will depend on the injured party seeking redress.[68] Exempt religious will ordinarily direct their plea to the Sacred Congregation of Religious.[69] Those religious, both the clergy and laymen, who are subject to the Sacred Congregation for the Propagation of the Faith will direct their request to that Congregation.[70] Other clerics and laymen will have recourse to the Sacred Congregation of the Council, the Congregation which is ordinarily competent in matters of precedence.[71]

On the other hand, if the controversy is to be settled judicially, the judge of the first instance is the ordinary of the place, even for exempt religious, if the quarrel is with some other religious or lay persons, or with the secular clergy;[72] If the controversy arises within the exempt institute of clerical religious, the provincial superior or the abbot (of an independent monastery) is the judge of the first instance.[73] If this controversy extends be-

65 Canon 1573, § 1.

66 Canon 106, 6°. Berutti, *Institutiones*, II, n. 27. "Obedire debet quousque superior competens non deciderit controversiam." — Jone, *Commentarium*, I, *sub canone* 106, 6°.

67 A recourse which is granted for a review of a nonjudicial precept does not ordinarily suspend the power of the superior. Thus, such a recourse is said to be *in devolutivo*. Such a procedure must be followed with the view to preserving the respect due to episcopal authority and the general order of diocesan organization. — E. Roelker, *Precepts*, p. 200.

68 Contra Ordinariorum decreta non datur appellatio seu recursus ad Sacram Rotam; sed de eiusmodi recursibus exclusive cognoscunt Sacrae Congregationes. — canon 1601. There is likewise no judicial appeal to the metropolitan. — Sipos, *Enchiridion*, p. 721.

69 Canon 251, § 1.

70 Canon 252, § 1.

71 Canon 250, § 1.

72 Canon 1579, § 3.

73 Canon 1579, § 1.

yond the boundaries of the province or the monastery, but remains within the institute, the supreme moderator for clerical exempt religious is the competent judge in the first instance.[74]

An appeal can be made from the decision of the judge of first instance;[75] but until a more favorable sentence is given, the litigant parties must abide by the decision of the judge of first instance. Canon 106, 6°, rules out any suspensive effect for appeals made in matters of precedence.[76]

Ordinarily exempt religious appeal their cases to the court of the Supreme Moderator of the institute or of the monastic congregation. Wherever the local ordinary is the judge in the first instance, as the law provides in canon 1579, §3, the norms of canon 1594, §§1, 2, and 3, must be observed: an appeal from the tribunal of a suffragan goes to the metropolitan; when the metropolitan is the judge of first instance the appeal is to be made to the ordinary whom the metropolitan has chosen *"semel pro semper"* with the approval of the Apostolic See; if the judge of first instance is an archbishop without suffragans or a bishop who is not subject to a metropolitan, the norms of canon 285 must be observed.

Although the controversy is settled for the time administratively, the nature of such a solution is transitory. In view of this aspect, a more definitive rule can be sought by the litigant parties.[77]

SECTION 4—THE FUNDAMENTAL RIGHTS OF PRECEDENCE REMAIN UNCHANGED AFTER A CONTROVERSY

Canon 106, 6°, provides specifically for the protection of the fundamental rights of precedence for both interested parties in the case wherein the local Ordinary has settled an urgent controversy. Therefore, no one may claim a new right to precedence based on this one instance, or on several similar solutions over a period of time. The controversial nature of repeated solutions of a similar pattern would rule out the possibility of acquiring any new right of precedence from quasi-possession.

74 Canon 1579, § 2.

75 Canons 1594, § 1; 1599, § 1.

76 Cf. canon 1889, § 2.

77 Beste, *Introductio in Codicem, sub canone* 106, 6°.

CHAPTER X

PRECEDENCE WITHIN THE PONTIFICAL HOUSEHOLD

Canon 106, 7°. *Circa personas quae ad Domum pontificalem pertinent, praecedentia moderanda est secundum peculiaria privilegia, regulas et traditiones eiusdem pontificiae domus.*

The privileges, rules and traditions of some of the papal household are available in two codifying papal documents, namely the *Inter multiplices* of Pius X in 1905,[1] and the *Ad incrementum* of Pius XI in 1934.[2] These two documents give detailed norms prescribing the duties, privileges, and rights of the various members of the papal household. *Inter multiplices* treats primarily of the four kinds of protonotaries; five paragraphs at the end are devoted to other prelates of the Roman Curia, some dignitaries, canons, and others who enjoy the privileges of prelates. Several of these specific norms for protonotaries were incorporated into the later constitution of Pius XI with particular references to sections of the *Inter multiplices.*[3] Where this is not specified in the *Ad incrementum* the legislation of Pius X is abrogated,[4] just as it in turn had abrogated all legislation for protonotaries which had been promulgated earlier.[5]

The papal household consists of clerics and laymen who are considered to be close to the Roman Pontiff because of their personal or domestic service, or because they hold some office in the Vatican Palace. Besides such members who give actual service, there are those who merely have the honorary title and accompanying privileges of such personal servants.[6] The members are also divided into those who are prelates, and those who do not have that title.[7] Some of the prelates form a college, and

1 Motu proprio, 21 febr. 1905 — *Fontes,* n. 655 (hereafter cited as *IM,* n. ....).

2 Apost. const. 15 aug. 1934 — *AAS,* XXVI (1934), 497 (hereafter cited as *AI,* n. ....).

3 See *AI,* nos. XXXVIII, XLIII, XLIV, LIV, LIV-LIX.

4 *AI,* paragraph *"Quam ob rem."*

5 *IM,* paragraph, *"Quam ob rem."*

6 Beste, *Introductio in Codicem, sub canone* 328.

7 Regatillo, *Institutiones,* I, n. 482.

receive their rights and privileges by appointment to such a college; others are named personally, and together with others of the same rank they do not form a college.[8] Some are engaged in the work of the Roman Congregations, others are occupied outside Rome itself, and hold their title as an honor.[9] Others, in addition to being domestic prelates, are also called protonotaries apostolic, or at least are in some degree equal to them.[10]

Article 1. The Kinds of Domestic Prelates

The dignity of domestic prelate, or prelate *di mantelletta*,[11] is a title of honor, conferred on deserving clerics. These clerics are members of the pope's household, with all the prerogatives of this dignity. Some are given the honor in virtue of the office they hold:

a) archbishops and bishops assistant at the throne;

b) protonotaries apostolic participating;

c) protonotaries apostolic supernumerary;

d) protonotaries apostolic *ad instar;*[12]

e) prelates of the College of the Prelature;

f) archbishops and bishops appointed domestic prelates before their promotion to the episcopacy.[13] Others are domestic prelates *ad instar, durante munere.*[14] A third group of domestic prelates receive their title by direct grant.[15]

---

[8] *AI*, n. LIII.

[9] The title of domestic prelate requires admission to membership in one of the colleges of prelates, or creation as a protonotary apostolic. It is concerned with a special ecclesiastical dignity, which joins the chosen person to the pontifical household with the right to use the prelatial garb and to attend functions in the papal chapel. — Nabuco, *Ius Pontificalium*, p. 32.

[10] "Domestic Prelates," *Annuario Pontificio* (1959), p. 1221.

[11] Regatillo, *op. cit.*, I, n. 482.

[12] These are appointed domestic prelates by means of a brief before their appointment as protonotaries. — *Annuario Pontificio* (1959), p. 1221.

[13] *Loc. cit.*

[14] These include the canons of the primatial church of Pisa, dignitaries of the metropolitan chapter of Catania, the senior of the canons of the Basilica of San Lorenzo in Damaso (Rome), the Archpriest of the Chapter of SS. Celsus and Julian (Rome), the auditors of the tribunal at the Apostolic Nunciature in Spain (these two received the title as a special concession from Pius XII), and the penitentiaries of St. Peter's Basilica. — *Loc. cit.*

[15] *Loc. cit.*

Not all of these are true prelates in the sense of canon 110, as exercising jurisdiction in the external forum. True prelates are those who either singly or as a member of a college are vested with some power to help the Roman Pontiff and the cardinals in governing the Church. These include the following:

a) prelates *a flocculis;*

b) assessors and secretaries of the Sacred Congregations;

c) the *Maestro di Camera,* the Secretary of the Apostolic Signatura, the Dean of the Rota, and the Substitute Secretary of State;

d) four colleges of prelates:

(i) Prelate Auditors of the Rota;

(ii) Clerics of the Apostolic Camera;

(iii) Prelates of the Apostolic Signatura *(Votantes);*

(iv) Prelates *Referendarii* of the Apostolic Signatura;[16]

e) metropolitans;

f) bishops, and all those listed as ordinaries in Canon 198;

g) vicars general, and

h) superiors general, provincial and local of exempt clerical religious institutes.[17]

Among the honorary prelates, who without any special power perform simple functions in the papal household or curia, or who without any special office enjoy all the honorific rights of prelates, are the following:

a) supernumerary protonotaries (if they were previously named domestic prelates);

b) protonotaries *ad instar participantium;*

c) titular or honorary protonotaries;

d) domestic prelates;

e) supernumerary privy or papal chamberlains (if they enjoy certain privileges and insignia of prelates).[18]

---

16 All the above named are domestic prelates and members of the papal family. — Sipos, *Enchiridion,* p. 200.

17 These are prelates in the strictly legal sense of canon 110. — Vermeersch-Creusen, *Epitome,* I, 235; Abbo-Hannan, *The Sacred Canons,* I, 163; Larraona, *CpR,* IV (1923), 75, 76.

18 Sipos, *Enchiridion,* p. 201.

From these lists and the general norms, it can be concluded that honorary domestic prelates will yield precedence to true domestic prelates on the basis both of jurisdiction and pre-eminence. In practice, then, an honorary domestic prelate will not take precedence over the vicar general. He will precede both protonotaries titular who are not vicars general,[19] and also papal chamberlains.[20] Commonly, the honorary domestic prelates will be preceded only by the ordinary of the place, by the vicar general, and by other bishops.

SECTION 1–ASSISTANTS AT THE PAPAL THRONE

Bishops received this title as early as the XI century. It was bestowed as a special sign of preference by the Pontiff when he honored some bishops by inviting them to take a place near the throne. This sign of preference was duly noted by the papal master of ceremonies, who then gave these assistants to the throne precedence over others who had not been so honored. Through the years patriarchs received this title *de iure*. At a later time archbishops and bishops also received the honor through a brief. Today the title is conferred by diploma together with various faculties and privileges. These assistants retain their rank even after the death of the pope who appointed them.[21]

Outside of Rome these assistants to the throne do not enjoy any special precedence over others who are not so honored; they take their regular place among the other patriarchs, archbishops, and bishops. It is only as a body, and in Rome (unless the pope is absent) that the college of assistants to the throne has any special right to precedence.[22] Beste further adds the explicit condition that these assistants be in attendance at a papal function in Rome, a fact not mentioned by other com-

---

19 Nabuco, *Ius Pontificalium*, p. 28 .

20 Papal chamberlains, although they enjoy some of the prelatial privileges, are not prelates. — Sipos, *Enchiridion*, p. 201.

21 "College of Patriarchs, Archibishops and Bishops Assistant at the Throne," *Annuario Pontificio* (1959), p. 1156.

22 S.R.C., *Urbe Collegii Episcoporum Assistentium*, 10 sept. 1816 — *D.*, n. 2571; Nabuco, *Ius Pontificalium*, p. 19.

mentators, but surely presupposed.[23] Within this college or body of domestic prelates so honored, the ranks of patriarch, archbishops and bishops are given their proper precedence.[24] Within each rank of archbishop and bishop, the right of precedence is to be based on the date the honor was received rather than on the date of promotion to the episcopacy.[25] When attending the papal functions in Rome, these assistants to the throne go just after the cardinals.[26]

SECTION 2—PROTONOTARIES

Notarii in Urbe were found as early as the III century, when they were engaged as recorders of the acts of the martyrs and of other ecclesiastical acts. By the V century they formed a college, whose head was the *primicerius notariorum.* These recorders at one time lived in common. By the XIV century they appear to be divided into regional protonotaries and the apostolic notaries. By the XV century a distinction was made between those who actually performed the duties of a notary, and those who merely held the title as an honor. This distinction remains today in the *motu proprio* of Pius X and the apostolic constitution of Pius XI.

Four grades of protonotaries are recognized today:

a) protonotaries apostolic *de numero participantium;*
b) supernumerary protonotaries;
c) protonotaries *ad instar;*
d) titular or honorary protonotaries.[27]

A. Protonotaries de numero participantium

These protonotaries constitute the only one of the four grades that forms a college of its own, with just seven members. They collect and care for some of the most important documents of the Church, from consistories, councils, canonization processes

---

23 *Introductio in Codicem, sub canone* 106, 7°.

24 Within the rank of patriarch, the common rules of precedence of patriarchs is to be followed, as given below, p. 263 ff. Cf. Nabuco, *op. cit.*, p. 20.

25 S.R.C., *decr. cit. D.*, n. 2571.

26 Nabuco, *op. cit.*, p. 19. Outside these functions, the prelates *"a flocculis"* come just after the cardinals. — Michiels, *Normae Generales,* II, 206, note 11.

27 "Protonotaries Apostolic," *Annuario Pontificio* (1959), p. 1168; *AI,* n. LIII.

and the like.[28] They take their place immediately before all ecclesiastics below episcopal rank; therefore, they precede all chapters of canons, even in the cathedral, and blessed abbots. They do not precede non-episcopal ordinaries of the place,[29] prelates *"a flocculis,"*[30] assessors or secretaries of the Sacred Roman Congregations,[31] and certain prelates with the title "Most Reverend Excellency."[32]

Even though this type of protonotary is found only in Rome itself, there are prelates in Rome and throughout the Church who enjoy the privileges (not the *right* of precedence)[33] of protonotaries *de numero,* although they are not in fact members of this select college:

a) assessors and secretaries of the Sacred Congregations;[34]

b) auditors of the Sacred Roman Rota;[35]

c) vicars and prefects apostolic who are not consecrated, but only within their own territory and while in this office, according to canon 308;[36]

d) apostolic administrators *"ad tempus dati"* who are not consecrated bishops, whether they are appointed to a diocese, prelacy or abbacy *nullius,* for the time of their assignment and

---

28 *AI,* nos. XXXI-XXXVII.

29 Canon 347.

30 These include the *vice-camerlengo,* the auditor-secretary of the Apostolic Camera, the Treasurer-General of the Apostolic Camera, and the prefect or Majordomo of the Apostolic Palace. — Nabuco, *Ius Pontificalium,* p. 120; cf. *Annuario Pontificio* (1959), pp. 1164, 1166.

31 Even though they are not bishops, the assessors and secretaries of the Congregations, *ratione muneris,* are preceded only by the prelates *"a flocculis"* in the Roman Curia. — *AI,* n. I. They precede even singly all archbishops and bishops with the exception of ordinaries of places in their own territory. — *AI,* n. XIX; Canon 347.

32 In addition to the assessors and secretaries of the Sacred Roman Congregations, these include the *Maestro di Camera,* the Secretary of the Apostolic Signatura, the Dean of the Sacred Roman Rota, and the Substitute Secretary of State. — *AI,* nos. XXI, L.

33 Compare AI nos. XIX and L.

34 *AI,* nos. XVII, XXIX.

35 *AI,* n. LXXIII; cf. n. LXXXI for precedence different from protonotaries *de numero.*

36 *AI,* n. XXX.

within their proper territory, according to canon 315, §2, 2°[37] It is to be noted, however, that the prefects, vicars and administrators apostolic *"ad tempus dati"* enjoy merely the insignia and privileges of the protonotary *de numero participantium.* Precedence is a right; the vicars and prefects apostolic, with the insignia and privileges of protonotaries *de numero,* nevertheless enjoy the rights and obligations of a residential bishop in his own diocese, according to canon 294. §1; therefore the same is true of the rights of the permanent apostolic administrator, according to canon 315, §1. The apostolic administrator *"ad tempus datus"* has the rights (of precedence) of a diocesan administrator, according to canon 315, §2.[38]

B. Supernumerary Protonotaries

The only way anyone becomes a supernumerary protonotary is by being named to one of the chapters of canons to which this special privilege has been given. These are the chapters of three patriarchal basilicas of Rome.[39] These canons have the title of protonotary supernumerary for life. There are other canon prelates of cathedral churches outside of Rome who have the same title as long as they are in office.[40]

In the papal chapels these supernumerary protonotaries take their places just behind the protonotaries *de numero.*[41] Supernumerary protonotaries take precedence over all clerics, priests, canons and dignitaries of chapters, even when these are present *collegialiter* (except the cathedral chapter) even outside the papal chapel.[42] They likewise precede all prelates regular[43]

---

37 *AI,* n. XXX.

38 The diocesan administrator has the *"iura honorifica"* of the vicar general as mentioned in canon 370. — canon 439 (cf. infra, pp. 275 ff.). The *index analytico-alphabeticus* of Cardinal Gasparri uses the term *"iura honorifica;"* the canons do not use the term.

39 St. Peter, St. John Lateran, and St. Mary Major — *AI,* n. LIV.

40 The Cathedrals of Concordia, Florence, Gorizia, Palermo (also the Palatine Chapel), Padua, Treviso, Udine, and Venice. — *AI,* n. LIV; cf. Coronata, *Institutiones,* V (3 ed.; Taurini-Romae: Marietti, 1951), p. 198, note 1.

41 *AI,* n. XX.

42 *IM,* n. 13.

43 This includes any religious superior with ordinary jurisdiction *in foro*

who do not enjoy the use of the *pontificalia.* Supernumerary protonotaries do not precede vicars general, vicars capitular, or abbots.[44]

C. *Protonotaries* ad instar participantium

Of this type of protonotaries, there are four groups. The canons of some collegiate chapters *(durante munere tantum)* have been given the title;[45] It has also been granted to former assessors and secretaries of the Sacred Congregations, for life.[46] Former protonotaries *de numero,* after they have left their office, unless they have been advanced to a position which is incompatible with the title of protonotary, become *ad instar* protonotaries.[47]

Finally, the Roman Pontiff may decorate some individual clerics with this title personally by means of a brief. These protonotaries are created for life. They are also counted among the domestic prelates, either because they had been previously elected to that honor, or because they are now elected in virtue of their nomination as protonotaries.[48]

Pronotaries *ad instar* have the same precedence as the supernumerary protonotaries mentioned above. In the papal chapel

---

externo. Cf. cc. 501, § 1; 875, § 1; 1313, 2°; 1320, 1338, § 1. — Larraona, "Commentarium Codicis," *CpR,* IV (1923), 76.

44 *AI,* n. LV, directs that the norms of *IM* are to be followed; they are given in *IM,* n. 21.

45 St. Mary of the Martyrs in Rome, the Cathedrals of Bologna, Caliari, Malta, Modena, and Esztergom. — Coronata, *op cit.,* p. 198, note 3.

46 Upon their leaving office, unless they are advanced to some other honor which is incompatible with the title of protonotary, they *ipso iure,* became protonotaries *ad instar* with all the rights and privileges attached to this title. — *AI,* n. XX.

47 If they have served as protonotaries *de numero* for at least ten years, they retain all the rights and privileges thereof for five years more after their retirement. After these five years, they become protonotaries *ad instar* for life, *ipso iure.* If they have been *de numero* protonotaries less than ten years, they become protonotaries *ad instar* immediately upon retirement. If, by special favor, they are declared *emeriti,* they retain all the privileges of protonotaries *de numero,* but not their rights. — *AI,* n. LVI, citing nos. XX and XXVIII.

48 Nabuco, *op. cit.,* p. 25; cf. "Domestic Prelates," *Annuario Pontificio* (1959), p. 1221.

all protonotaries, except those who are merely titular or honorary, form one body and proceed as one body.[49]

This is the only type of protonotaries in the United States, besides the titular protonotary who is such because he is also vicar general or diocesan administrator.

D. *Titular or Honorary Protonotaries*

These protonotaries are priests who were chosen for the honor either by an apostolic nuncio or by the College of Protonotaries *de numero*.[50] The Code gives this title of honor with its insignia and privileges to the vicar general and the vicar capitular if they do not already have some higher title of honor.[51] This title, too, is sometimes given to the members of chapters of canons. Titular protonotaries all are prelates residing outside of Rome, but they are not members of the papal family. Nabuco states that these titular or honorary protonotaries have nothing in common with the other types of protonotaries. He would prefer to call them titular prelates outside of Rome.[52]

In processions titular protonotaries take their place immediately after the domestic prelates (since titular protonotaries are not in themselves [*per se*] of the rank), unless they are vicars general or capitular;[53] as vicar general or diocesan administrator, a titular protonotary would precede all the other clergy of the diocese who are not bishops, including supernumerary protonotaries, domestic prelates and papal chamberlains. By their honorary title, other titular protonotaries also precede the canons of collegiate chapters who are present singly. They do not precede superiors general of Regulars, or abbots, or prelates of the Roman curia.[54]

If the titular protonotary is also a domestic prelate, as may happen in the case of a vicar general or vicar capitular (diocesan administrator), the two honors can be reconciled; the vicar general or vicar capitular will wear the purple garb of the

49 *IM*, n. 57.

50 Once each year this college is entitled to name one titular or honorary protonotary according to an old tradition recognized in *AI*, n. XXXVIII.

51 Canons 370, § 2; 439. *AI*, n. LVIII.

52 *Ius Pontificalium*, p. 27.

53 Nabuco, *op. cit.*, p. 28.

54 *IM*, n. 66.

domestic prelate. If, however, the titular protonotary is a privy (papal) chamberlain, he may not use the purple cassock and *mantellone;* he should wear the black prelatial habit which is proper to the titular protonotary.[55] This seems to imply that the rank of titular protonotary is higher than that of the privy or papal chamberlain. In the absence of any other criteria, a titular protonotary would precede a papal chamberlain.

If any titular protonotary should leave the position to which this honor is attached, he automatically loses the honorary title, along with its accompanying privileges and rights.[56]

Article 2. Supernumerary Privy Chamberlains of His Holiness

There remains one other group of the papal family which is of practical interest in this country: the *cubicularii intimi seu secreti,* otherwise known as privy or papal chamberlains. These chamberlains of the papal household are divided into lay and clerical groups.[57]

The supernumerary chamberlains are appointed through a *biglietto* from the Secretariat of State; these chamberlains lose their office (or honorary title) at the death of the pope. The original appointment requires confirmation from the new Pontiff. Aside from this difference, the privileges and rights of all chamberlains are the same.[58]

In processions they come after the domestic prelates and titular protonotaries.[59]

---

55 Nabuco, *loc. cit.*

56 *IM,* n. 76.

57 The lay chamberlains include participating privy chamberlains of sword and cape, *de numero* and supernumerary privy chamberlains of sword and cape, and *de numero* and supernumerary honorary privy chamberlains of sword and cape.

The clerical chamberlains include the eight participating privy chamberlains, the supernumerary privy chamberlains, the honorary chamberlains, and the honorary chamberlains outside the City. — Nabuco, *op. cit.,* pp. 34-35; cf. *Annuario Pontificio* (1959), pp. 1211, 1230, 1235, 1239, 1240.

58 Nabuco, *op. cit.,* p. 35.

59 Canon 106, 3°. The privy chamberlains are listed after the domestic prelates in the arrangement of the *Annuario Pontifico.* One might also argue from the fact that the prefect of the College of Masters of Pontifical Cere-

Article 3. The Precedence of the Prelates of the Roman Curia

In brief, the precedence of the members of the Roman Curia is as follows:

a) cardinal-bishops of the sub-urbicarian sees;

b) cardinal-priests;

c) cardinal-deacons, (with all in each of these two classes according to the order of their creation in consistory);

d) (in the papal chapels) the college of assistants to the papal throne:

- i. patriarchal assistants, in the order commonly followed among the patriarchs;
- ii. archiepiscopal assistants, and
- iii. episcopal assistants, in the order in which they were named to the college;

e) prelates "*a flocculis*":

- i. *vice-camerlengo;*
- ii. auditor general of the Apostolic Camera;
- iii. treasurer general of the Apostolic Camera;
- iv. prefect of the Apostolic Palace;

f) assessors and secretaries of each Congregation, in the order observed among the Congregations;

g) the five prelates considered equal with assessors or secretaries of the Congregations;

h) archbishops and bishops (including those who are assistants to the papal throne. if the function takes place outside a papal chapel) in the order of their promotion to the rank of archbishop or bishop;

i) college of protonotaries *de numero*;

j) abbots general, or generals of religious orders;

k) the college of auditors of the Sacred Roman Rota;

l) the college of the Clerics of the Apostolic Camera;

m) the college of Prelates of the Apostolic Signature together with the Prelates *Referendarii* of the same college.[60]

---

monies is a domestic prelate; all other members of this college are papal chamberlains. — *Annuario Pontificio* (1959), p. 1230.

60 Nabuco, *op. cit.*, pp. 38-39; *AI*, n. I, lists (i) to (m) in the above precedence also.

CHAPTER XI

THE SPECIAL NORMS OF PRECEDENCE ALLUDED TO IN CANON 106

Canon 106. *Circa praecedentiam inter varias personas seu physicas seu morales, serventur normae quae sequuntur, salvis normis specialibus, quae suis in locis traduntur.*

Gasparri's analytico-alphabetical index to the Code of Canon Law lists no fewer than fifteen special norms of precedence for various persons in the Church. Most of these have been discussed briefly in the earlier sections. Some of them require more detailed treatment for the sake of clarity and unity. The following were treated in some detail at the given places:

a) archbishops and bishops, pp. 133-34; 115; 230;
b) pastors and vicars, pp. 232-35;
c) the secular clergy, pp. 186-92;
d) religious, pp. 155-222.

Lay associations of the faithful, lay patrons and cathedral chapters do not form a part of this study. The special norms of the following will be discussed in this chapter: cardinals, papal legates, patriarchs, primates, bishops in their own dioceses, the vicar general and the diocesan administrator, and the vicar forane.

Article 1. The Sacred College of Cardinals

Canon 239, §1, 21°. *Praeter alia privilegia quae in hoc Codice suis in titulis enumerantur, Cardinales omnes a sua promotione in Consistorio facultate gaudent: . . . Praecedendi omnibus Praelatis etiam Patriarchis, imo ipsis Legatis Pontificiis, nisi Legatus sit Cardinalis in proprio territorio residens; Cardinalis autem Legatus a latere praecedit extra Urbem omnibus aliis.*

The Sacred College of Cardinals as it exists today is the result of several facets of historical development. Originally the cardinals were the priests or deacons of Rome, plus the seven suburbicarian bishops. They all served as counsellors to the pope. After 1150 they formed a college, with the Bishop of Ostia as their dean.[1] They were made the exclusive electors of the pope in 1179. About the same time it became the practice to select even prelates residing outside of Rome for membership in the college. From this time also cardinals began to have precedence over bishops and archbishops. Two reasons were given: the cardinals were the papal electors; frequently, too, they were the pope's legates to councils and other occasions. As legates they were given the same honor as their principal, the Roman Pontiff. This developed into a rather common acknowledgement of the position of cardinal itself, even outside of a council or aside from his role as legate.[2] In the fifteenth century their traditional precedence over patriarchs was confirmed by Pope Eugene V in the bull *Non mediocri.*[3]

The number of members in the college has varied considerably through the centuries. Under Pope Honorius II (1124-1130) there were in 1125 only fifty cardinals. Boniface VIII (1294-1303) had only twenty in his college. It was Paul IV (1555-59) who first brought the membership of the college up to the number of seventy. He later increased this number to seventy-six. It was the decision of Paul V (1605-21) to limit the college to seventy after the example of the seventy elders elected by Moses.[4] The full number of the Sacred College remained at seventy until 1958, when Pope John XXIII named twenty-three new cardinals. This brought the number to seventy-five. Before the Consistory took place on December 15, however, the Cardinal-Primate of Chile had died, leaving the college with only seventy-four members. With appointment of additional members in December, 1959, and February, 1960, the Sacred College reached a record-breaking total of eighty-five members.

SECTION 1–THE DIVISION OF THE COLLEGE OF CARDINALS

Canon 231, §1. *Sacrum Collegium in tres ordines distribuitur: episcopalem, ad quem soli pertinent sex cardinales dioecesibus*

---

1 "The Sacred College of Cardinals," *Annuario Pontificio* (1959), p. 36; Rupprecht, *Notae Historicae universi Iuris Canonici,* tit. xxxiii, *de majoritate et obedientia,* n. 9.

2 Petra, *Commentaria,* I, 89.

3 Anno 1439 — *Fontes,* n. 50; *Bull. Lux.,* I, 332.

4 Verano, *Iuris Canonici Universi Commentarius Paratitlaris,* I, *de majoritate et obedienta,* § *XIII, de majoritate cardinalium,* n. 2.

suburbicariis praepositi; presbyteralem, qui constat Cardinalibus quinquaginta; diaconalem, qui quatuordecim.

The entire college of cardinals is ordinarily considered to be one of the grades or ranks in the Church for which precedence can be determined according to the norms of canon 106, 3°: he who belongs to the higher rank precedes him who belongs to the lower rank. It is commonly agreed today that because of the important role the college plays in the election of the pope and in the ruling of the Church, there is no higher rank in the Church than that of cardinal. Within this grade, howere, there are various degrees of higher or lower ranks of importance commonly referred to as orders, as the above quoted canon indicates: the orders of cardinal-bishop, cardinal-priest, and cardinal-deacon.

The cardinal-bishops are the six cardinals who are the ordinaries of the seven suburbicarian Sees of Rome.[5] By the very nature of their office as ordinaries, these cardinals are *de facto* bishops. The cardinal-priests are traditionally bishops also (not cardinal-bishops, but bishops who are cardinals).[6] This tradition was evidenced very clearly when Monsignor Tardini was named titular archbishop the day before his name was to be published in the consistory of December 15, 1958, as a cardinal-priest.[7] Besides being consecrated bishops, cardinal- priests are often ordinaries of dioceses throughout the world. It is within this order that the universal representation of the Church is best accomplished in the college.

The cardinal-deacons are, at least in the present day, almost always priests; they are never bishops.[8]

SECTION 2—THE CREATION OF CARDINALS

In view of canon 239, §1, which grants the special faculties (including precedence) of cardinals only from the time of their

---

5 Ostia (which is always joined with the See held by the dean of the college), Albano, Frascati, Palestrina, Porto and Santa Rufina, Sabina and Poggio Mirteto, and Velletri. — *Annuario Pontificio* (1959), p. 76.

6 Vito, *Note Canoniche Sulla Precedenza,* p. 15.

7 Cf. *Annuario Pontificio* (1959), p. 71.

8 Vito, *loc. cit.*

creation or promotion in consistory, it is important to determine this moment. For upon it, in most cases, depends the precedence of the cardinals.

Cardinals are created and published by the pope in consistory; from this moment of publication they enjoy all the rights and privileges of cardinals. The bestowal of the red hat and other ceremonies are of no consequence as regards these privileges and rights. There is an exception, however.

It is possible for the Roman Pontiff to create a cardinal outside of consistory, since it is the pope's will alone that makes a cardinal. The law requires, for juridic purposes, that a public pronouncement be made, so that it may known who has the rights and privileges. Therefore, it is possible to have a cardinal created not in consistory, but "*in petto*," or "*in pectore*" some time before a consistory is called. He may not exercise his new rights and privileges until he is announced in the consistory, however, oncee he has been announced, he may use the date of creation "*in pectore*" to determine his preecedence.[9]

SECTION 3—THE PRIVILEGE OF OPTION FOR CARDINALS

When cardinals are first created in consistory, it is the expression of the will of the pope alone. Such cardinals will ordinarily belong either to the order of cardinal-priest or cardinal-deacon.[10] The law provides that the curial cardinal deacon or cardinal priest may request that he be transferred to a different titular church, or that he be advanced to a higher order in the college under certain conditions: this is the privilege of option.[11] Cardinal-deasons then have the right of option to the rank of cardinal-priest; certain cardinal-priests may make an option to the rank of cardinal-bishop.

---

9 Canon 233, § 2.

10 Wernz-Vidal, *Ius Canonicum*, II, n. 471.

11 Canon 236. The Code specifically requires a curial position only for option to a suburbicarian see in canon 236, § 3. Coronata, however, extends this requirement to the option to the rank of cardinal-priest also. — *Institutiones*, I, n. 323. In view of the present practice of naming only curial cardinals as cardinal-deacons, this requirement is obvious and superfluous. [Wernz-Vidal (*Ius Canonicum*, II, n. 471) extend the right of option to a different titular church to non-curial cardinals.]

The option on a different titular church is not of particular interest here. The right to take an option on a higher rank will affect precedence, however.

After a cardinal-deacon has been in that Order for ten years, or less by special concession of the Roman Pontiff,[12] the law gives him the right of option to the rank of cardinal-priest, with the approval of the pope.[13] If more than one cardinal-deacon qualifies for this option, priority of promotion to the rank of cardinal-deacon will be the decisive factor.[14]

If the Roman Pontiff approves this option, the fact is announced in consistory. At that moment the former cardinal-deacon becomes a cardinal-priest. He takes his precedence with the other cardinal-priests according to the date he was first made a cardinal-deacon, not from the date he was promoted to the rank of cardinal-priest.[15] In this way the cardinal-deacon who becomes a cardinal-priest precedes all other cardinal-priests who were named to the Sacred College after his original nomination as a cardinal-deacon. Other cardinal-deacons who had been his seniors by promotion to the college and had transferred to the rank of cardinal-priest before him, would still have precedence over him according to the original date of first promition to the rank of cardinal. Basically, the law determines that the difference in matters of precedence arises not from the fact that the individual was named to the rank of cardinal-priest, but from the fact that he was named a cardinal, i.e., a member of the Sacred College in the rank either of deacon or of priest.

Cardinal-priests who are present in the Roman curia, or absent from it only because of a special assignment from the pope, have the right of option when one of the suburbicarian sees becomes vacant. The law provides no time period, such as the ten years for cardinal-deacons. Here, too, if more than one cardinal-priest is eligible for the right of option, the priority of promotion to the college will determine who may use the

12 Wernz-Vidal, *loc. cit.*

13 From what has been said above, this seems also to imply nomination as a titular bishop by the pope.

14 Canon 236, § 1.

15 Canon 236. The same is true if the privilege of option was used before ten years elapsed. — PCI, 29 maii 1934 — *AAS,* XXVI (1924), 493.

right.[16] When the cardinal-priest has taken such an option, and, with the approval of the Roman Pontiff, is announced in consistory, he becomes a cardinal-bishop His precedence within this rank will be determined according to the norms for cardinal-bishops discussed below.

Cardinal-bishops have no right of option to transfer from one suburbicarian see to another. However, the cardinal-bishop who becomes dean according to canon 237, §1, will add to his own see that of Ostia.[17]

SECTION 4–THE PRECEDENCE OF CARDINALS AMONG THEMSELVES

Following the norms of canon 106, 3°, the cardinal-bishops precede the cardinal-priests, who in turn precede the cardinal-deacons. Within each order, the precedence is determined as follows:

a) Cardinal-bishops determine their priority from the date of their promotion to the rank of cardinal-bishop, as ordinary of the suburbicarian see. This norm is clear in the law for determining the senior cardinal-bishop for the rank of dean of the Sacred College; it is also implied as the norm for the selection of the sub-dean.[18] In addition, it appears, from the order in which they are listed in the *Annuario Pontificio,* to be the curial practice for all other cardinal-bishops. There is a note to that effect on the first page of the list in the *Annuario Pontificio: "L'anzianità degli Emi et Rmi Signori Cardinali Vescovi dipende dalla data della loro opzione alla sede suburbicaria."*[19] This is in keeping with the general norm of precedence for bishops, as explained above.[20]

b) Cardinal-priests, even those who have used the right of option to be transferred from the order of cardinal-deacon, determine their precedence from the date they were named to the College of Cardinals, as either priests or deacons.[21]

---

16 Canon 236, § 3.

17 Canon 236, § 4.

18 Canon 237; cf. Wernz-Vidal, *Ius Canonicum,* II, n. 468.

19 Page 39 (1959 edition); cf. Coronata, *Institutiones,* I, n. 323; Hynes, *The Privileges of Cardinals,* p. 35 .

20 Pages 142-43.

21 Canon 239, § 1; canon 236, § 2.

c) Cardinal-deacons determine their precedence among themselves from the date of their promotion to the College of Cardinals also.[22]

Cardinals are anywhere preceded only by a cardinal legate *a latere,* by any other cardinal legate in his own territory,[23] by another cardinal of a higher order, within the same order by a cardinal of greater seniority in the college, or by a cardinal of the same order in his own territory if the latter is a residential bishop.

In or outside of Rome, Cardinals precede all others of any rank or rite, with a due observance of the norms of their mutual precedence as stated above. It appears to the present writer that, by analogy with the cardinal legate in his own territory, and with the ordinary in his own diocese, a cardinal-priest who is a residential bishop would be preceded in his own diocese only by a cardinal-bishop, not by another cardinal-priest, even if the latter had greater seniority in the college, and certainly not by a cardinal-deacon.[24] By force of canon 106, 1°, the cardinal-priest who is a residential bishop would also have to yield to a cardinal legate, either *a latere* or otherwise, if the latter were in his own territory.[25]

To put these conclusions into schematic form would result in the following arrangement:

a) cardinal legate *a latere;*

b) cardinal legate in his own territory;

c) cardinal-bishop in his own territory;

d) cardinal-bishop, dean of the College;

e) cardinal-bishop, sub-dean;

f) other cardinal-bishops, according to the time of their promotion to their suburbicarian sees;

g) cardinal-priest, ordinary of the place in his territory;

h) other cardinal-priests, in the order of their entry into the college of cardinals;

i) cardinal deacons, in the same order.

---

22 Canon 239, § 1.

23 Canon 239, § 1, 21°; canon 106, 1°.

24 Canon 347.

25 Canon 239, § 1, 21°; canon 347.

ARTICLE 2. THE PRECEDENCE OF PAPAL LEGATES

Canon 239, §1, 21. *Praeter alia privilegia quae in hoc Codice suis in titulis enumerantur, Cardinales omnes a sua promotione in Consistorio facultate gaudent: . . . Praecedendi omnibus Praelatis etiam Patriarchis, imo ipsis Legatis Pontificiis, nisi Legatus sit Cardinalis in proprio territorio residens; Cardinalis autem Legatus a latere praecedit extra Urbem omnibus aliis. . .*

Canon 269, §2. [*Legati*] *licet forte charactere episcopali careant, praecedunt tamen omnibus Ordinariis qui non sint cardinalitia dignitate insigniti.*

Even from the very earliest times the Roman Pontiffs were represented in councils and on other important occasions by their legates, This assignment as representative of the Roman Pontiff came to be filled more frequently by cardinals, who were at first called *"de latere."* Some residential archbishops were given a permanent assignment as a representative and were called *"legati nati."* If there was some special matter, often of minor importance, the representative was called a *"nuntius."* By the XVI century nunciatures were established on a more permanent basis, and nuncios were accredited to a kingdom, a republic, or some other form of state with duties similar to those of the legates *a latere*. The latter were then reserved for most unusual cases. The permanent nuncios were often given judicial authority to handle certain degrees of appeal, and were empowered to handle political affairs.[26]

When a nunciature was vacant because of some longlasting impediment of the incumbent, the person who replaced him was called an internuncio. It will be seen below that the nature of these legates is somewhat changed at the present time.

SECTION 1–THE PRECEDENCE OF LEGATES *A LATERE*

These legates *a latere* are the highest form of personal representative the pope can send.[27] As such they are honored as if they were the pope himself. On this same basis they have

---

26 "Apostolic Nuncios and Internuncios and Envoys Extraordinary of the Holy See," *Annuario Pontificio* (1959), pp. 1090-91.

27 Canon 266.

precedence, according to canon 106, 1°, over everyone else in the Church when they are actng as legates *a latere*.[28]

These legates are cardinals, as canon 239, §1, 21°, states. Ordinarily they are created as legates in a consistory. Sometimes they are created while they are in the country where they will carry out their mission. They are then excused from coming to Rome.[29] If they are created in consistory, their special privileges do not become effective until they are away from the side *(a latere)* of the Pontiff. This is a reasonable interpretation of the rule governing all proxies, namely that they have no authority when the principal is present. Therefore, only after they leave Rome itself do these legates enjoy their special privileges. In Rome they take their precedence as cardinals among the other cardinals according to the norms proper to their rank and order.

Outside of Rome the norms of canon 239, §1, 21°, are very simple to apply: cardnal legates *a latere* precede everyone anywhere on any occasion, just as the pope himself would. They precede even other cardinals who may be of a higher order or of greater seniority of promotion to their rank or order. There are no exceptions to this rule of precedence.

SECTION 2—THE PRECEDENCE OF *LEGATI MISSI*

The second class of legates of the Roman Pontiff are called *legati missi* in contradistinction to the third class, known as the *legati nati*. The former are sent from the pope; at the present, the latter are residential bishops of such privileged sees as Prague and Lyons,[30] who have merely the honorary title of legate. They become legates by the very fact of their appointment to their sees. These *legati nati* do not derive any particular rights from their title, either in matters of precedence, or otherwise. The *legatus natus* of Esztergom, Hungary, is an exception.[31]

---

28 Canon 239, § 1, 21°; cf. Nabuco, *Ius Pontificalium,* p. 15.

29 Nabuco, *ibid.,* p. 12.

30 Vito, *Note Canoniche sulla Precedenza,* p. 14, note 1.

31 Canon 270; cf. *infra,* p. 267; cf. Vermeersch-Creusen, *Epitome,* I, n. 386.

The *legati missi*, however, play a very important role in the relations of the Apostolic See with countries throughout the world. Canon 265 recognizes the pope's power to send such delegates, with or without ecclesiastical jurisdiction, with or without diplomatic powers and privileges.

A. Apostolic Nuncios

These delegates of the Pontiff, in addition to their ecclesiastical function, have a diplomatic mission as ambassador to the civil government to which they are sent.[32] By the terms of the Congress of Vienna (1815), these nuncios are the deans of the diplomatic corps accredited to the government to which they are sent.[33] When this right is not extended to them, the Holy See will not send a legate or a nuncio.[34]

B. Apostolic Internuncios

In addition to their ecclesiastical function, the internuncios also have a diplomatic mission. Wernz-Vidal compare nuncios and internuncios to ministers first and second class in diplomatic circles. The *Annuario Pontificio* states that the internuncio has the rank of a Minister Plenipotentiary.[35] Internuncios are commonly sent to non-Catholic countries or countries of lesser importance.[36]

C. Apostolic Delegates

Apostolic delegates are representatives of the pope who do not have the diplomatic status of the legates mentioned above. They are merely to watch over ecclesiastical affairs and keep the Roman Pontiff informed. The title "apostolic delegate" was definitely clarified in the communique of the Secretary of State

---

32 Vermeersch-Creusen, *ibid.*, n. 387.

33 Acts of the Congress of Vienna (1815), Art. IV, Appendix XVII, cited by Nabuco, *Ius Pontificalium*, p. 17, note 18.

34 "Id etiam explicat cur gubernium anglicum, quod suum legatum conservat apud Sanctam Sedem, nuntium apostolicum tamen non recipit ex eo quod ipsi praecedentiam dare noluit." — Nabuco, *loc. cit.* Note, however, that England has had an apostolic delegate since 1938. — *Annuario Pontificio* (1959), p. 1101.

35 *Ius Canonicum*, II, n. 515; 1959 Ed., p. 1091.

36 Vermersch-Creusen, *loc. cit.*

on May 9, 1916, which confers this title on papal representatives who are without diplomatic status.[37]

D. Precedence

Most of the apostolic nuncios prior to 1957 were at least titular archbishops or bishiops.[38] Since that time, however, and beginning with the appointment of the internuncio to Ethiopia, both nuncios and internuncios have been appointed who were not archbishops or bishops: nine of them are only domestic prelates.[39] If they are not consecrated, they have the privileges of a protonotary apostolic, but their precedence remains the same as that of other *legati missi*.[40] By reason of the person they represent, they precede all ordinaries of the place or metropolitans, unless either of these is a cardinal, and the legate or nuncio is not. If the legate is a cardinal, he precedes everyone in his territory except a cardinal legate *a latere*.[41]

A procession would find the hierarchy around the legate arranged in this order:

a) the cardinal legate *a latere* (outside Rome);

b) the cardinal legate in his own territory;

c) the cardinal ordinary of the place (if there is one);

d) the patriarch in his own territory at ceremonies or divine offices proper to his own rite, unless the legate has an explicit mandate granting him precedence;[42]

e) the apostolic nuncio, internuncio, or delegate (if he is not a cardinal, and even if not a bishop);

f) the patriarch other than in his own territory or at a service conducted in a rite different from his own;

g) the primates;

h) the metropolitan in his own territory;

i) the ordinary of the place in his own territory

---

37 Ex Audientia SSmi die 8 maii 1916 — *AAS*, VIII (1916), 213.

38 Nabuco, *Ius Pontificalium*, p. 14; Wernz-Vidal, *Ius Canonicum*, II, n. 515.

39 *Annuario Pontificio* (1959), pp. 1093-99.

40 Canon 269, § 2.

41 Canon 239, § 1, 21°.

42 Cf. discussion about patriarchs below, p. 263, ff. for explanation.

j) In the United States, the archbishop of Baltimore;[43]
k) the other archbishops in the order of their promotion, and
l) the other bishops in the order of their promotion.

Article 3. The Precedence of Patriarchs

Canon 271. *Patriarchae aut Primatis titulus, praeter praerogativam honoris et ius praecedentiae ad normam Can. 280, nullam secumfert specialem iurisdictionem, nisi iure particulari de aliquibus aliud constet.*

Canon 280. *Patriarcha praecedit Primati, Primas Archiepiscopo, hic Episcopis, salvo praescripto can. 374.*

The Latin Code gives very little to guide the determination of precedence for patriarchs. Canon 271 merely states that the Latin patriarchs have no jurisdiction unless particular law provides otherwise;[44] they have only the prerogative of honor and the right of precedence according to canon 280. This canon gives to patriarchs a right of precedence over all primates, archbishops and bishops, even the ordinaries of places in their own territories.[45] Canon 239, §1, 21°, indicates that patriarchs are preceded by cardinals.

These norms indicate that the patriarch has a rank or grade. The general norms of canon 106, 3°, require accordingly that

---

43 Cf. *infra*, p. 268 ff., for discussion of the precedence of the Archbishop of Baltimore.

44 The Latin patriarchs of Jerusalem and Alexandria are only Western patriarchs with jurisdiction, and not merely a title. — A. Coussa, *Praelectiones in Librum Secundum Codicis Iuris Canonici de Personis, de Clericis in Specie* (Typis Monasterii Exarchici Cryptoferratensis, 1953), n. 157; cf. Pius IX, const. *Nulla celebrior*, 23, iulii 1847 — *Pii IX Pontificis Maximi Acta,* (7 vols. in 9, Vol. I, part 1; Roma, 1857) p. 59; cf. also Wernz-Vidal, *Ius Canonicum,* II, n. 517.

45 Blat comes to this conclusion with this line of reasoning: Although the fact that canon 347 does not make an exception for patriarchs or primates, and inasmuch as the term "archbishop" in that canon does not include patriarchs or primates, the ordinary of the place must yield to either of them. They are not included in the term "archbishop," because canon 280 gives the three of them (patriarch, primate and archbishop) different rights of precedence. The phrase ". . . *salvo praescripto can. 347* . . ." must be understood as limiting only the last phrase of canon 280, . . . *hic* [*Archiepiscopus*] *Episcopis, salvo prescripto can. 347*. . . ." — *Commentarium,* II, 314.

precedence among patriarchs (who are of the same grade or rank) be determined by the prior promotion to that rank. In view of the small number of patriarchs in the Latin rite (six), it is not likely that any two of them have been promoted to that rank on the same day. If they have been thus promoted, the norms of canon 106, 3°, seem to supply the distinguishing norm: two people promoted to the same rank on the same day determine their precedence according to the priority of ordination. However, this norm of prior ordination (consecration) is not used in the case of bishops, and it appears from the laws of the Oriental Code that it should not be used for patriarchs either. Canon 219 of *Cleri sanctitati*[46] determines that, after promotion to rank, the next criterion should be the personal seniority or age of the patriarch. It may happen, as at a general council, that patriarchs of both Oriental and Latin rites will attend. In such a case it seems that both may determine their precedence according to the same norms, i.e., by using the factor of age as the secondary criterion. The more detailed norms of precedence of patriarchs of the Oriental rites will be discussed briefly here with a view to determining if these norms of patriarchal precedence can be considered interritual law.

In his own church or anywhere else in the performance of services in his own rite, the Oriental patriarch of that rite has precedence over all other patriarchs,[47] and even over a papal legate (who is not *a latere* or a cardinal)[48] unless the legate (even if not a bishop) has an explicit mandate from the pope giving him precedence over the patriarch in specific conditions.[49]

At first this exceptional norm could seem to apply to the patriarchs of the Latin rite, at least to the jurisdictional patriarch of Jerusalem, for he most closely resembles the jurisdictional Oriental patriarchs.[50] But to give the Latin titular patriarchs

46 Pius XII, *motu proprio,* 2 iunii 1957 — *AAS,* XLIX (1957), 433 ff.

47 *Cleri sanctitati,* canon 219, § 3, 1°. — *Loc. cit.*

48 Canon 239, § 1, 21°; *Cleri sanctitati,* canon 185, § 1, 21°.

49 This was an official interpretation of the Oriental canon 215, § 2, of *Cleri sanctitati,* given by the Code Commision, June 23, 1958 — *AAS,* L (1958), 550.

50 *Cleri sanctitati,* canon 216. — *Loc. cit.*

this special precedence appears to derogate from the Latin Code's provision for legates of the Roman Pontiff.[51] The response of the Oriental Code Commission based its interpretation of the Oriental Norm on the fact that the original Oriental canon gave precedence to the legate over all hierarchs. The Oriental patriarch is explicitly not a hierarch.[52] On the other hand, the Latin Code gives legates precedence over all ordinaries who are not cardinals, and the patriarchs of the Latin Church are commonly ordinaries because they are residential bishops.[53] For this reason, the Latin patriarchs appear to have an obligation to yield precedence to the legate.[54]

The second norm given for the precedence of patriarchs in the Oriental legislation is the presence or absence of patriarchal jurisdiction: jurisdictional patriarchs precede titular patriarchs.[55] This norm clearly points to the interritual nature of this particular section of the Oriental canon for the precedence of patriarchs; for all Oriental patriarchs have jurisdiction.[56] To speak of titular patriarchs, therefore, is to speak of the patriarchs of the Latin rite. To include the Latin patriarchs in one norm would seem to warrant including them in other norms for patriarchal precedence. Yet the legislator in canon 219 of the Oriental legislation explicitly states twice that the norms are ". . . *inter antiquas patriarchales* orientis *sedes* . . ." and ". . . *inter* hos *patriarchas* . . ." and "*Inter ceteros* orientis *Patriarchas*. . . ."[57]

The third section of canon 219 clarifies the point, however, by referring to "*Patriarcha omnis* . . ." in a definite departure from the explicit references to Oriental patriarchs in the first

---

51 He precedes all ordinaries who are not cardinals. — Canon 269, § 2.

52 Compare canon 215, § 2, of *Cleri sanctitati* and canon 306, § 4, of Pius XII, *motu proprio, Postquam apostolicis litteris,* 9 febr. 1952 — *AAS,* XLIV (1952), 65 ff.

53 Canon 198, § 1.

54 Canon 269, § 2.

55 *Cleri sanctitati,* canon 219, § 3, 2° — *Loc. cit.*

56 *Ibid.,* canon 216. Cappello (*Summa Iuris Canonici,* I, 335, note 9) and Beste (*Introductio in Codicem, sub canone* 271) state that the Latin patriarchs of Jerusalem and Alexandria are both jurisdictional patriarchs.

57 Sections 1 and 2 of canon 219 of *Cleri sanctitati.*

two sections. It is only in this section that Latin patriarchs seem to be clearly included. The present writer maintains that this is the only part of the Oriental norms for patriarchal precedence which can be considered interritual. Even a Latin titular patriarch, therefore, in his own church or in divine services in his own rite, precedes all other patriarchs, even if the others are jurisdictional or from one of the four privileged Sees of Constantinople, Alexandria, Antioch or Jerusalem, or enjoy prior promotion to their rank.

To distinguish patriarchs as jurisdictional and titular, as canon 219 does, is to create two groups. Within either of these groups the following norm is the next criterion for Oriental patriarchs: among the jurisdictional patriarchs, those of the four privileged sees will precede all other jurisdictional patriarchs, and in the order named above.[58] Within the rank of titular (Latin) patriarchs the same norm is to be applied, but not because of the Oriental Code. The same norm was established for the Latin patriarchs of these four sees by the IV General Council of the Lateran (1215).[59]

Other jurisdictional or titular patriarchs in each group will follow these four privileged patriarchs according to the order of their promotion to the rank of patriarch. If this does not provide sufficient criteria, the seniority or age of each Oriental patriarch will next determine his precedence.[60]

Schematically, these norms will determine the precedence of patriarchs in this order:

a) a patriarch (jurisdictional or titular, Latin or Oriental) in his own territory or in services of his own rite;

b) jurisdictional patriarchs (within each group, according to the date of promotion):

(i) Constantinople (all Oriental);
(ii) Alexandria (Oriental and Latin);
(iii) Antioch (all Oriental);
(iv) Jerusalem (Oriental and Latin);

58 *Cleri sanctitati,* canon 219, § 1, 1°.

59 Canon 5 — Schroeder, *Disciplinary Decrees of the General Councils,* p. 246.

60 *Cleri sanctitati,* canon 219, § 1, 2°.

c) jurisdictional patriarchs of other sees, in the order of their promotion to that see, then according to age;

d) titular patriarchs, first in the order of the four privileged sees, then followed by all others in the order of their priority of promotion, and finally according to their age.[61]

Article 4. The Precedence of Primates

Canon 280. *Patriarcha praecedit Primati, Primas Archiepiscopo, hic Episcopis, salvo praescripto can. 347.*

Primates are metropolitan archbishops whose sees were the first of a particular region or nation. They are, therefore, the oldest sees in the given territory. The title of primate is either conferred by the Apostolic See, or confirmed by it when from time immemorial the see has been considered and called primatial.[62]

In the present-day law, a primate has only a prerogative of honor and his special precedence as a result of his title.[63] Some primates are also given the title of *legati nati* to the Apostolic See. The Primate of Esztergom (Strigonia), Hungary (at the present time Cardinal Mindszenty) is the only one to have any special jurisdiction because of his primacy; he is the only Latin primate *de iure* and *de facto*.[64]

Canon 280 permits patriarchs to precede primates, and primates to precede archbishops. Archbishops, in turn, precede bishops, with due regard for canon 347, which grants special precedence to ordinaries of places when they are in their own territories. In this matter of the precedence of a primate (or a patriarch) over the local ordinary, Blat argues that the saving clause of canon 280 applies only to the archbishop. The patriarch and primate are given their own special precedence. Canon 280, therefore

61 Besides the four sees, there are also titular Latin patriarchs (or there may be) at Venice, in the West Indies (the major chaplain of the Spanish Army, the Bishop of Madrid), in the East Indies (the Archbishop-Primate of Goa), and at Lisbon. — *Annuario Pontificio* (1959), p. 92.

62 Nabuco, *Ius Pontificalium,* p. 39.

63 Canon 271.

64 This is the exception of particular law allowed for in canon 271; cf. Nabuco, *op. cit.*, p. 44.

gives precedence to both the patriarch and the true primate over the local ordinary, even in his own territory.[65]

Nabuco lists twelve primates in Europe, one in Africa, and nine in the Americas. Some of these have never been confirmed officially; others have only implicit confirmation in view of the place which was among other primates assigned to them in the Vatican Council.[66] The late Archbishop of Chile, Cardinal Caro Rodriguez, had the title of primate *ad personam*.[67] The same personal privilege was given to the late Archbishop of Caracas.[68]

Two Archbishops are listed by Nabuco as honorary or titular primates *ad instar*,[69] the Archbishop of Baltimore and the Archbishop of Westminister.[70]

The I Plenary Council of Baltimore (May 19, 1852) sent a request to the Apostolic See with the acts of the Council, seeking some form of recognition for the Archbishop of Baltimore by reason of his occupancy of the first residential see in the United States.[71] Although their request was denied, the Conciliar Fathers

---

65 Cf. p. 263, note 45. Nabuco, however, says that a primate does not in consequence of the ruling in canon 347 have such precedence over either the episcopal ordinary of the place or the metropolitan. — *Op. cit.*, p. 39.

66 Eg., the Archbishop of San Salvador of Bahia, Primate of Brazil.

67 S. C. Consist., decree, 11 oct. 1950 — cited by Nabuco, *op. cit.*, p. 45.

68 S. C. Consist., decree, 23 apr. 1952 — cited by Nabuco, *op. cit.*, pp. 44-47.

69 This title was found only in Nabuco, *Ius Pontificalium*, p. 47.

70 Pius X, const. ap. *Si qua est*, 5 nov. 1911 — *AAS*, IV (1911), 553. For the sake of peace, since the Archbishop of Canterbury was originally the primate of all England, the Archbishop of Westminster does not enjoy the use of the title or the privileges. — Nabuco, *loc. cit.*

71 Established April 6, 1789 — *Annuario Pontificio* (1959), p. 148. The Conciliar Fathers based their petition on the wording of the decree which raised the diocese to the rank of a metropolitan see, April 8, 1808, and referred to Baltimore as the "*. . . caput aliarum ecclesiarum Americae totius Foederatae. . . .*" This petition was Decree XXVIII of the original draft of the acts of the I Plenary Council (Baltimore Archdiocesan Archives, 32 B, D-1):

> Pius VII sa.mem. in Bulla erectionis Sedis Metropoliticae Baltimorensis die octavo Aprilis Anno Salutis MDCCCVIII data, eam constituit et designavit "caput aliarum ecclesiarum Americae totius Foederatae," eique subjecit "tamquam membra capiti, ecclesias omnes in posterum erigendas in eisdem Americae Foederatae partibus." Quum autem Sedes metropoliticae plures erectae sint et in posterum forsan erigendae, praesules huius plenarii Concilii suppli-

were encouraged by the Congregation for the Propagation of the Faith to ask for a different sort of privilege for their Archbishop of Baltimore. This they did in the IX Provincial Council in 1858.[72] This petition states that an earlier request had been made "*. . . pro quibusdam privilegiis Sedi Baltimorensi . . .*" by the Fathers of the I Plenary Council. There is also an allusion

---

> candum duxerunt Summo Pontifici, ut ordinem et unitatem custodiendi causa declarare dignetur suprema sua auctoritate, Sedem Baltimorensem adhuc esse caput aliarum sedium, etiam Metropolitiarum totius Americae Septentrionalis Foederatae."

When the original acts were returned with the Instruction of the Sacred Congregation for the Propagation of the Faith, Decree XXVIII was struck out, and therefore never appeared in the printed editions of the Council (I Plenary Council appeared in printed editions with only twenty-five decrees). For completeness' sake, and because the present writer believes the instruction in regard to the request of the Council has not appeared in print elsewhere, it is given in full here:

> Quominus ad sublimiorem gradum eveheretur sedes Baltimorensis juxta preces exhibitas in decreto XXVIII adjectoque supplici libello, satis graves rationes obstiterunt. Metropolitanis enim constitutis, provinciarum regimini satis consulitur; quoad vero indicendos eminentiores gradus experientia docuit caute ad modum esse procedendum. Licet vero compertum existat qua orto studio Amplitudo Tua ceterique Praesules Catholicae unitati adhaereant, quandoque obsequie Apostolicam Sedem prosequantur, attamen non ex eo tantum re est adjudicanda, potissimum vero aliarum regionum ratio habenda, ubi simile aliquid haud sine gravissimo periculo concederetur. Quae porro ex litteris apostolicis s.m. Pii VII adducuntur ad metropoliticam dignitatem potius pertinent, cum de pluribus isthic efformandis provinciis Ecclesiis serius admodum cogitavi [?] coeperit. Porro Ssmus. Dmns. Noster in eam propendis sententiam ut Sedi Baltimorensi honorificum aliquod privilegium tribuat, quod a ceteris illam distinguat ac memoriae tradata eam Ecclesiam omnium ferme per foederatas istas Provincias matrem fuisse. Sententia Tua circa modum exquiritur, quemadmodum aperire etiam poterit si quae alia suppetant ad unionem fovendam atque uniformitatem in praecipuis nonnullis capitibus facilius servandam. — "Instructio S. Congregationis de Propaganda Fide circa Decreta Concilii Plenarii Baltimorensis, 28 sept. 1852, n. 13" — Baltimore Archdiocesan Archives, 32 C, J-6.

72 In the first private congregation held on May 3, it was suggested that the tenor of the answer to the first petition had been that the Holy See was willing to grant some form of privilege; it was only for the American hierarchy to determine what form this privilege would take in place of a declaration as a primatial see. The Conciliar Fathers then proposed "*. . . ut honoris locus inter omnes Archiepiscopos Foederatarum Provinciarum Baltimorensi tribuatur, nulla habita ratione temporis promotionis. . . .*" — *Concilium Baltimorense Provinciale IX* (Baltimori, 1858), p. 11; cf., for full petition, pp. 33-34.

to the answer from the Sacred Congregation for the Propagation of the Faith that serious reasons stood in the way of elevating the see to a more honorable level. In addition, the fact is mentioned that Pope Pius IX thought that some kind of honorific privilege should nevertheless be given to distinguish this see as the Mother See from the other sees of the United States. This time the Conciliar Fathers specified that they sought the prerogative of place for the Archbishop at all councils, meetings, and gatherings of whatever kind. They indicated that because of this privilege they expected the Archbishop of Baltimore to have precedence and the main place in a seating arrangement over all other archbishops of the provinces of the United States, apart from any and all consideration of the time of his promotion or ordination (consecration).

This second petition was answered, and granted in the exact words of the petition:

> . . . censuerunt expedire ut loci praerogativa Sedi Baltimorensi concedatur, ita ut in Conciliis, coetibus, et comitiis quibuscumque Archiepiscopo Baltimorensi pro tempore existenti praecedentia, princepsque in sedendo locus supra quosvis istarum Provinciarum Archiepiscopos, si qui adsint, nulla habita ratione promotionis seu ordinationis, tribuatur. . . .[73]

Several conclusions may be drawn from the granting of this privilege of place. The Apostolic See intended to mark the Archbishop of Baltimore with a special dignity to distinguish him from all other archbishops in the country, ". . . *supra quosvis istarum Provinciarum Archiepiscopos. . . .*" It explicitly made an exception to the current law only in regard to the date of promotion to the rank of archbishop and the date of ordination (consecration). It may be presumed that all other norms of the current law were supposed to remain in effect. It seems, then, that the ordinary of the place will still take his special precedence in virtue of canon 347, as would the metropolitan in his own province by way of analogy. This norm of precedence for the Archbishop of Baltimore over the ordinaries of places in the

[73] S. C. de Prop. Fide, *decretum, De Praerogative Loci* — 15 aug. 1858 — *ibid.*, pp. 34-35; *Concilii Plenarii Baltimorensis II, Acta et Decreta* (2.ed.; Baltimorae, 1894), Appendix XVIII, pp. 307-308.

United States differs from the norm adopted above for primates (from Blat) because of the specific wording of the decree, and because the Archbishop of Baltimore is recognized as a primate only in the broadest sense of the word: a titular primate *ad instar*. If an analogy may be used, it seems proper that the precedence of such a primate should be lower or less than that of other titular primates, just as the precedence of protonotaries *ad instar* is less or lower that that of protonotaries *de numero*.

Cardinals would likewise retain their rank over those who are not cardinals, even if one of the non-cardinals should have this pre-rogative of place; the Archbishop of Baltimore would therefore yield to the cardinals, unless he himself were a cardinal, just as a true primate or a full titular primate must yield to a cardinal.[74] In this case it seems that the Archbishop of Baltimore, if he were a cardinal, would likewise precede all other archbishops of the United States who were cardinals; for the privilege makes an exception to the norm of prior promotion, which is the basis for precedence among the cardinals also, in regard to their promotion to the Sacred College. The Archbishop of Baltimore, however, would not precede another Archbishop in his own diocese, whether both were cardinals or both were not. If the Archbishop of Baltimore was a cardinal, he would have precedence over any ordinary who was not a cardinal, even in the ordinary's own diocese.

It is interesting to discuss the possibilities of the Archbishop of Baltimore taking precedence over other archbishops outside the limits of the United States. The wording of the grant states specifically that this special precedence is over the archbishops of the provinces of the United States. There seems to be little doubt that if the American hierarchy as a body attended some function outside the country, the Archbishop of Baltimore would be within his rights to make use of this special privilege just as he must in this country, preceding all who were not cardinals, or everyone if he were a cardinal. It seems that in any other circumstances such a right of precedence would not exist. Just as the special precedence of ordinaries of places and also of metropolitans ceases once they are outside their territory inas-

74 Canons 280; 239, § 1, 21°.

much as the reason for special precedence has ceased, so does the basis of this privilege seem to cease outside the United States. Like these ordinaries and metropolitans, the Archbishop of Baltimore would take his place among all other archbishops according to the time of his promotion.

If the occasion were a general council, the solution might be different. Perhaps the forthcoming general council and the order of seating therein will provide a norm of precedence for the American titular primate *ad instar* as the order of seating for the Vatican Council did for the primates in general.[75] It seems unlikely, however, that such a recognition would be given in this instance, because nowhere is the privilege referred to in the decree itself as a primatial privilege; it is only a prerogative of place. The term "titular primate *ad instar*" was found only in the work by Nabuco.[76]

The following outline would represent the conclusions reached in this article as they are applicable in the United States:

a) the apostolic delegate (if a cardinal);

b) the archbishop of Baltimore (if a cardinal);

c) in his own territory the archbishop who is a cardinal;

d) other archbishops who are cardinals, in the order of their creation as cardinals;

e) the apostolic delegate (if not a cardinal);

f) the archbishop metropolitan of the territory (if not a cardinal);

g) the ordinary of the place, even if not a bishop;

h) the archbishop of Baltimore (if not a cardinal);

i) other archbishops, in the order of their promotion, and

j) other bishops, in the order of their promotion.

Article 5. The Precedence of the Bishop in His Own Diocese

Canon 347. *In suo territorio Episcopus praecedit omnibus Archiepiscopis et Episcopis, exceptis Cardinalibus, Legatis Pontificiis*

---

75 Pius IX, brief, *Multiplices inter,* 27 nov. 1869 — *Coll. Lac. VII, Acta et Decreta Sacrosancti Oecumenici Concilii Vaticani,* p. 726, b, in Congregatione XXV.

76 Page 47.

et proprio Metropolita; extra territorium serventur normae traditae in canone 106.

In some ways this special norm of precedence is one of the most outstanding in the Code, for it gives to ordinaries of the place, who may not even be bishops, prcedence over others who may even be archbishops. Only three exceptions are made to the special rule of canon 347: the metropolitan precedes all the suffragan bishops within the province; the papal legate precedes all ordinaries who are not cardinals; and cardinals precede everyone except cardinals of higher rank, such as cardinal legates *a latere* or other cardinal legates in their own territory, or cardinal-bishops.[77]

Who is included in this special norm under the term *"episcopus"*? Since precedence is a right according to canon 106, 2°, 6°, and canon 478, and not a mere privilege, a list of those who enjoy this same precedence in their territories is quickly compiled. Any ordinary of the place who is also a bishop will be certainly included. But the Code provides for the inclusion of others, even if they are not consecrated bishops. Canon 215, §2, puts abbots and prelates *nullius* in the same category as bishops. Canon 294. §1, gives to vicars and prefects apostolic the same rights and faculties in their territories that residential bishops enjoy in their diocese, unless some special reservation is made by the Apostolic See. The same is true of the apostolic administrator who is permanently assigned to a territory.[78]

The temporary apostolic administrator is given the rights of the diocesan administrator,[79] who, in turn, enjoys the rights and privileges of the vicar general[80] as mentioned in canon 370: this includes precedence over all the clergy of the diocese, unless one of them is a bishop and the vicar general (or capitular) is not. Any one of these three, if he were a bishop, would be preceded in his own diocese by someone who is a bishop. Since this rule is applicable if one of the diocesan clergy is a bishop, it seems to be all the more applicable with reference to a bishop

77 Canons 280, 347, 269, § 2, and 239, § 1, 21°.

78 Canon 315, § 1.

79 Canon 315, § 2, 1°.

80 Canon 439.

from outside the diocese. In either case it is an application of canon 106. 3°: two persons in the same grade (ordinaries of the place) determine their precedence by the higher order. If the apostolic administrator is a bishop, he has the precedence of canon 347.

By analogy, if the bishop of a diocese is given special precedence in his own territory, the archbishop *a fortiori* should enjoy the same special precedence in his territory, the province. The same rule appears to be all the more applicable if the archbishop is likewise a cardinal, as was noted above.[81]

These norms would establish the same order as several of the schematic outlines indicate at the end of earlier articles,[82] where the condition of being an ordinary in his own territory was added to some member of the hierarchy.

For some occasions, on a diocesan level, the precedence will follow this order:

a) the cardinal legate in his own territory, except for the cardinal *a latere:*

b) the archbishops who are cardinals, headed by the archbishop of the province in which the function is taking place, and the archbishop of Baltimore if he is a cardinal;

c) the metropolitan (who is not a cardinal) in his own province;

d) the ordinary of the place (or the permanent apostolic administrator; also the temporary apostolic administrator, or the diocesan administrator, if either be a bishop);

e) the archbishop of Baltimore (unless he is a cardinal);

f) the other archbishops according to the time of their promotion to this rank;

g) the vicar general, if he is a bishop;

h) the other bishops in the order of their promotion to this rank, including consecrated abbots and prelates *nullius,* and vicars and prefects apostolic who are bishops;

i) the vicar general, the temporary apostolic administrator, or else the diocesan administrator, if they are not bishops;

j) the abbots and prelates *nullius* who are not bishops;

---

81 Page 258.

82 Pages 133, 258, 262, 266, 272.

k) the vicars and prefects apostolic who are not bishops;
l) the major religious superiors;
m) the vicars forane;
n) the local religious superiors;
o) the pastors, preceded by the pastor of the cathedral, and
p) the vicars in the order named in canon 478.

Article 6. The Precedence of the Vicar General and of the Vicar Capitular

Canon 439. *Quae in can. 370 de Vicario Generali praescripta sunt, eadem de Vicario quoque Capitulari dicta intelligantur.*

Canon 370, §1. *Praesente etiam Episcopo, Vicarius Generalis publice privatimque praecedentiae ius habet super omnibus dioecesis clericis, non exclusis dignitatibus et canonicis ecclesiae cathedralis, etiam in choro et actibus capitularibus, nisi clericus charactere episcopali praefulgeat, et Vicarius Generalis eodem careat.*

What is to be said in this article about the vicar general is equally true for the vicar capitular (diocesan administrator in the United States and other places where there are no cathedral chapters) and the vicar delegate in mission territory.[83] It is possible that the first two will have the episcopal character; it is equally possible that they will not. In either case, the three of them will have the same precedence.

There will be no question of determining the mutual precedence of the vicar general, and the diocesan administrator, in view of the very nature of their offices. There is a vicar capitular only when the see has been left vacant; when the see is vacant, the vicar general loses his office, accordingly also the corresponding basis for his precedence.[84]

The vicar general has precedence for a twofold reason: in virtue of canon 106, 1°, he has precedence as the bishop's proxy or *alter ego;*[85] in virtue of canon 106, 3°, he has precedence over the other clergy of the diocese because he has authority over them in the same way the bishop does in matters of adminis-

83 S.C. de Prop. Fide, 8 dec., 1919 — *AAS,* XII (1920), 120
84 Canon 371, and canon 430, § 3, 1°.
85 Canon 366, § 3.

tration (ordinarily not in judicial matters, unless he holds the office of *officialis* cumulatively).[86] The diocesan administrator is the proxy, not of the bishop, but of the board of diocesan consultors.[87] His authority in the diocese is the same as that of the bishop except in those things which are expressly forbidden him by the law itself.[88]

It seems the more probable opinion that the vicar general has his special precedence over the clergy of his own diocese only within the limits of the diocese.[89] The same may be said of the diocesan administrator by analogy. If either of them is a bishop, then by reason of his consecration (or even of his election alone) he would precede the other clergy of his own diocese even outside the territory, unless one of them was also a bishop. In conclusion, neither the vicar general nor the diocesan administrator has any precedence outside the diocese, *ratione officii.*

The practice regarding the precedence of the vicar general was quite confused before the legislation of the Code was promulgated. Possibly this was due to the fact that it was not clear just how the vicar general differed from the archdeacon, and which of the two was to receive the higher rank. In the Code, no provision at all is made for the archdeacon (the historical predecessor of the present-day vicar general).[90] With the Code legislation and a resolution of the Sacred Congregation of the Council, it has become clear that the office is regulated now solely by the norms in the Code.[91]

Canon 370 specifically gives the vicar general precedence over the entire body of the diocesan clergy, including the cathedral chapter with its dignitaries and canons, even in choir and in capitular acts. The only exception made by the law occurs in the case when one of the diocesan clergy is a bishop, and the vicar general is not. If the vicar general is also a bishop, then

---

86 Canons 1573, § 1; 368; Coronata, *Institutiones,* I, n. 421.

87 Canon 432, § 1.

88 Canon 435, § 1.

89 Cf. *supra,* pp. 111 ff., for a discussion of this point.

90 Regatillo, *Institutiones,* I, 583.

91 S.C. Conc., resolutio, *Cunen. et Utinen.,* 17 maii 1919 — *AAS,* XI (1919), 349.

he is preceded in the diocese only by the ordinary himself. The vicar general will, therefore, precede the pastor of the cathedral,[92] all prelates of lesser dignity than a bishop,[93] and protonotaries supernumerary and *ad instar*.[94] Smith (1845-1895) maintained in his pre-Code commentary that the vicar general of the metropolitan would precede one of the suffragan bishops.[95] From the nature of the exception made in canon 370, §1, it seems that this opinion is no longer tenable, except perhaps in the case wherein the metropolitan's vicar general was a bishop (even though a junior by promotion to any of the suffragans). Even this does not seem very probable in view of the opinions expressed in the discussion on pages 111 and the following in regard to the nature of the precedence of the vicar general outside the diocese, when it is based on the notion of his authority. It might be conceded that the episcopal vicar general of the metropolitan would precede one of the suffragans if the metropolitan himself were not present. In that case the vicar general would be acting as the proxy of his ordinary, the metropolitan, who certainly takes precedence over all the suffragans.[96]

There is some controversy over the exact meaning of the words ". . . *omnibus dioecesis clericis*. . . ." in canon 370. Beste maintains it would not include an exempt abbot;[97] Augustine, on the other hand, maintained that it did include even the exempt abbot.[98] There could be no doubt about the abbot's precedence if he were consecrated, and the vicar general were not. This will be true of most abbots and prelates *nullius* who are nearly always consecrated. It will rarely be true of the abbots *de regimine* or of independent monasteries, who most often are only blessed.

When the vicar general who exercises ordinary power vicariously, and the blessed abbot who exercises it in his own right, are both in a procession, precedence would seem to go to the

92 S.C. Prop. Fide, 16 ian. 1924 — *AAS*, XVI (1924), 243.

93 Zitelli, *Apparatus Iuris Ecclesiastici*, Appendix, lib. I, cap. V. art. 1.

94 *IM*, n. 57 and *AI*, n. LV.

95 *Elements of Ecclesiastical Law*, I, 218.

96 Canon 347.

97 *Introductio in Codicem, sub canone* 106, 2°, and 370, § 1.

98 *Commentary*, II, 404; cf. Vito, *Note Canoniche sulla Praecedenza*, p. 29.

abbot.[99] However, both Michiels and Jone would put all major religious superiors[100] after the vicar general and before the vicar forane.[101] Such a norm may seem to be more in keeping with the rank of the diocesan administrator than with that of the vicar general, but canons 370 and 439 make no such distinction.

The diocesan administrator is not given the same right to precedence as the bishop himself. Vicars and prefects apostolic, on the other hand, even though not bishops, have all the rights of bishops (including the special precedence allowed for them in canon 347).[103] The pro-vicars and pro-prefects, as mentioned in canon 309, §1, do not have any power from the Code during the lifetime of the vicar or the prefect apostolic. Therefore, they are not entitled to any special precedence as based on authority, unless they have been given that authority by the vicar or the prefect himself.[104] Once the vicar or the prefect apostolic dies or is impeded in the manner contemplated in canon 429, §1, the pro-vicar and the pro-prefect assumes full power until the Holy See provides for a successor.[105] Juridically, these two are appointed as temporary successors; in the law, they are not sharers of the power of the vicar or the prefect as the vicar general is. This type of office belongs to the vicar delegate. He has a position distinct from that of the pro-vicar or the pro-prefect. Like the vicar general, he constitutes one person together with the vicar or the prefect apostolic. It seems logical, then, that he should have the precedence of the vicar general also.[106]

The diocesan administrator, however, is given the precedence of the vicar general in canon 370. In view of this, canon 347

---

99 Cf. *supra*, p. 134.

100 The abbot primate, the abbot president of a monastic congregation, the abbot of an independent monastery, the supreme religious moderator, the provincial superior, and their vicars, and all who possess authority equivalent to that of a provincial superior. — canon 488, 8°.

102 Jone, *Commentarium*, I, *sub canone* 106, 3°; Michiels, *De Personis*, p. 691.

103 Canon 294. § 1.

104 Canon 309, § 2.

105 Canon 309, § 2.

106 S.C. Prop. Fide, 8 dec. 1919 — *AAS*, XII (1920), 120; Regatillo, *Interpretatio, sub canone* 309, *annotationes*.

does not seem to apply to the administrator, for neither is he included under the term "*episcopus*" in the Code[107] nor is he given the rights of a residential bishop.[108] In view of these facts it is evident that an administrator who is not a bishop would have to yield precedence to any bishop, whether from the diocese or from outside.

Vicars general, temporary apostolic administrators, and diocesan administrators, therefore, share an identical right of precedence together with the vicar delegate of mission lands. This right gives them precedence over all the other clergy of the diocese, and, according to some authors, also over major religious superiors. Only their Ordinary and a bishop precede them when they themselves are not bishops.

ARTICLE 7. THE PRECEDENCE OF THE VICAR FORANE

Canon 450, §2. [*Vicarius foraneus*] *Praecedit omnibus parochis aliisque sacerdotibus sui districtus.*

The vicar forane (the rural dean) is to the deanery what the vicar general is to the diocese, as far as precedence is concerned.[109] With regard to power, however, there is this difference: the vicar general has ordinary power; the vicar forane has only delegated power.[110] Another difference is this: the vicar general is not limited in his right of precedence to those occasions at which he is present as vicar general; some authors would make this limitation on the vicar forane, and accordingly give him the special precedence of his office only when he is exercising it within his deanery;[111] at the diocesan synod, or in a provincial council. Otherwise the vicar forane is subject to the general norms of precedence, according to these two authors.

At least one official interpretation on the precedence of the vicar forane has been made since the promulgation of the Code

107 Canon 215, § 2.

108 Canon 294, § 1.

109 Vito, *Note Canoniche sulla Precedenza,* p. 50, note 1.

110 Canons 366, § 1, and 447, § 1.

111 Cappello, *Summa Iuris Canonici,* I, n. 486; Augustine, *Commentary,* II, 504.

concerning the vicar forane who is also a member of a collegiate chapter. It was declared that he has no special precedence in this circumstance, *ratione vicariati.*[112] This seems to give some validity to the opinion expressed above.

Canon 450, §1, certainly protects the rights of precedence for the vicar forane within his district. It does not forbid him to have precedence outside his deanery, however. In view of this, the recommendation of the III Plenary Council is still timely: ". . . oportet ut Ordinarii . . . aliquam praeeminentiam inter rectores conferant."[113] Such a recommendation was made by the present writer when he treated of the ordinary's power to determine precedence within his diocese.[114]

The Code law definitely grants precedence to the vicar forane at all deanery meetings, such as the clergy conference on the deanery level.[115] He would likewise be acting in his official capacity when the diocesan faculties or statutes appoint him the usual delegate of the ordinary for the installation of pastors in his deanery.

Basically, then, since the precedence of the vicar forane is based on his authority over the clergy of his deanery; his precedence is limited, by the law, to the same territory, that is the deanery, to which also his authority is restricted.

112 PCI, 10 nov. 1925 — *AAS,* XVII (1925), 582.

114 Cf. *supra,* p. 232.

115 Canon 448, § 1.

CONCLUSIONS

1. Precedence is a right, not a privilege. As such it cannot be denied to any person except as a punishment, nor is the individual fundamentally *(per se)* violating any virtue in demanding his right (p. 74).

2. The "*conventus*" as mentioned in canon 106, 1°, must have the nature of a deliberative meeting or gathering, and accordingly resembles a council (pp. 106-108).

3. Grade or rank, in canon 106, 3°, is determined very vaguely on almost any basis except direct authority, sacramental Orders, or age. Any other reason which carries with it some notion of pre-eminence, or some participation in or resemblance to authority, even if it is only by way of title, provides a sufficient basis for rank (pp. 127-31).

4. Order is to be understood as the effect of a sacramental rite, except in the specific provisions for non-sacramental orders in the college of cardinals and in chapters of canons (pp. 130-31).

5. The application of each criterion of canon 491, §1, results in a juridically different species of religious institute. Within each species there is no grade or further subdivision, as there is in some other kinds of moral persons. (p. 155-56).

6. Quasi-possession of the right of precedence will frequently not be a satisfactory criterion for determining the precedence of moral persons of the same species in the United States. Recourse will be necessary, in nearly every case, to the date of foundation either in the place (broadly interpreted) or in the universal Church. Thus the order of religious institutes given in the *Annuario Pontificio* (the norm followed in Rome) will ordinarily be a safe criterion, unless some controversy occurs. From an investigation of the allegations, it may be discovered that quasi-possession or prior foundation in a place can be proved. In this case, such prior claims must be recognized. (pp. 195, 199).

7. Latin patriarchs are bound by the norms of the Oriental Code for patriarchs only insofar as jurisdictional patriarchs should precede titular patriarchs. (pp. 265-66).

8. The Archbishop of Baltimore is not a true primate with approval of primatial status by the Holy See. He has only the prerogative of precedence over other archbishops of the United States with due regard for the norms of canon 347, namely that a bishop in his own territory precedes all other Archbishops and bishops except cardinals, papal legates, and his own metropolitan. (pp. 268-72).

9. Titular archbishops and titular bishops take the same precedence as they would if they were residential bishops, under all due safeguarding of the special norms for the ordinary of the place in his own diocese. Thus the date of their promotion may put them before residential bishops (pp. 137-41).

10. Diocesan consultors in the United States when present as a body have the same precedence as do cathedral chapters in the Code (p. 135, footnote n. 159).

11. The precedence which is enjoyed by retired pastors, like that which is enjoyed by bishops, is not lost in virtue of their retirement. Their precedence is still determined on the basis of their first promotion to the rank of pastor. (p. 232).

12. Although the pastor of the cathedral has precedence over all other pastors, assistants *(vicarii cooperatores)* of the cathedrals in the United States do not have such precedence by law over all other diocesan clergy or over the other assistants. (p. 234, note 45).

13. Military chaplains and chaplains of Veterans' Administration Hospitals take their precedence with pastors as equals, according to the time of their promotion either to the rank of pastor or chaplain, whichever came first. (p. 232, note 41).

BIBLIOGRAPHY

Sources

Acta Apostolicae Sedis, Commentarium Officiale, Romae, 1909-29; Civitate Vaticana, 1929—

Acta Ecclesiae Mediolanensis, Lugduni, 1683.

Acta et Decreta Concilii Plenarii Baltimorensis Tertii, A.D. MDCCCLXXXIV, Baltimorae, 1886.

Acta et Decreta Sacrorum Conciliorum Recentiorum, Collectio Lacensis, 7 vols., Friburgi Brisgoviae, 1870-92.

Acta Sanctae Sedis, 41 vols., Romae, 1865-1908.

Bouscaren, T. Lincoln, *The Canon Law Digest,* Vols. I-III; Bouscaren and James O'Connor, Vol. IV; Milwaukee: Bruce, 1934-58.

Bruns, H. T., *Canones Apostolorum Conciliorum Saeculorum IV-VII,* 2 vols., Berolini, 1839.

Bullarium Ordinis F.F. Praedicatorum, ed. Thomas Ripoll et Antonius Bremond, 8 vols., Romae, 1729-40.

Bullarum Diplomatum et Privilegiorum Romanorum Pontificum Taurinensis Editio, 24 vols. and Appendix, Augustae Taurinorum, 1857-1872; 5 vols., Neapoli, 1867-85.

Codex Iuris Canonici Pii X Pontificis Maximi Iussu Digestus, Benedicti XV Auctoritate Promulgatus, Praefatione, Fontium Annotatione et Indice Analytico-Alphabetico ab Emo Petro Card. Gasparri Auctus, Romae: Typis Polyglottis Vaticanis, 1917; reimpressio, 1933.

Codicis Iuris Canonici Fontes, cura Emi Petri Card. Gasparri editi, 9 vols., Romae (postea Civitate Vaticana): Typis Polyglottis Vaticanis, 1923-1939. (Vols. VII-IX, ed. cura et studio Emi Iustiniani Card. Serédi.)

Collectanea in Usum Secretariae Sacrae Congregationis Episcoporum et Regularium, Romae, 1863.

Concilium Plenarium Totius Americae Septentrionalis Foederatae, Baltimori Habitum, A.D. 1852, Baltimori, 1853.

Concilii Plenarii Baltimorensis II, A.D. MDCCCLXVI . . . Acta et Decreta, 2. ed., Baltimorae, 1894.

Concilium Tridentinum: Diariorum, Actorum, Epistularum, Tractatuum Nova Collectio, edidit Societas Goerresiana, 13 vols., Friburgi Brisgoviae: B. Herder, 1901—

Corpus Iuris Canonici, ed. Lipsiensis secunda, post Aemilii Richteri curas . . . instruxi Aemilius Friedberg, 2 vols., Lipsiae: Tauchnitz, 1879-1881, ed. anastatice repetita, Graz: Akademische Druck-u. Verlagsanstalt, 1955.

Corpus Iuris Civilis, 3 vols., Vol. I, *Institutiones* quas recognovit P. Krueger; *Digesta,* quae recognovit T. Mommsen et retractavit P. Krueger, ed. stereotypa 15; Vol. II, *Codex Iustinianus,* quem recognovit et retractavit P. Krueger, ed. stereotypa 10; Vol. III, *Novellae Constitutiones,* ed. stereotypa 5, a R. Schoell; Berolini; Apud Weidmannos, 1928-29.

Corpus Scriptorum Ecclesiasticorum Latinorum, editum consilio et impensis Academiae Litterarum Caesareae Vindobonensis, 70 vols., incomplete, Vindobonae, 1866—

Decisiones Sacrae Romanae Rotae coram Ansaldo, 8 vols., Romae, 1711-77.

Decisiones Sacrae Romanae Rotae coram Clemente, Romae, 1781.

Decisiones Sacrae Romanae Rotae coram de Herrera, Romae, 1731.

Decisiones Sacrae Romanae Rotae coram Marco et Catalan, 2 vols., Romae, 1829.

Decisiones Sacrae Romanae Rotae coram Molines, 5 vols., Romae, 1728.

Decisiones Sacrae Romanae Rotae Nuperrimae, 10 vols., Romae, 1751-71.

Decisiones Sacrae Romanae Rotae coram Otthobono, Romae, 1657.

Decisiones Sacrae Romanae Rotae Recentiores, 25 vols., ed. Farinaccio, Rubeo, et Compagno, Venetiis, 1697.

Decisiones Sacrae Romanae Rotae coram Rezzonico, 3 vols., Romae, 1759-62.

Decreta Authentica Sacrorum Congregationis Rituum, 7 vols., ed. Gardellini, Romae, 1807-27.

Decreta Authentica Congregationis Sacrorum Rituum, 5 vols., Romae, 1898-1901; Vol. VI, 1912; Vol. VII, 1927.

Decretales D. Gregorii Papae IX, suae integritati una cum glossis restitutae, cum privilegio Gregorii XIII, Pont. Max., et Aliorum Principum, Romae, 1582.

Decretum Gratiani emendatum et notationibus illustratum cum glossis, Gregorii XIII, Pont, Max., iussu editum, 2 vols., Romae, 1582.

Hardouin, Jean, *Acta Conciliorum et Epistolae Decretales ac Constitutiones Summorum Pontificum,* 12 vols., Parisiis, 1714-15.

Jaffé, Philippus, *Regesta Pontificum Romanorum ab condita Ecclesia ad annum post Christum natum MCXCVIII,* ed. 2. correctam et auctam auspiciis Gulielmi Wattenbach curaverunt, S. Loewenfeld, F. Kaltenbrunner, P. Ewald, 2 vols., Lipsiae, 1885-88.

Leonis XIII Pontificis Maximi Acta, 23 vols., Romae: Ex Typographia Vaticanna, 1881-1905.

Magnum Bullarium Romanum, seu eiusdem Continuatio, 19 vols., Luxemburg, 1727-58.

Mansi, Joannes, *Sacrorum Conciliorum Nova et Amplissima Collectio,* 53 vols. in 60, Parisiis, 1901-27.

Manuale Decretorum Sacrorum Rituum Congregationis, Ratisbone, 1873.

Migne, J. P., *Patrologiae Cursus Completus, Series Latina,* 221 vols., Parisiis, 1844-55.

Monumenta Germaniae Historica, incomplete, Hannoverae, 1826—

National Catholic Almanac, The, Paterson: St. Anthony's Guild Press, 1904—

Official Catholic Directory, The, New York: P. J. Kennedy and Sons, 1912—

Ordo in Concilio Plenario Servandus, Typis Polyglottis Vaticanis, 1946.

Pallottini, S., *Collectio Omnium Conclusionum, et Resolutionum Quae in Causis Propositis apud Sacram Congregationem S. Consilii Tridentini Interpretum Prodierunt ab eius Institutione Anno MDLXIV ad MDCCLX, Distinctis Titulis Alphabetico Ordine per Materias Digestas,* 18 vols., Romae, 1868-95.

Pii IX Summi Pontificis Acta, 9 vols., Romae, 1854-78.

Potthast, Augustus, *Regesta Pontificum Romanorum inde ab anno post Christum natum MCXCVIII ad annum MCCIV,* 2 vols., Berolini, 1874-75.

Rituale Romanum Pauli V. Pont. Max. Iussu Editum Aliorumque Pontificum Cura Recognitum atque ad Norman Codicis Iuris Canonici Accommodatum SS. mi D. N. Pii XII Auctoritate Ordinatum et Auctum.

Schroeder, Henry J., *Canons and Decrees of the Council of Trent,* St. Louis: Herder, 1941.

——— *Disciplinary Decrees of the General Councils,* St. Louis: Herder, 1937.

Turner, Cuthbertus H., *Ecclesiae Occidentalis Monumenta Iuris Antiquissima, Canonum et Conciliorum Graecorum Interpretationes Latinae,* 2 vols. in 9, Oxonii: e Typographia Clarendoniana, 1899-1939.

Reference Works

Adone, Aloysius, *Synopsis Canonico-Liturgica,* Neapoli, 1886.

Abbo, John—Hannan, Jerome, *The Sacred Canons,* 2 vols., rev. ed., St. Louis: Herder, 1957.

Augustine, Chas. [Bachofen], *A Commentary on the New Code of Canon Law,* 8 vols., London, 1919-22.

Ayrinhac, H. A., *Constitution of the Church in the New Code of Canon Law,* New York: Longmans, Green and Co., 1930.

Baart, Peter, *Legal Formulary, A Collection of Forms to be Used in the Exercise of Voluntary and Contentious Jurisdiction,* New York, 1898.

Bassi, Franciscus, *Bibliotheca Iuris Canonico-Civilis Practica (seu Repertorium),* 4 vols., Mutinae, 1758.

Bender, Ludovicus, *Potestas Ordinaria et Delegata,* Romae: Desclée et Socli, 1957.

Benedictus XIV, *De Synodo Dioecesana,* 2 vols., 2 ed., Parmae, 1764.

Bernardus Papiensis, *Summa Decretalium,* Ratisbonae, 1860.

Berutti, Cristoforo, *Institutiones Iuris Canonici,* 5 vols., Taurini: Marietti, 1936-1943.

Beste, Udalricus, *Introductio in Codicem,* 4. ed., Collegeville: St. John's Abbey Press, 1956.

Blat, A., *Commentarium Textus Codicis Iuris Canonici,* 5 vols. in 6, Romae, 1919-1927.

Boeckhn, Placidus, *Commentarium in Ius Canonicum Universum,* 3 vols., Salisburgi, 1776.

Boich, Henricus, *In Quinque Decretalium Libros Commentaria,* Venetiis, 1576.

Bouscaren, T. Lincoln—Ellis, Adam C., *Canon Law, A Text and Commentary,* 2 rev. ed., Milwaukee: Bruce, 1951.

Cappello, F. *Summa Iuris Canonici,* 3 vols., Vol. I, 5. rev. ed., Romae: Aedes Universitatis Gregorianae, 1951.

Catalani, Josephus, *Commentarium in Caeremoniale Episcoporum,* 2 vols., Parisüs, 1860.

Chelodi, J., *Ius Canonicum de Personis,* 5. ed., Vicenza: Societa Anonima Tipografica, 1947.

Cicognani, A. G., *Canon Law,* 2. rev. ed., Westminster: Newman Press, 1934.

Cocchi, G., *Commentarium in Codicem Iuris Canonici ad usum scholarum,* 8 vols. 3. ed., Taurinorum Augustae: Marietti, 1925-1940.

Conte a Coronata, M., *Institutiones Iuris Canonici ad usum utriusque cleri et scholarum,* 4 vols., 4. ed., Taurini-Romae: Marietti, 1950-56; Vol. V, 3. ed., 1951.

Coussa, Acacius, *Praelectiones in Librum Secundum Codicis Iuris Canonici de Personis, de Clericis in Specie,* Typis Monasterii Exarchici Cryptoferratensis, 1953.

Creusen, J., *Religious Men and Women in the Code,* 5. ed rev. by Adam Ellis, Milwaukee: Bruce, 1953.

DeAngelis, Philippus, *Praelectiones Iuris Canonici ad Methodum Decretalium Gregorii IX Exactae,* 5 vols. in 9, Romae, 1877-91.

DeHerdt, J. B., *Praxis Pontificalis,* 3 vols., 2. ed., Lovanii, 1873.

De Institutis Saecularibus, 1 vol. incomplete, cura et studio *Commentarium pro Religiosis,* Romae, 1951.

Dictionary of the American Hierarchy, ed. Joseph B. Code, New York: Longmans, Green and Co., 1940.

Doheny, William J., *Canonical Procedure in Matrimonial Cases,* 2 vols., Vol. I, *Formal Judicial Procedure,* 2. ed., Milwaukee: Bruce, 1948.

Droste, F.— Messmer, S. G., *Canonical Procedure in Disciplinary and Criminal Cases of Clerics,* New York, 1887.

Eichmann, E. and Moersdorf, K., *Lehrbuch des Kirchenrechts,* 3 vols., 7. ed., Paderborn: Verlag Ferdinand Schoeningh. 1953-1954.

Engel, Ludovicus, *Collegium Universi Iuris Canonici, servato ordine Decretalium,* 7. ed., Venetiis, 1733.

Fanfani, L., *De Iure Religiosorum,* 3. ed., Rovigo: Istituto Pandano di Arti Grafiche, 1949.

Ferraris, L., *Prompta Bibliotheca, Canonica, Iuridica, Moralis, Theologica, necnon Ascentica, Polemica, Rubricistica, Historica,* ed. Migne, 9 vols., Romae, 1885-99.

Fortescue, Adrian, *The Ceremonies of the Roman Rite Described,* 8. ed., rev. by J. B. O'Connell, Westminster: Newman, 1949; 10. ed., 1958.

Giraldi, Ubaldus, *Expositio iuris pontificii,* 2 vols., Romae, 1769.

Gonzales-Tellez, Manuel, *Commentaria perpetua in singulos textus quinque Librorum Decretalium Gregorii IX,* 5 vols., Lugduni, 1673.

Goyeneche, S., *Quaestiones Canonicae de Iure Religiosorum,* 2 vols., Neapoli: M. D'Auria, Pontificius Editor, 1954-55.

Haydt, John J., *Reserved Benefices,* The Catholic University of America Canon Law Studies, n. 161, Washington, D. C.: The Catholic University of America Press, 1942.

Heintschel, Donald E., *The Medieval Concept of an Ecclesiastical Office,* The Catholic University of America Canon Law Studies, n. 363, Washington, D. C.: The Catholic University of America Press, 1956.

Hilling, N., *Das Personenrecht des Codex Iuris Canonici,* Paderborn, 1924.
——— *Procedure at the Roman Curia* (trans. from the German), New York, 1907.

Holböck, Carolus, *Tractatus de Jurisprudentia Sacrae Romanae Rotae,* Vindobonae: In Officina Libraria Styria, 1957.

Hostiensis, Cardinalis (Henricus de Segusio), *Commentaria in Quinque Decretalium Libros,* 5 vols. in 3, Venetiis, 1581.

Hynes, Harry G., *The Privileges of Cardinals,* The Catholic University of America Canon Law Studies, n. 217, Washington, D.C.: The Catholic University of America Press, 1945.

Innocentius IV, *In V. Libros Decretalium Commentaria,* Venetiis, 1570.

Jone, H., *Commentarium in Codicem Iuris Canonici,* 3. vols., Paderborn: Officia Libraria F. Shoeningh, 1950-55.

Kurtscheid, Bertrandus, *Historia Iuris Canonici,* Vol. I, *Historia Institutorum, Ab Ecclesiae Fundatione usque ad Gratianum,* Romae: Officium Libri Catholici, 1941.

Landon, Edward H., *A Manual of Councils of the Holy Catholic Church,* Edinburg, 1909.

Lauer, Arcturus, *Index Verborum Codicis Iuris Canonici,* Civitate Vaticana: Typis Polyglottis, 1931.

Lemoine, Robert, *Le Droit des religieux du Concile de Trente aux Instituts séculièrs,* Bruges: Desclée de Brouwer, 1956.

Leurenius, Petrus, *Forum Ecclesiasticum in quo ius canonicum universum librorum ac titulorum ordine explanatur,* Venetiis, 1729.

Luca, Joannis Card. de, *Theatrum veritatis et iustitiae,* 16 vols., Colonia Agrippina, 1706.

Manrique, Michaele F., *Tractatus de Praecedentiis et Praelationibus Ecclesiasticis ordine alphabetico digestus,* Lugduni, 1635.

Maroto, Ph., *Institutiones Iuris Canonici ad Normam Novi Codicis,* Vol. I., 3. ed., Matriti, 1921.

Matulenas, Raymond, *Communication—A Source of Privileges,* The Catholic University of America Canon Law Studies, n. 183, Washington, D. C.: The Catholic University of America Press, 1943.

McManus, Frederick R., *The Congregation of Sacred Rites,* The Catholic University of America Canon Law Studies, n. 352, Washington D. C.: The Catholic University of America Press, 1954.

Metz, John E., *The Recording Judge in the Ecclesiastical Collegiate Tribunal,* The Catholic University of America Canon Law Studies, n. 287, Washington, D. C.: The Catholic University of America Press, 1949.

Michiels, Gommarus, *Normae Generales Iuris Canonici,* 2 vols., 2. ed., Parisiis: Desclée et Socii, 1949.
——— *Principia Generalia de personis in Ecclesia, Commentarius libri II Codicis canonici, Canones praeliminares,* 2. ed., Romae: Desclee et Socii, 1955.

Moretti, Aloisius, *Caeremoniale iuxta Ritum Romanum seu De Sacris Functionibus,* 4 vols., Taurini: Marietti, 1936-39.

Murphy, Francis J., *Legislative Powers of the Provincial Council,* The Catholic University of America Canon Law Studies, n. 257, Washington, D. C.: The Catholic University of America Press, 1947.

Nabuco, Joachim, *Ius Pontificalium, Introductio in Caeremoniale Episcoporum,* Parisiis: Desclée et Socii, 1956.

——— *Pontificalis Romani Expositio iuridico-practica,* 3 vols., Petròpolis, Brasilia, 1945.

Ojetti, B., *Commentarium in Codicem iuris canonici,* 4 vols., Romae, 1927-31.

——— *Synopsis Rerum Moralium et Iuris Pontificii,* 4 vols., 3. ed. rev., Romae, 1909-14.

Panormitanus, Abbas (Nicolaus de Tudeschi), *Commentaria in Quinque Libros Decretalium,* 5 vols. in 7, Venetiis, 1588.

Perathoner, A., *Kurze Einfuehrung in das neue kirchliche Gesetzbuch,* Brixen, 1919.

Petra, Vincentius Card., *Commentaria ad Constitutiones Apostolicas,* 5 toms. in 2 vols., Venetiis, 1729.

Pirhling, E., *Universum Ius Canonicum secundum titulos Decretalium distributum nova methodo explicatum,* 5 vols. in 4, Dilingae, 1674-77.

Poblete, Elias Olarte, *The Plenary Council,* The Catholic University of America Canon Law Studies, n. 372, Washington, D.C.: The Catholic University of America Press, 1958.

Praxis Synodalis, Manuale Synodi Diocesanae ac provincialis Celebrandae, New York, 1883.

Ramstein, Matthew, *A Manual of Canon Law,* 2. rev. ed., Hoboken, N. J.: Terminal Printing and Publishing Co., 1948.

Regatillo, Eduardus, *Institutiones Iuris Canonici,* 2 vols., 5. ed., Santander: Sal Terrae, 1956.

——— *Interpretatio et Iurisprudentia Codicis Iuris Canonici,* 3. ed., Santander: Sal Terrae, 1953.

Reiffenstuel, Anacletus, *Ius Canonicum Universum,* 6 vols., Venetiis, 1735.

Roberti, Franciscus, *De Processibus,* 2 vols., Romae: apud Aedes Facultatis Iuridicae ad S. Apollinaris, 1926.

Roelker, Edward, *Precepts,* Paterson: St. Anthony Guild Press, 1955.

Rufinus, Magister, *Summa Decretorum,* ed. H. Singer, Paderbornae, 1902.

Rupprecht, Theodorus M., *Notae Historicae in universi iuris canonici,* Venetiis, 1764.

Sabelli, Marcus A., *Summa Diversorum Tractatuum,* Venetiis, 1692.

Schaefer, T., *De Religiosis ad Norman Codicis Iuris Canonici,* 2. ed., Muenster: Ex Officina Libraria Aschendorff, 1931.

Schmalzgrueber, Franciscus, *Ius Ecclesiasticum Universum,* 5 vols. in 12, Romae, 1843-45.

Sipos, S., *Enchiridion Iuris Canonici,* 6. ed. rev. by Ladislaus Galos, Romae: Orbis Catholicus-Herder, 1954.

Smith, S. B., *Elements of Ecclesiastical Law,* Vol. I, 6. ed., New York, 1887.

Stickler, Alphonsus M., *Historia Iuris Canonici Latini: Historia Fontium*, Vol. I, unicum, Torino: Augustae Taurinorum, 1950.

Tangl, M., *Die paepstlichen Kanzleiordnungen, von 1200-1500,* Innsbruck, 1894.

Toso, Albertus, *Ad Codicem Iuris Canonici Commentaria Minora,* 5 vols., Romae, 1921-27.

Van Hove, Alphonse, *Commentarium Lovaniense in Codicem Iuris Canonici,* Vol. I, *Prolegomena,* 2. ed., Mechliniae-Romae: H. Dessain, 1945.

Vasto, Bernardus A., *De Communicatione Privilegiorum,* Dissertatio historico-canonica ad lauream in facultate Iuris Canonici Pontificiae Universitate Gregorianae, n. 161, Aquilae in Vestinis, 1936.

Verano, Gaetanus, *Iuris Canonici Universi Commentarius Paratitlaris,* 5 vols., Monachii, 1703-1708.

Vermeersch, A.,—Creusen, I., *Epitome Iuris Canonici,* 3 vols., 7. ed., Rome: H. Dessain, 1949-1956.

Vito, Pasquale, *Note Canoniche sulla Precedenza,* Verona, 1924.

Walsh, Donnell, *The New Law on Secular Institutes,* The Catholic University of America Canon Law Studies, n. 347, Washington, D.C.: The Catholic University of America Press, 1953.

Wernz, Franciscus, *Ius Decretalium,* 6 vols., Romae et Prati, 1898-1914.

Wernz, F.—Vidal, Petrus, *Ius Canonicum,* 7 vols. in 8, Vol. II, 3. ed. 1943; Vol. III, 1933; Romae, Apud Aedes Universitatis Gregorianae.

Woywod, Stanislaus—Smith, Callistus, *A Practical Commentary on the Code of Canon Law,* 2 vols., 7th printing, New York: Wagner, 1943; rev. ed., 1957.

Zitelli, Z., *Apparatus Iuris Ecclesiastici in Usum Episcoporum et Sacerdotum praesertim Apostolico Munere Fungentium,* Romae, 1886.

Articles

Kuttner, Stephan, "Cardinalis: The History of a Canonical Concept," *Traditio,* III (1945), 189.

Larraona, Arcadius, "Consultationes," *Commentarium pro Religiosis,* I (1920), 77-82.

——— "Commentarium Codicis," *Commentarium pro Religiosis,* II (1921), 275-287; IV (1923), 168-173; 210-218; 273-280; 331-335; 360-367.

"Lex Propria Confoederationis Ordinis Sancti Benedicti," *Commentarium pro Religosis et Missionariis,* XXXIII (1954), 1-14.

Periodicals

Commentarium pro Religiosis, Romae, 1920-1934; *Commentarium pro Religiosis et Missionariis,* Romae, 1935—

Periodica de Religiosis et Missionariis, Brugis, 1905-1919; *Periodica de Re Canonica et Morali, utilia praesertim Religiosis et Missionariis,* Brugis, 1920-27; *Periodica de Re Morali, Canonica, Liturgica,* Brugis, 1927-1936; Romae, 1937—.

Traditio, New York, 1943—.

Unpublished Thesis

Graves, Lawrence P., *Precedence,* Typewritten Licentiate Thesis in the Catholic University of America Canon Law Studies, The Catholic University of America, Washington, D. C., 1947.

ABBREVIATIONS

AAS—*Acta Apostolicae Sedis.*

AI—*Ad incrementum,* ap. const. Pius XI, 1934.

ASS—*Acta Sanctae Sedis.*

Bruns—*Canones Apostolorum etOunciliorum.*

Bull. Lux.—*Magnum Bullarium Romanum, seu ejusdem Continuatio.*

Bull. Rom. Taur.—*Bullarum Diplomatum et Privilegiorum Romanorum Sanctorum Pontificum Taurinensis Editio.*

Coll. Lac.—*Acta et Decreta Sacrorum Conciliorum Recentiorum Collectio Lacensis.*

CpR(M)—*Commentarium pro Religiosis (et Missionariis).*

CSEL—*Corpus Scriptorum Ecclesiasticorum Latinorum.*

D—*Corpus Iuris Civilis, Digesta Iustiniani.*

D.—*Decreta Authentica Congregationis Sacrorum Rituum.*

de M. et O.—Decretals of Gregory IX, Lib. I, tit. xxxiii, *de maioritate et obedientia.*

Ferraris—*Prompta Bibliotheca.*

Fontes—*Codicis Iuris Canonici Fontes,* Gasparri-Serédi.

Friedberg—*Corpus Iuris Canonici.*

Hardouin—*Acta Conciliorum et Epistolae Decretales ac Constitutiones Summorum Pontificum.*

IM—*Inter multiplices,* motu proprio of Pius X, 1905.

Jaffé—*Regesta Pontificum Romanorum* (to 1198)

Mansi.—*Sacrorum Conciliorum Nova et amplissima Collectio.*

MGH—*Monumenta Germaniae Historica.*

MPL—Migne, *Patrologiae Cursus Completus, Series Latina.*

Pallottini—*Collectio Omnium Conclusionum . . . apud S. C. Concilii Tridentini* (1564-1860).

PCI—Pontifical Commission for the Authentic Interpretation of the Code.

Potthast—*Regesta Pontificum Romanorum* (1198-1304).

S.R.C.—Sacorum Rituum Congregatio.

S.R.R. Decis Nuper.—*Sacrae Romanae Rotae Decisiones Nuperrimae.*

S.R.R. Decis Recent.—*Sacrae Romanae Rotae Decisiones Recentiores.*

s.v.—sub verbo.

ALPHABETICAL INDEX

The page references in bold face type indicate where the individual canon is given major treatment. References to footnotes are labelled with page number followed by "n".

The page references in bold face type indicate where the individual canon is given major treatment. References to footnotes are labelled with page number followed by "n".

The page references in bold face type indicate where the individual canon is given major treatment. References to footnotes are labelled with page number followed by "n".

The page references in bold face type indicate where the individual canon is given major treatment. References to footnotes are labelled with page number followed by "n".

The page references in bold face type indicate where the individual canon is given major treatment. References to footnotes are labelled with page number followed by "n".

The page references in bold face type indicate where the individual canon is given major treatment. References to footnotes are labelled with page number followed by "n".

The page references in bold face type indicate where the individual canon is given major treatment. References to footnotes are labelled with page number followed by "n".

The page references in bold face type indicate where the individual canon is given major treatment. References to footnotes are labelled with page number followed by "n".

The page references in bold face type indicate where the individual canon is given major treatment. References to footnotes are labelled with page number followed by "n".

The page references in bold face type indicate where the individual canon is given major treatment. References to footnotes are labelled with page number followed by "n".

The page references in bold face type indicate where the individual canon is given major treatment. References to footnotes are labelled with page number followed by "n".

The page references in bold face type indicate where the individual canon is given major treatment. References to footnotes are labelled with page number followed by "n".

The page references in bold face type indicate where the individual canon is given major treatment. References to footnotes are labelled with page number followed by "n".

The page references in bold face type indicate where the individual canon is given major treatment. References to footnotes are labelled with page number followed by "n".

The page references in bold face type indicate where the individual canon is given major treatment. References to footnotes are labelled with page number followed by "n".

The page references in bold face type indicate where the individual canon is given major treatment. References to footnotes are labelled with page number followed by "n."

The page references in bold face type indicate where the individual canon is given major treatment. References to footnotes are labelled with page number followed by "n."

The page references in bold face type indicate where the individual canon is given major treatment. References to footnotes are labelled with page number followed by "n."

The page references in bold face type indicate where the individual canon is given major treatment. References to footnotes are labelled with page number followed by "n."

The page references in bold face type indicate where the individual canon is given major treatment. References to footnotes are labelled with page number followed by "n."

The page references in bold face type indicate where the individual canon is given major treatment. References to footnotes are labelled with page number followed by "n."

The page references in bold face type indicate where the individual canon is given major treatment. References to footnotes are labelled with page number followed by "n."

The page references in bold face type indicate where the individual canon is given major treatment. References to footnotes are labelled with page number followed by "n."

The page references in bold face type indicate where the individual canon is given major treatment. References to footnotes are labelled with page number followed by "n."

The page references in bold face type indicate where the individual canon is given major treatment. References to footnotes are labelled with page number followed by "n."

The page references in bold face type indicate where the individual canon is given major treatment. References to footnotes are labelled with page number followed by "n."

The page references in bold face type indicate where the individual canon is given major treatment. References to footnotes are labelled with page number followed by "n."

The page references in bold face type indicate where the individual canon is given major treatment. References to footnotes are labelled with page number followed by "n."

The page references in bold face type indicate where the individual canon is given major treatment. References to footnotes are labelled with page number followed by "n."

The page references in bold face type indicate where the individual canon is given major treatment. References to footnotes are labelled with page number followed by "n."

The page references in bold face type indicate where the individual canon is given major treatment. References to footnotes are labelled with page number followed by "n."

The page references in bold face type indicate where the individual canon is given major treatment. References to footnotes are labelled with page number followed by "n."

INDEX OF CANONS

The page references in bold face type indicate where the individual canon is given major treatment. References to footnotes are labelled with page number followed by "n".

The page references in bold face type indicate where the individual canon is given major treatment. References to footnotes are labelled with page number followed by "n".

The page references in bold face type indicate where the individual canon is given major treatment. References to footnotes are labelled with page number followed by "n".

BIOGRAPHICAL NOTE

Paul Frederick Schreiber was born September 21, 1928, in Olmitz, Kansas. After graduating from St. Ann's Parochial School in Olmitz, he entered the preparatory seminary of the Pontifical College Josephinum, Worthington, Ohio, in 1942. He received the Bachelor of Arts degree in 1950. In 1954, he was ordained to the priesthood in the Josephinum Chapel on May 8. After two years of parish work in the Diocese of Dodge City, he was appointed by the Most Reverend John B. Franz, D. D., first Bishop of the Diocese of Dodge City, to pursue graduate studies at the School of Canon Law of the Catholic University of America, where he received the Baccalaureate in Canon Law in June, 1957, and the Licentiate in Canon Law in June, 1958.

CANON LAW STUDIES *

402. Chyang, Rev. Peter B., M.A., J.C.L., Decennial faculties for ordinaries in quasi-dioceses.
403. Gossman, Rev. Francis J., A.B., S.T.L., J.C.L., Pope Urban II and canon law.
404. Love, Rev. Paul L., A.B., J.C.L., The penal remedies of the Code.
405. McLeaish, Rev. Donald C., A.B., S.T.L., J.C.L., The laws of the State of Texas affecting church property.
406. Rodriguez, Rev. Manuel J., Ph.B., S.T.L., J.C.L., The laws of the State of New Mexico affecting church property.
407. Sampson, Rev. Robert G., Ph.B., S.T.L., J.C.L., A comparative study of the First Provincial Council of Milwaukee and the Code of Canon Law.
408. Schreiber, Rev. Paul F., A.B., J.C.L., Canonical precedence.
409. Welsh, Rev. Maurice L., M.A., J.C.L., The laws of the State of Nevada affecting church property.

* For a complete list of the available numbers of this series apply to the Catholic University of America Press, 620 Michigan Ave., N.E., Washington (17), D.C., for a general catalogue.

www.ingramcontent.com/pod-product-compliance
Lightning Source LLC
LaVergne TN
LVHW050259080826
844660LV00012B/657

* 9 7 8 0 8 1 3 2 2 5 6 7 8 *